The Art of
Sprinting

The Art of Sprinting

Techniques for Speed and Performance

WARREN DOSCHER

McFarland & Company, Inc., Publishers
Jefferson, North Carolina, and London

LIBRARY OF CONGRESS CATALOGUING-IN-PUBLICATION DATA

Doscher, Warren, 1930–
    The art of sprinting : techniques for speed and performance /
Warren Doscher.
        p.   cm.
    Includes bibliographical references and index.

    ISBN 978-0-7864-4314-7
    softcover : 50# alkaline paper ∞

    1. Sprinting.   2. Sprinting—Training.   I. Title.
    GV1069.D67   2009
    796.42'2—dc22   2009009454

British Library cataloguing data are available

Cover photograph ©2009 Fotosearch

Manufactured in the United States of America

McFarland & Company, Inc., Publishers
  Box 611, Jefferson, North Carolina 28640
    www.mcfarlandpub.com

2

INJURY

Before beginning our look at how to run faster, let us take a moment to consider the risk of injury. If you truly intend to do your very best in a sport, all training routines should be performed, and for that matter your lifestyle should be mostly lived in a manner that truly reduces your risk of injury. Almost any injury will have a detrimental effect upon your training, and subsequently upon your athletic performance. We do not get to choose when or where injuries will take place. We can only attempt to minimize the opportunity for them to occur.

Perhaps the best deterrent to injury, from a sprinter's perspective, is proper warm up and conditioning of the primary muscles used in running. This is addressed in a later chapter. A close second to warm up is the use of well-designed, properly-fitting shoes. In addition to heel support, pay particular attention to the area of the forefoot. The shoe (we are talking about the training shoe here because this is the one you wear the most) should provide good support for the foot without any bunching of the toes. It should also provide good cushioning for the high pressure exerted by the ball of the foot.

Try on shoes in several models and by more than one manufacturer before deciding which one is the best for you. Seek the advice of a knowledgeable salesperson to ensure you get the shoe with the proper characteristics for your particular foot and the event for which you will be training. Do not be in a rush to make your purchase; try on both the left and the right shoe. If you use orthotics, make certain you check out each shoe with the orthotic inserted. A clean pair of socks, of the weight you use in training, should also be part of your shoe-shopping venture. A distance runner might reverse the order of importance and rate the shoe as being more important than the warm up. But here, we are speaking of the sprinter.

If, when on the track, you are going to be practicing some short speed bursts, these can be done on the back side of the track which is usually less immediate sense, apologies are offered that it wasn't clearer and a re-reading is encouraged.

The honing of the sprinter will be described for the more serious athlete. Techniques that can enhance one's sprinting ability are examined; and just as importantly, factors that limit a sprinter's speed are explored so their negative influences may be mitigated. The physics involved will also be brought to light in order to provide a better understanding of how to best implement a described technique.

Not everyone will agree with everything contained between the covers of this book, and that's fine. The intention is to have you, the runner, think about *your* endeavor into running. Think about every detail. Think about how those details are put together. Think about the finished product. How can it be improved? You may want to utilize some of the techniques discussed herein; you may not. Keep trying to improve your performance. Improve any part of your game and you improve your entire game. You have to develop your own race. You will have one lane, 100 meters long, to demonstrate what you can do. Think your race through. Develop what works best for you. Put it all together and make it happen!

Ahead, we will look at the several stages of the sprint. Runners, on your marks!

CONTENTS

PREFACE

Sprinting is probably the oldest sport in which we humans engage. In the past century, we have come to understand better ways to run faster. Using experience and modern science we can now sprint faster than ever before. And using more experience and better science, we will be able to sprint still faster in the future. *The Art of Sprinting* opens the door just a bit wider so we can better see how to improve our present sprint abilities.

This is not a history of where the sport has been, nor is it a theoretical treatise on where it might be at some time in the future. The runner is shown how it is possible to run faster the next time he is on the track, and the next time he is on the starting line.

Much of what is covered here is not to be found in a single volume elsewhere. This book embraces information ranging from that which is so basic there seems to have previously been little need to put it into print to concepts that are technical and totally new to the sport of sprinting. It also explains not only what works and what doesn't, but draws on physics to explain how and why these actions perform as they do. This further step has added considerably to the length of the study, but it better reveals the advantages of infusing certain techniques into one's sprint.

The 100-meter and 200-meter races are directly addressed, but many of the techniques discussed are applicable to races of other lengths, both longer and shorter. This book has been written by a sprinter for the support and benefit of other sprinters, their coaches and also the administrators of the sport.

The Art of Sprinting does not cover the necessary physical conditioning and accompanying drills to optimize one's physical and neurological attributes; this information is available in well-conceived works by other authors and is not repeated here. This book stresses how one can achieve the best performance from her body regardless of its present state of conditioning. The runner is accepted in her current physical status, and offered direction on how to best perform the sprint on race day.

1

Chapters cover areas of particular interest to the sprinter: items to be addressed prior to the race; the warm up; special techniques for the start; detailed procedures for attainment of top speed; considerations that are unique to the curve; approaching the finish line; and critiquing one's race as a preparation for the next race.

During the author's endeavor to become a better sprinter, bookstores and library shelves were searched for publications that would provide advice on the running of a faster race. The information gained compared to the hours spent searching for it seemed to present an obstacle to the general advancement of the sport. Many of the author's racing techniques were, therefore, developed through his own experimentation. That experience, gained over a period of nearly a decade of failures and successes, is brought together for the benefit of others who are searching for ways to improve their sprint.

The material that has been assembled is authentic in that it documents the author's own thoughts, observations, efforts and experiences. It may, or may not, be conceptually new to the reader. On occasion, it is indicated that an observation has been made of a well-known individual utilizing the technique under discussion. It is the author's intention to be neither critical nor complimentary about any individual's performance. But if someone of prominence has utilized the technique under discussion, perhaps the reader has also noticed or would benefit from an understanding of it.

Experience now provides a better understanding and awareness of what works well, what does not, why the techniques work as they do and how each affects the total picture. If running success has come to you by using your natural running form, that's wonderful and the author tips his cap to you. A *natural* runner has the instincts to employ those actions best suited to obtaining the desired end result—speed.

Such has not been the case for the author; he had very poor form and had to work diligently to improve it. Having been forced to consciously study and develop each of the various running techniques, the author is now able to specifically describe those techniques and explain their effects on one's overall running form and speed. Running has been experienced both with and without good form. The beneficial consequence is now a keen awareness of the difference.

In the development of better form, the author utilized the approach wherein problems are reduced to their basic elements so that the pieces can then be sorted through and analyzed separately without regard for other influences. Once the individual parts are thoroughly understood, they can be prioritized. Necessary tradeoffs are made and the parts reassembled in a manner that provides the best result.

This process, which was influenced heavily by the author's engineering training, forces one to think more clearly and more thoroughly when evaluating a situation or solving a problem, and was applied to the sprint. Subsequently, the results of each analysis have been taken to the track for evaluation. After all the parts are assembled and put into motion, the process of re-analyzing, re-testing, re-thinking, and tweaking continues. This process never ends in our continuing quest for more speed.

The author has a deep-seated fundamental desire to understand, and thereby better appreciate, those things that are approachable by the natural senses. He also, after many years' experience in track and field, is a firm believer that better technique in the sprint will lead to faster times. The reason behind the author's search for better sprint technique was his basic desire to fully understand the actions of the runner and the vagaries that control his times on the racecourse. What developed from this was a study of the sprint that could not have been envisioned at the outset. As more knowledge of the sprint was gained, more questions that demanded further study came up.

The author's own sprinting career was unexpectedly abbreviated by a spinal injury, and he is no longer competitive, but there were years that allowed experimentation on the track of techniques that looked promising on paper. Some of those techniques turned out to be disappointments, but they all added to the author's growing store of knowledge. It was during this period that major strides were made toward arriving at a better style of the sprint. Notes were kept and techniques were honed in the hope he might return to the starting line. It eventually became obvious that a return was not going to happen, and the idea of publishing the results of those studies for the benefit of others evolved.

I would like the opportunity to express my regrets to my wife, Jeanne, for the time that the writing of this book took from our lives. Her patience, love and understanding were extraordinary, and my true appreciation of them—always understated. If I had known how limited her remaining time was to be, this book would never have been written. Her presence is sorely missed.

It is not possible for me to adequately express my gratitude to those who offered their advice, and more importantly their encouragement, as I pursued my running career. Without their generous support, my running abilities would not have advanced to the point where I became sufficiently experienced to write this book. To each, I say, "Thank you! You are welcome to share the pride I feel in having compiled the chapters that follow."

INTRODUCTION

Are you interested in the sport of sprinting? Probably so. That's the reason you picked up a book titled *The Art of Sprinting*. Do you enjoy running fast? Again, probably so. All sprinters enjoy the thrill of running swiftly. Would you like to run faster than you do presently? An unequivocal "Yes!" Inherently, all sprinters want to run still faster. Would you like to explore ways you can increase your sprint speed? The author hopes so, because that is precisely what this book offers you. The premise of this book is the search for ways to improve your running game. In pursuit of this objective, the crafting of a sprinter is explored in fresh detail.

If you are an accomplished runner, you can probably attribute your achievements, in large part, to extensive training and dedication to your sport. You can look inwardly and find gratification in your awareness of your improved condition and overall sense of well-being. But what about your aspirations for tomorrow? How will you achieve those goals of which you dream? Will you really get there? How will you get there? Is the route to those achievements just more time to be spent doing more intensive drills? Or are there some other elements that could, when properly implemented, help you achieve a greater reward from your dedicated training?

The author believes there is an additional requirement, beyond repetitive training, that is needed in order to reap the maximum benefit from your physical conditioning. It is *knowledge*, in this case the knowledge of what you want each of your various body parts to do so that the entire body will reach the finish line the quickest.

The routines that an athlete practices during training should provide a dual benefit. First, the athlete should achieve an overall greater degree of fitness. Second, the athlete should become more efficient through the repetition of particular routines which are designed to produce a carryover effect to race day. But what if the carryover effect is not producing the desired result? If the athlete does not fully understand what comprises the finished product, it will be only hit-or-miss if the training routines produce their fully intended result. *The Art of Sprinting* takes the hit-or-miss aspect out of the picture.

During the author's search for improvements in the mechanics of sprinting, an effort was made to set aside the inertia of thought that accompanies the general acceptance of what is considered to be *conventional wisdom* and find fresh ideas that can be applied to this age-old sport. The author's thoughts about running faster do not always follow established standards for the sport. Adherence is made to only one standard: the fullest expression of the author's beliefs of what makes a runner fast—or faster! Hopefully this information will contribute to *your* ability to run faster.

The 100-meter sprint is the shortest running event conducted in the national and international sport of outdoor track and field. As the shortest race, it inherently requires the attainment of the highest speed and requires the sprinter to possess certain skills, some natural and some acquired. At a world or Olympic championship, the winner of this race is generally acclaimed as the world's fastest male or female. This is often the showcase event of the competition.

There is evidence that as far back as the Olympic Games in 776 B.C., contestants ran a foot race the length of the stadium. Logically enough, the event was called the stade. Foot races continued to be held throughout the centuries, and when the Olympics were revived as the modern games in Athens 1896, the 100m was established as one of the events. The first intercollegiate track meet took place in 1864 between Cambridge and Oxford. Women were excluded from running events for several more decades. It was not until 1928 that women were allowed a handful of running events that included the 100m in the Amsterdam Olympics.

Conditions are much better today. Track and field is a major sport in most high schools and universities across the country with equal opportunities for both girls and boys. Private clubs abound for those who want to pursue their running careers after leaving school. Competitions are offered to athletes through their senior years.

If it appears you will not advance as far as you would like in another sport, you may find, instead, a rewarding experience in a track and field event. Evaluate your assets and enter events in which you believe you might do well. Until you try, you won't really know your capabilities.

There is little doubt that the best way to improve one's performance is developing a better-conditioned body to bring to the starting line. That is a long and tedious journey. The runner's best friend in this journey is the coach. The coach is in the best position to confirm that the athlete is participating in the proper event, determine the best training routines and see the athlete through the more taxing drills. The more circumspect coach will see things that the athlete cannot. The athlete who has a coach is very fortunate and enters a competition from a more favorable position than the athlete who goes it alone.

This book is for the coach and the sprinter, but it is especially valuable to the sprinter who has no coach. *The Art of Sprinting* spells out the do's and don'ts and tells the reader exactly what to do in the short sprints to get the most speed from his body and reach the finish line the quickest. The concepts and techniques put forth are universal in their application—men and women, young and old, novice and experienced all can use them. They are based upon fundamental principles of physics.

If you want to be a faster sprinter, this book is for you!

1

A NEW LOOK

While one's position at the finish line is ultimately the most important aspect of a race, it is not the only aspect of the race. Let's disassemble the 100m race and consider three different capabilities of a competitor in this event. First, there is the ability to accelerate off the starting line and be in good position at the 25-meter mark. Second, there is the ability to achieve a higher speed than one's competitors in the central portion of the race. Third, there is the ability to conjure up a final burst of speed and potentially improve one's position over the last 10 meters.

Just because an athlete has just won a race does not necessarily mean that she performed better than her competitors in all three areas. It is entirely possible that a runner, not known for having good starts, could be in the middle of the pack at the 25-meter mark but have sufficient high-end speed to grind out a win. A runner with consistently good starts could establish such a commanding position at the 25-meter mark that other runners with greater high-end speed are still unable to overtake her. A runner could dramatically improve her finishing position with an unexpected burst of speed late in the sprint.

Finding the upper limits of your capabilities is certainly a magnificent goal, but it cannot be attained without a major share of self-confidence, of knowing that within you there are still untapped resources that need only to be found, nurtured and released. It's only a matter of cutting through the chaff and inquiring of your coach, and yourself, to discover what is lacking from your running form. Once the mechanics of high-speed running are understood, and incorporated into your running form, then the many hours of training will pay off. At the end of the day, the frustration of not having performed better will be replaced by the gratification of knowing that the performance was to your full ability.

It is presupposed that you already have some running experience, good physical fitness, and no medical or physical conditions that would inhibit performance. It is also expected that those disciplines which as a runner you know contribute to your success are being practiced and that you will bring to the track a genuine desire to improve your running skills. If all the above are not true, stop and regroup. Remember, this is a sport that demands the very best from you.

Even if you do not fulfill all the above conditions, you may still glean much from the following chapters. The degree to which you are willing to, and able to, practice a runner's lifestyle will vary widely. It can range from the world and Olympic class runner to the once-a-week individual who has other of life's demands to meet but still enjoys the thrill of running as swiftly as possible. This book is for the person who is anywhere within these limits and wants to get still more from his body when he steps to the starting line on race day. It is written for the person who is ready to take on the challenge of putting herself on the line in sportsmanlike competition and doing her best.

And if you are not presently a member of the running community, it is hoped that, after reading this book, you will want to try sprinting. After all, you will be ready to begin your venture by utilizing the mechanics that can give you the most reward from your efforts. This will put you a *leg up* on the seasoned runner who would have to go through a changeover process if it is deemed his current running style should be modified. Of course, a thorough medical checkup and consultation with a qualified physician is a recommended prerequisite of any physically demanding endeavor. You should follow up with your physician as needed.

Normally, one set of techniques is presented as being the most advantageous for most runners, but it is acknowledged that all runners are not alike. Therefore, in addition to what the author sees as the preferred technique, alternative techniques are often presented.

Because of the dependency of one body motion on another, discussion of one technique requires mention of others, and the reader may find some techniques referred to in more than one chapter. Reference to a subject in one place does not necessarily preclude it from appearing more explicitly in another location.

This book should be read in its entirety from start to finish; understanding the content of one chapter forms the basis for the next chapter and so on. In a situation wherein one person is explaining something to another person, and the listener's response is a blank stare, the person doing the talking knows that a connection was not made. At that point, there is the opportunity to try again. The author will try to not create too many of those blank stares in this reading audience. However, if a passage doesn't make

crowded. Distance runners, hurdlers and coaches tend to congregate on the front side of the track. This makes it more difficult for someone practicing speed work. A sudden stop, or change in direction to avoid an unexpected obstacle, not only ruins what might have otherwise been a rewarding exercise, but could also cause injury both to you and to others.

Once you have picked out *your spot* on the track, walk that section of track and clear it of any debris. Pick up any pebbles, lost spikes, etc. Walk the lane again in the opposite direction. Your eye will spot different things with a different angle of sunlight. Sometimes the most innocent-appearing object, such as a cylindrical twig, can roll under your shoe and thereby put an unexpected strain on muscles, upon which you are already calling to do their maximum. The author does not view mishaps that result from this sort of thing as accidents; these are *preventables.*

Some athletic fields are equipped with lightning warning devices. You should determine if the field on which you regularly train, or the field that you will be visiting, is equipped with such a safety device. As an alternative to the permanently installed equipment, an official on the field may have a hand-held device. When one of these devices emits a warning that a lightning strike could occur, all personnel should immediately leave the field and take cover.

However, many athletic fields have no such warning devices. The responsibility for your own safety can never be shirked. Stay alert and be aware of the conditions around you. Safety is everyone's full-time job. If you feel the hair on your body stand up, it's too late. The lightning bolt is about to be delivered.

If a track is not available for your everyday training, choose a level surface that is not too hard. A softer surface is easier on the feet and the knees. If you run on grass, check the location carefully for ruts and other irregularities. An uneven surface can cause a twisted ankle or knee and thereby cause more trouble than if you had run on a harder but more level surface. If you must train on a bituminous or a concrete surface, you may want to slip some additional padding into those shoes.

If you've made it through training without injury, and have now completed your race day sprint, still in good shape, don't get careless after crossing the finish line. Putting on the brakes can put a greater strain on the legs than did the run that you just completed. Coast gradually to a stop, well beyond the finish line. A longer walk back is a small price to pay in order to save your legs from that final punishment.

Beyond the finish line the lane markings begin their curve. Beyond the finish line some runners decelerate while remaining within their assigned lane.

Other runners decelerate while continuing in a straight line. Perhaps our governing body could issue some guidelines or regulations relative to proper protocol here. Hopefully, it will not require a career-threatening injury to a high profile athlete to precipitate some regulation in this regard. Safety of the athletes should be of paramount concern to all. Regulation or not, stay alert. Do not get involved in a collision after having successfully completed your race. An injury here could be just as debilitating as one occurring anywhere else.

If a professional athlete, or an athlete who is recognized as being on the road toward becoming a world-class competitor, becomes injured, the immediate concern is, "How can the injury be most effectively corrected?" If surgery is required, this is often scheduled within days, or sometimes within hours, of the injury. Everyone understands top athletes must be given every relief modern medicine can offer.

But on the other hand, if a similar injury were to occur to someone who is not on the aforementioned road to athletic stardom, the approach is often much different. This individual, whom we shall typify as Sam Sidestreet, has athletic ambitions that are still unrealized, his talents not yet demonstrated. He may still earn his livelihood in a more traditional and mundane manner. The urgency to repair this individual is just not the same as with his more famous counterpart. Surgery is often relegated to the "if all else fails" category. Regimens of medicine, therapy, modified therapy, and so on are explored ad infinitum. These alternative treatments sometimes help but often never completely cure the problem.

Sam is expected to adjust to his newly imposed physical limitations. He may have to cut back some on his athletic endeavors. And, if necessary, this person who also has other talents can undoubtedly find a fulfilling lifestyle in some other pursuit, or so he is told. Sam, whose athletic ambitions were no less fervent than his more well-known counterpart, is now relegated to forever wandering the nondescript side streets of a less fulfilling lifestyle. He will never realize what could have been his full capability. The message here is to do everything reasonably possible to avoid injury in the first place.

One of the more serious injuries to a sprinter is injury to a hamstring. As a sprinter demands more and more from the body, the risk of injury escalates. In general, the hamstring does not seem to fail when the runner is at top speed. It seems more prone to injury when the runner has just come fully erect and is in the final stage of acceleration to top speed. While the speed is high at this point, the change in speed (acceleration) is quite small, but to the sprinter who is attempting to save a few hundredths of a second, still important. At this stage of the race, the runner is trying to *pull* the body forward during that extremely brief portion of the foot plant that occurs immediately *before* the body advances to a position whereby the foot can begin pushing the runner from behind.

This brief period of maximum stress on the hamstring is when it is most likely to fail. Failure does not occur because of a lack of stretching, lack of strength, lack of conditioning, or lack of anything. The stronger the hamstring, the more the runner will demand from it. During those few strides just before reaching top speed, we take everything the hamstring will give us, and are still searching for more in order to accelerate the quickest.

The author knows of no way to avoid this injury other than to avoid the use of the hamstring in this manner in the first place. Our competitive instincts do not allow us to only partially engage our strengths at such a critical time. The alternative then is to employ the final running form as soon as one is fully erect thereby eliminating this particular high-risk action. The final running form utilizes a softer foot plant and less hamstring stress. We would now have to accept whatever time penalty is associated with not achieving the maximum acceleration during this short interval of a few strides.

The decision whether to include or omit this injury-prone period from your race must be made before the race begins, when you can evaluate the bigger picture and properly weigh the risk vs. the gain. You cannot wait to make this decision until you are in the race and the moment of this action arrives. The injury can strike with absolutely no warning no matter how well one is prepared for the race. A severe hamstring injury can sideline a runner for six months or longer. (The author is speaking from experience here.)

This brings to mind the race that included Michael Johnson and Maurice Greene in the highly anticipated meeting of these two great athletes in the 200m event of the 2000 Olympic Trials in Sacramento. In the final, both runners went out strong. To the dismay of all onlookers, both suffered an injury before reaching the top of the straightaway. Both these men came in as favorites and it was a forgone conclusion that both of them, among the best 200m runners in the world, would qualify for the Olympic Games. It was just a matter of who would be first and who would be the other finisher. (We don't seem to put much stock in 2nd place, no matter how great the accomplishment.) Because of the injuries suffered here, both men were unable to complete the race and lost the opportunity to compete in this event at the Olympic Games.

The author has no firsthand knowledge of how the injury to either of these men came about. No inference is intended that these injuries occurred in the same manner that one specific injury was described earlier. This illustration is offered only to underscore the adverse effects an injury can have.

The intent has been to point out the devastating results of an injury, and thereby possibly save another runner a similar agony.

Even lesser impairments such as cramped muscles, smashed toes or hands, digestive tract disorder, colds and infections, all have a negative effect upon one's training. If you want to train and to compete at your best, the entire body must be at its best.

The sprint stresses the running muscles to the maximum; this includes their associated tendons and attachments. In many sports, it is possible to compete even though one may have an injury and not be at 100 percent of one's capability. Not so in the sprints. Any attempt to compete with a leg injury will almost certainly prove futile, and may further aggravate the injury thereby delaying recovery.

Most importantly, one must be cognizant of the fact that injury is the worst enemy of virtually every athlete. It is the individual's responsibility to distance oneself as much as possible from this unpleasant acquaintance. Do not lull yourself into the false mindset that injury is always someone else's problem. It can happen to YOU. The conscientious athlete must take a proactive stance in its avoidance. Do your warm ups and proper race preparations. Accept the cutoff point for the day when your body is becoming too tired to safely engage in a maximum-exertion effort. When the body is tired, it is more prone to injury. The longer you remain injury free, the shorter will be the time line to reach your next milestone. Water aerobics has been shown to be a useful tool to the healthy athlete and also during the rehabilitative period to one who is injured.

The effects resulting from an injury can be enormous. One must treat the risk of injury with all the respect it deserves. If not career threatening it will, at the very least, significantly slow you down in your quest to become the very best that you can be. Of all the training routines, the one called "Injury Recuperation" is unique; it makes one slower, not faster. Train at only the exertion level your body is prepared for and will benefit from. Overexertion can lead to injury. No one is immune from being attacked by this adversary. Do not let down your guard. Remain alert for circumstances that could lead to injury. Remember to engage the brain before engaging the body.

3

THE BASICS

The basic goal of the short sprint is to attain one's highest speed as quickly as possible and thereby move one's body from the starting line to the finish line in the shortest possible time. In order to achieve this goal, we must require every part of the body to make its maximum contribution to the effort. No part of the body should be exempt from this responsibility. No body part should be just *along for the ride*.

Here, we will begin to look at what contribution each of our many body parts can offer and also, how we can most effectively evoke that contribution in order to achieve the best possible end result: SPEED, from start to finish.

Checking One's Pulse Rate

To reach our objective, we must train effectively. It is quite customary for one who is exercising to keep track of his pulse rate. Convenient pulse rate monitors are available that perform this function very well. But, a word of caution: during a pronounced swinging of the arms, centrifugal force will cause the blood to momentarily pool in the fingertips at each swing of the hand. If one's monitor is of the type that attaches to a finger, it may register the hand swing rate rather than the pulse rate. Stopping the hand swing for a few seconds will allow the monitor to register the pulse rate.

You may, however, be one of the many who, during the course of their training, check the pulse manually by placing a finger on a prominent artery. One practice calls for the person to count the number of pulse beats over a 10-second period, and then mentally extrapolate that figure to arrive at the number of beats per minute. The author never found the mental arithmetic that is required to perform that calculation particularly easy. Therefore, an error was sometimes committed in the process. In an alternate method of taking a 15-second count and doubling it twice, the arithmetic is easier. But accuracy is somewhat diminished because of the slowing of the pulse rate that occurs during this 15-second period.

By nature, the author is one who looks for better ways of doing things, particularly if the present way is not working well. While sitting in solitude one day, the following approach to this nagging problem was developed.

The pulse beats over a 12-second period are counted. This figure is halved to obtain what the pulse count would be for a 6-second period, and then multiplied by ten to obtain the pulse count for a 60-second period. As an illustration: over a timed 12-second period, 26 pulse beats are counted. Mentally divide by 2 and obtain 13 beats. Move the decimal point one place to the right (same as multiplying by ten) and arrive at a pulse rate of 130 bpm. For the author, this mental arithmetic is much quicker and easier. Therefore, the result is more reliable.

If one should count an odd number of pulse beats over the 12-second interval, say 27, use the next smaller even number (26). Divide that number by 2 and multiply by 10 as before. Then add 5 to that result to account for the odd number counted. In this case, the pulse rate is determined to be 135 bpm.

One could also count the number of pulse beats in a 6-second interval and multiply that number by 10 to arrive at one's pulse rate. This would be simpler but an inaccuracy of counting just one beat would produce an error of ten in the result. In the 12-second count, an inaccuracy of one beat produces an error of only five in the result.

If working with a 10-second or 15-second pulse count is not to your liking, you might try this routine of a 12-second count.

Allow Rebuilding Time

After a day of strenuous workout, allow the body sufficient time to rebuild itself. This includes ample sleep time, which is when the body does most of its rebuilding. During a restful sleep the muscles are relaxed and more blood, with its rebuilding nutrients, is admitted to the muscles. If insufficient time is allowed for recuperation, additional strenuous exercise will only detract from the body's performance rather than enhance it. Following a day of strenuous exercise, a day of light exercise, rather than a day of zero exercise, will improve blood flow to the muscles and aid in the rebuilding process. But don't overdo it and again tear down those muscles before they have had the opportunity to completely recover.

If you should find that a day of zero exercise is really necessary, you may want to do some very mild stretching on that day. Not enough that will give the body something to repair, but just enough to stimulate additional blood flow to the muscles that are being rested. In this manner, the blood flow will be improved and the muscles will also get their needed rest. Seniors should accept an additional day of light exercise after a day of strenuous exercise to allow the body opportunity to fully recuperate and prepare for its next challenge. If the body needs still more recovery time than that, you probably exercised too strenuously, for too long a period, for best overall benefit.

Practice Correct Breathing

Correct breathing is important, even when competing in (and training for) short distance events. Breathing through the open mouth promotes only shallow breathing. This accomplishes good air exchange in only the upper chest. Even though one may be breathing faster and harder, less oxygen may actually be getting to the blood because the lower portions of the lungs are not being effectively utilized.

Use of the diaphragm should be accentuated in order to breathe deeply. The proper mechanics of inhalation can be checked by placing one hand just below the belly button and the other hand on the side of the chest. When making a maximum inhalation, the lower hand should feel the abdomen swell forward. Near the completion of the inhalation, and only then, the upper hand should feel the front face of the chest expand forward as the final amount of air is drawn into the lungs.

And just as the inhalation began with the diaphragm, so should the exhalation end with the diaphragm. It is exceedingly important to expel the maximum amount of air from the lungs in order to make room for the maximum amount of incoming fresh air. In actuality, only deep, diaphragm-controlled breathing should be utilized. An inhalation involving the upper chest should be discouraged.

Breathing deeply and utilizing the lower portions of the lungs can best be accomplished by breathing through the nose. This forces the diaphragm muscle to control the action. One should make a strong effort to continue breathing through only the nose even as the exertion level increases and more oxygen is needed. Adhesive strips designed to expand the nostrils can be of help here. Breathing through the mouth should only be initiated when the narrow nasal passages do not allow the passage of sufficient air to meet demand. Even when breathing through the mouth, breathing deeply from the diaphragm is still imperative.

When doing a resistance workout in the exercise room, breathing should be done in the same tempo as the exercise; exhaling through pursed lips and creating a pressure within the lungs during the muscle contraction portion of the exercise, and inhaling during the muscle extension portion. The creation of pressure within the lungs aids in getting oxygen into the blood stream, and then to the working muscles. This will also assist the athlete to continue working within his aerobic zone, the work zone where oxygen deprivation does not become a controlling factor.

One must acknowledge that there is a health risk involved when the breathing apparatus is intentionally altered (such as exhaling through pursed lips) in order to increase pressure within the body. Later, this technique will also be relied upon during specific phases of the sprint. This could put some individuals at risk for a catastrophic circulatory failure. Prior to using this technique, the runner should discuss it thoroughly with one's medical professional.

When sprinting (with some exceptions that will be detailed later), we have a totally different condition for optimal breathing than we had when doing resistance exercises. One should not attempt to apply breathing rules used in the exercise room to this event. Sprinting is an anaerobic event. Here, the athlete is using up oxygen at such a rate that it is impossible for the pulmonary/cardiovascular system to replace the oxygen as fast as it is being consumed. Much of the race is run utilizing the oxygen stores that are already in the body. The athlete builds up an oxygen deficit and then replaces it after the race is over. Of course, the runner begins the replacement of oxygen while still running the race.

The first several steps of the race will be made while holding one's breath. The steps taken for this early acceleration are extremely forceful. One will naturally hold in that final pre-start inhalation as an aid to getting the most from the body during those first several steps. Temporarily holding one's breath can be utilized to cause a rise of one's internal pressure and thereby provide a short-term maximum output of body strength. Do not consciously hold the breath longer than the body naturally wants to.

Subsequently, after normal breathing has been resumed for several steps, a single conscious and forceful exhalation will promote both deep breathing and relaxation. This exhalation should be made as forcefully as possible and be completed as quickly as possible. Then, just relax and let the lungs refill naturally. One does not have to force the lungs to refill with air. They will do that quite well without any conscious effort to bring it about.

When running, the most efficient cycle of breathing has absolutely nothing to do with the most efficient cycle of leg turnover. Any attempt to coordinate the tempo of the two would only result in one, or both, changing to a less efficient rate. Make no attempt to coordinate an exhalation with a foot plant. They are separate bodily actions. Let them occur at tempos that are best suited for them individually. Also, do not attempt to take excessively large inhalations. Once you are up and running, let your breathing apparatus do its thing—naturally. Your attention is now better directed toward making your four limbs achieve their best racing action.

Check Out the Feet and Legs

Now, let us look at basic body mechanics. We will start with the feet. For this demonstration we need to take off the shoes and socks, then stand erect on a hard level surface. Let's take a close look at those feet.

Place the feet together side by side, toes pointing straight ahead, ankles touching each other. Now raise up onto the toes; I mean put some serious weight onto the pads of the toes. Now look down at your feet. Those pathetic little toes on the outer sides of the feet are struggling to do what you have asked of them. Not a very reassuring sight. OK, back down onto the heels. Now spread the feet apart sideways leaving 8 or 10 inches clear between them, making certain they continue pointing straight ahead. Now raise up onto the toes again. The larger more powerful toes on the inner sides of the feet have assumed most of the load, and are handling it with ease. Now tell me, if you're looking for a strong powerful push off from your foot, which foot position would you use? This is not a difficult choice. Remember these images while on the track and deciding the lateral distance between foot plants with which you will run. We will address this issue again in a later chapter. Oh yes, back down onto your heels again.

Our next parlor demonstration will require a heavy object such as a brick. Place the brick on the floor and stand facing it. Raise one foot off the floor and balance on the other. (It's OK to hold onto something for balance.) With the free foot, try to slide the brick sideways across the floor by using only the side of the big toe. Not the side of the foot, the side of the toe. Careful, don't struggle too hard; you may injure yourself. An attempt to move the brick in the opposite direction with the side of the little toe would prove even more futile. It is apparent that our toes (and by the same reasoning, our feet) have relatively little strength in a sideways direction. Now stand just in front of the brick. With the under side of the big toe, push the brick backward. Same brick. Same toe. Suddenly, the task has become very easy.

The lesson here is to use the foot in the manner and direction of its greatest natural strength. Just as the hands and fingers have their greatest strength in the clenching action, so do the feet and toes have their greatest strength when pushing in the rearward direction. If the foot is turned sideways to any degree, the runner becomes dependent upon a more sideways use of the foot and toes during push off. The full power of the foot cannot be developed if it were to be used in that orientation. Use the foot in the manner it works best, pointing straight ahead.

So, think about your foot plant. Better yet, think of what orientation you want for the foot as it pushes off from the track. Hopefully, you are convinced you want the push off to take place with the toes pointing straight ahead. Therefore, you must be absolutely certain that you orient the foot with the toes pointing straight ahead at the moment of touchdown. The spikes on the shoes prevent any reorientation of the foot between touchdown and takeoff.

Take stock of your running muscles. The combined mass and strength of all these muscles is quite large. But take note. If the power of these running muscles is to be used to propel you forward, their drive must be channeled through that small portion of the foot between the ball and the ends of the toes. That is the only part of the body that comes in contact with the track, and only on a momentary basis at that. The handling of all that power, in addition to the impact caused by the body's weight, is a lot to ask of that small portion of the body. Treat it with respect. Plant the foot on the track so it can properly do its job and give you the powerful push forward you are looking for.

Sprinting is not a sport for only the legs. It requires a full effort from all of the body. Do not undermine the effort of your entire body by directing its power through foot muscles that were not intended to take this load. Ensure the foot plant is made so that all power will be most efficiently directed to the track. The toes should be pointing straight ahead, the foot location should move outward from the body centerline and pass under the hip joint, and maximum use should be made of the stronger muscles located on the inner side of the foot. Note that incidental contact of the runner's heel is discounted for the purpose of this discussion since it applies virtually no weight to the surface of the track.

Let us begin to move our focus upward. Your foot placement is critical, but even if you do it correctly, its value can be quickly negated if one permits the knee to splay outward. It is not uncommon to see a runner's knee point outward, particularly at the start of a race.

To illustrate, hold onto a stationary object for balance. Stand erect with the feet several inches apart, pointing them straight ahead. Raise one foot only one inch off the ground by flexing the knee. Now, while keeping the foot in that same location, move that knee outward. As you can see, if you were to make or break contact with the track with the leg in this orientation, the lower leg would be at an angle to the track. You would be forcing yourself to run on the small outer toes instead of the large inner toe. Your push off power would be reduced. Power is also further lost because it must follow the bent path from the foot, outward to the knee and back in again to the hip, instead of traveling in a straighter path directly under the hip. More bad news, the outward splayed knee also adds a twisting tendency to the torso.

Keep toes, ankle, knee and hip joint in alignment. This is the most efficient conduit for the transfer of power between body and track. If any portion of that system strays sideways, quickness and power will be lost. Keep the path as straight as possible.

As a check on yourself to see how well the legs are kept in alignment, put on shorts and stand facing a full-length mirror. Do a few rapid high knee lifts. Check to see if the hip, knee and foot all remain in a vertical plane. While not necessarily so, if they stay in alignment here they will hopefully also do so when running. But we must acknowledge, it is much more difficult to maintain this form under the pressure of running. Primarily use the mirror practice to get the feel of what it's like when done correctly. For comparison, feel what it's like when done incorrectly (knees splayed outward). At the track, explain to a friend that you would like to check your knee alignment. Have the alignment viewed from the front during a high-speed run. If there is a problem with the knees, it's back to the mirror and more high-speed practice.

Learn to get the feel of doing it right and carry that mental information with you when you return to the track. Leg strengthening exercises done with the leg in correct alignment can be a big help here. Powerful legs are a necessity for good speed, but once you've developed the power don't waste it. Keep all in alignment. Everything you own should be pointing toward the finish line. That's the direction in which you want to propel your body.

Check Out the Arms

When one is running, the legs move alternately forward and backward. As each leg moves, it develops a momentum that also alternates forward and backward. These actions, if left unchecked, would introduce an alternating twisting action to the torso, first clockwise then counterclockwise. This twisting action would be counterproductive to the running effort.

The main role of the arms is to develop a momentum that acts in the opposite direction from the legs, so the torso twist is reduced to zero. We must therefore use the arms in such a manner as to best perform this function. We will delve into momentum of the limbs in greater detail in a later chapter, but for now let us proceed on the basis that this function of the arms seems reasonable. The torso should remain stable with only the arms and legs moving.

While it is true the arms do not directly move us down the track as do the legs, do not underestimate their importance. The author believes there are many sprinters who have unnecessarily limited their maximum speed, not because their legs will carry them no faster, but because of improper use of the arms. An insufficient swinging action of the arms will limit the speed with which your legs can drive you forward. How then can we maximize the effectiveness of the arms in this role? Two basic ways to improve effectiveness of the arm motion are as follows.

The first way is to make a conscientious effort to swing the upper arm further to the rear. The shoulders must be kept low in order to maximize this rearward swing. Greater amplitude of the upper arm swing will increase the effectiveness of the arm. As part of a long-range training program, and also as part of the daily warm up, one should work toward keeping the shoulder joint flexible. The more nearly one can raise the upper arm to a horizontal position rearward, the greater and the freer will be the arm swing.

The second way to improve effectiveness of the arm is to move the arm swing *slightly* further away from your side. Note that as one experiments with a wider foot plant, the elbows must also move slightly outward. As the swinging momentum of the legs moves outward from the body centerline, so also must the swinging momentum of the arms. Allow a little more air to pass between the elbows and the sides.

When a change is made to the swinging path of the elbow, a similar change must be made to the swinging path of the forearm. If the elbows move slightly outward, the wrists must move outward with them. The forearm must be maintained in one vertical plane and pointing forward. The runner should not let any arm crossover creep into the running form. Any sideways motion will steal fore-and-aft effectiveness from the arm swing. On the other hand, do not move the wrists too far outward. The path of the wrist should *never* be permitted to be further from one's side than is the path of the elbow. Do not permit hands or elbows to flail about; keep all under control and in alignment.

It would be wise to check the equality of your arm swings. If you are right-handed, stand with your right side facing a mirror. Move the right arm slowly in a running motion, looking for correct form. Make sure the elbow travels the full distance to the rear; keep the complete arm in fore-and-aft alignment. The hand should be carried lower on the back swing and higher on the forward swing. Now increase the turnover rate until you reach your maximum without losing form or decreasing the amplitude of the swing. Get the feel of this motion while using your stronger arm. This will set the standard to which you will compare the next routine.

Now turn around and perform the same routine with the other arm. This nondominant arm will most probably be less able to perform this exercise as well as the dominant arm. Strength and coordination will, in all likelihood, not be present to the same degree in both arms. Some differences should be expected here. But, if one should discover a large difference, some attention should be given to this aspect of the running picture. If one arm has significant difficulty with this exercise, it needs to be practiced. Remember, even a basic inequality such as this can be improved if practiced regularly and conscientiously.

Exercise by moving both arms in a precise pattern. Strive to make the movement in both arms, although alternating, identical. Without good strength and coordination in *both* arms, one will have difficulty developing the necessary swinging momentum needed from these upper limbs. This examination may seem extremely elementary, but it will take only a few minutes of your time and should be checked. You may find cause for concern about a problem that you did not know existed. If necessary, the arms can be worked with and improved, in order to maintain a smooth relaxed form when running at the higher speeds. If you don't take the time to check your swing, what you don't know *can* hurt you. Remember, if you find a deficiency, it can be improved.

If, at times, you have a tendency to drift to one side of your lane, do not overlook the possibility that unequal arm action could be responsible for unequal leg action. If the two leg actions are not equal, it can be difficult to run in a straight line.

It may also be worth your while to evaluate the turnover rate of your arm swing. Try this exercise. Stand facing the mirror to make certain the form of your arm swing remains in conformity with typical running motions. On this occasion, you will rapidly perform a given number of arm swings and note the time required to complete these swings. Do you know the number of strides you take when running the 100m? Utilize this number if you know it; otherwise take your best guess, perhaps 50, 55?

Utilizing a clock or watch that indicates seconds, time how long it takes you to complete the number of arm swings that corresponds to the number of strides you take when running the 100m race. (It may be easier to count the swings of just one arm and read the clock when the count reaches one half the total number of strides required to run 100 meters.) In this exercise, the objective is to swing the arms as rapidly as possible while still maintaining optimum form. The time registered would represent the best 100m time that your arms could support if you had a flying start and ran full speed the entire way. Add perhaps one second to this time to compensate for real world conditions of running 100 meters from a standing start.

These are approximate figures only, but if the result of this exercise shows that the time that has elapsed in order to accomplish the above noted number of arm swings is anywhere near that which you actually clock when running the race, you then must logically ask yourself the question, "Is it possible that my arm turnover rate is curtailing my leg turnover rate and thereby controlling my race time?" This would indeed be a strange circumstance for an event we have always called a foot race. The arms have an important job to do. Do not overlook their conditioning.

Utilize the Weight Room

One should make extensive use of the weight room. Here, we can concentrate on those arm and leg muscles that are directly used in running. One should not forget the kickback action. Include exercises that challenge both the folding and the unfolding of the knee when in the fully flexed position. These exercises should include the position with the foot nearly touching the buttock, replicating the action encountered in running. Exercises for the quadriceps and the hamstring are a must. It is important to develop exercises that mimic as closely as possible those motions that will be used when running.

This book loosely refers to upper quadriceps and lower quadriceps muscles. Quadriceps is the term applied to the set of four muscles that run the full length of the thigh. The Vastus Lateralis and the Vastus Medialis muscles have their meaty portion at their lower ends and are referred to as the lower quads. The Vastus Intermedius and the Rectus Femorus muscles have their meaty portion at their upper ends and are referred to as the upper quads. However, do not concentrate on only those muscles used to pull a limb in one direction. Proper balance must be maintained between opposing muscles. An imbalance of muscle power is not only detrimental to optimal performance, it can also lead to injury.

One should not overlook the benefits of strengthening the arms and shoulders. With one's back to the weight machine, take a handgrip in each hand. The starting position for this exercise is with the arm extended well to the rear. Keeping the arm straight, but the elbow unlocked, the hand is swung forward in an arc against a resistance until it is well out in front, then returned to the starting position. The intent of this exercise is to provide sufficient strength in the shoulder and upper arm so the runner will be capable of swinging the forearm further rearward and still be able to return it forward at a sufficiently fast pace so as to not inhibit the turnover rate. An under appreciation of arm action may lead to an underperformance of leg action. Work conscientiously with the arms. Swinging both arms in an alternating motion while the torso remains unsupported will simultaneously incorporate one's core muscles into this exercise.

Do not concentrate on strengthening the limbs to the exclusion of the body trunk. Core strength is vital if the full potential of strong limbs is to be realized. The limbs do not work completely independent of each other; they are interconnected through the body hub. A strong central body is essential if limb strength is to be transformed into speed. Good core strength provides a firmer platform for support of the working limbs. This allows for a crisper movement of the arms and legs, optimizing their effectiveness.

Proper breathing must be incorporated as part of each resistance exercise. A generous inhalation is performed during the muscle extension portion of the exercise. Then, a measured exhalation through pursed lips during the muscle contraction portion of the exercise. This is intended to elevate the air pressure in the lungs and enhance one's oxygen absorption into the blood. Get to feel comfortable with this routine of breathing; it will enhance your maximum-exertion actions.

Exercise is intended to improve and enhance our physical capability. (It will also improve overall health, increase mental alertness and provide a psychological boost.) If there is a specific goal you want to achieve through exercise, one's exercise should be conducted with that goal in mind. For a runner, the accomplishment of lifting a certain amount of weight or of performing a particular number of repetitions is not the end goal. Running faster is the end goal. We only exercise so that we can reach our *running* goal. Therefore, when fatigue caused by an exercise exceeds the body's ability to properly respond to it, the exercise is no longer performing its intended function. Too strenuous an exercise can be detrimental to achieving our goal of running faster. It can even be potentially dangerous. We sometimes allow our competitive urges to surpass our sense of good judgment. Keep in mind that common sense and objectivity should never be surrendered just to accomplish a meaningless number in the weight room. Make certain your exercise routine is doing its intended job.

Exercise Outside the Weight Room

Remember, sprinting is a sport in which the entire body is utilized and it must therefore be properly conditioned in its totality. But all strengthening exercises do not necessarily have to be performed in the weight room. Much good work can also be done at home. One exercise that has been found helpful in strengthening the abdominal and upper quad muscles is the balanced crunch. In this exercise, one lies flat on the back with legs extended, and with no other support simultaneously raises and brings together the upper legs and the torso. The body weight remains balanced on the buttocks. As the legs are brought upward, the knees are flexed progressively more so that they are fully bent when the upper legs and the torso come together in a nearly vertical position. The arms do not actively participate in this exercise but are utilized only to maintain balance. When doing reps of this exercise, the arms and legs do not touch the floor.

Diagonal crunches are a good exercise for the abdomen. These are done lying face up on the floor. The feet are flat on the floor, in close to the buttocks. With the hands clasped behind the neck, the shoulders are raised off the floor while keeping the soles of both feet firmly planted on the floor. Do not attempt to keep the upper body straight; starting with the head, the spine should begin to roll up like a rug. As the shoulders begin to rise, a twist at the waist is performed so that one shoulder is pointed toward the opposite knee. At the same time, the knees are leaned sideways in the direction opposite from the shoulders, to accentuate the twist at the waist. The succeeding crunch will twist oppositely.

A different version of the crunch, the high crunch, can be performed as follows. One sits on the floor with knees bent approximately 90° and the feet placed comfortably on the floor. The starting position is with the torso vertical. The exercise begins by twisting the upper body in one direction as much as one's flexibility will allow. In this twisted position, lean backward and then recover to the vertical. During this exercise, the torso muscles are continuously stressed in order to maintain the maximum degree of twist. Repeat. The intent here is to exercise the abdominal muscles in the contracted mode rather than being extended as in the standard crunch. Then, the same when twisted in the opposite direction.

The back muscles can be strengthened by lying face down on the floor with the arms extended overhead. The exercise is to repeatedly arch the back and raise arms and legs off the floor. A more challenging form of this exercise is to hold the back in the arched position and repeatedly swing the arms and legs out sideways while not letting them touch the floor.

The sides of the torso can be strengthened with an exercise that starts with the runner lying on one side on the floor. From here, the free leg is kept straight and raised as high as possible. Hold for a count of 5 and then lower the leg. Aim for the highest lift possible at each leg raise. A suitable weight can be added to the ankle to make this more challenging.

For strengthening the lower quads, deep knee bends are an excellent exercise. These can be performed either two-legged or one-legged, depending upon the advancement of the individual. One should not let a lack of balance detract from the performance of this exercise. To remove the aspect of balance, one can stand in a standard 3-foot wide doorway and face into either room. Move slightly backward so that the toes are just an inch or two behind the doorway (into the room at the athlete's back). The arms, which are extended downward, are swung outward and forward until the fingertips make contact with the corner of the doorway.

Do not place the feet too close together; a foot position directly under each hip is good. Now, raise up onto the toes and with a slight forward lean, the fingers will supply a steadying force as they press against the near corners of the doorway. Now the deep knee bends can be performed, concentrating only on the building of strength in the legs. If one is doing this exercise utilizing both legs, it is important to concentrate upon making both legs contribute an equal amount to the effort. If one leg is stronger, this exercise will help close the gap between the stronger and the weaker one. Do not allow the knees to point outward. Keep the knees and the feet pointing straight ahead, the same configuration we want to maintain during the sprint. If one's balance is good, doing deep knee bends *free* is even better.

When building leg strength, a few partial deep knee bends performed on just one leg are infinitely better than just doing a greater number of full deep knee bends on both legs. Utilize the depth of bend that most challenges your present leg strength. Do not go so low that you cannot recover to a standing position. But, do not settle for a position where the knees are bent merely 90 degrees if you are capable of going deeper.

If you are going to do squats, do them in a manner whereby you will derive the maximum benefit from them. Do a full squat; lower yourself all the way down s-l-o-w-l-y. Your quads will feel the difference, and you will thank them for their performance on race day. When raising up from a full squat, the objective is to make the action as quick and as explosive as possible. This is what will enable you to drive your way out of the blocks in a posture that enhances rapid acceleration. When raising up from each full squat, think quick; think strength; think winning.

Another suggested exercise is to face a wall and place both hands flat against the wall. Back the feet away from the wall approximately 3' or 4'. This will incline the body while the arms are held horizontal from the shoulder to the wall. With the feet flat on the floor, adjust the angle of the elbows to control the angle of lean and lean forward. One should feel a good stretch in the back of the lower leg. After performing this stretch, adjust the angle of lean so that there is only a light stretch in the lower leg.

Now, while in this incline, stand on only one foot. Raise quickly up onto the toes, then let yourself back down slowly. At the instant the heel touches the floor, raise up again as quickly as possible. Repeat. A quick strong upward motion is what we are looking for here. Raise up as high as possible, putting as much weight onto the pads of the toes as they can handle. Do similarly with the opposite leg. This is good practice for the push off action of the running stride.

Shoulder strength can be improved with a simple 6-count exercise. Stand erect and keep the arms straight throughout this exercise. Starting with the arms down at the sides: 1—Raise arms to the horizontal, pointing outward. 2—Raise arms so they point vertically upward. 3—Swing arms down to the horizontal position 1. 4—Swing arms forward so they point straight ahead. 5—Swing arms back to position 1. 6—Return arms to the sides. Repeat the sequence. Each arm movement should be brisk and distinct, with a momentary hold in each position. One motion per second is a good pace. This exercise can be made sufficiently challenging by holding an appropriate weight in each hand.

Pushups are also useful in improving general arm and shoulder strength.

Swinging the arms rapidly forward and backward in a running motion more specifically targets the muscles used in running. Holding weights in the hands will enhance this exercise. Opt for lighter weights and a faster swing rather than heavier weights and a slower swing.

Another exercise can be performed while seated. Raise the legs and lock the knees with the legs extended horizontally forward. Keeping the leg muscles tensed, separate the legs so that the feet are perhaps 2' apart. Now close the legs so that the feet are about 6" apart. Repeat the opening and closing of the legs. This motion is now sped up. The objective here is to alternately open and close the legs in as rapid a motion as possible. This action uses the weight of the legs and brings into play those muscles on the sides of the legs that might otherwise be overlooked in your exercise regimen.

Another exercise can also be done while seated. Bend the foot downward as far as possible, then upward as far as possible. Repeatedly move the foot to its extreme up and down positions with a short hold at each extreme position. This can improve one's oft overlooked but much needed foot strength. The runner will find that opportunities also exist to perform many of these exercises in the work place. Training does not have to stop when one leaves the track.

When doing a particular exercise, the accomplishment of a high number of reps should not be one's goal. On the contrary, the derivation of most benefit from each rep should be one's goal. This, most probably, will result in a fewer number of reps being accomplished. The number of reps is not a goal; it is a tool to measure one's progress. Do not exercise for the sake of a tool; exercise for the sake of improving your running ability.

Running up stadium steps, two at a time, is a good exercise to improve one's drive power when coming out of the blocks. Maintain a high knee action during this routine. If difficulty is encountered in discerning which of the many steps is the next correct one to land on, and if the stadium is equipped with bench-type seating, running up the seats can be substituted for running up the steps. There are fewer objects for the eye to deal with here; therefore, it is easier to pick out the next point of touchdown.

Vertical jumping is an exercise that can be done almost anywhere. In inclement weather, it can be done indoors.

Springing sideways, alternately to the left and to the right, as if jumping from one side of a trampoline to the other, promotes quickness of foot.

Bicycling can afford a welcome change from running routines. This can be done as lightly or as vigorously as one chooses. When done lightly, bicycling can fit in nicely on the day following a strenuous running routine. This will provide the legs with an easy but stimulating exercise.

Jumping jacks will employ muscles that might otherwise be overlooked.

On practice days, episodes of jogging backward are good monotony breakers. They serve as an exercise to assist the body in its tune up phase. They also seem to fit in well as part of the cool down process and help reduce post-exercise stiffness. Unfortunately, this appears to be an underutilized routine.

Whether it is pushups or running laps, there must be a purpose to the exercise you are performing. And that purpose must always be central in your mind; do not waste your time by exercising with the body's senses in neutral. In this way, each exercise will be performed better and the desired result reached sooner. You are devoting a great deal of time and effort to this training. Make certain you conscientiously control it. Aim it in a manner that will reward you with the most improvement to your running.

The fast twitch fibers of the muscles are involved in a role that can be easily overlooked. Besides their use in propelling one forward, they are also called upon for the mundane duty of support. During the airborne portion of a runner's stride, the body is receiving no support from the track through the legs. Consequently, at the moment of touchdown, the body will be descending. This descending motion, when suddenly stopped upon touchdown, creates a stress we call impact. This impact force is in addition to the runner's weight. From a free-swinging non–weight-bearing motion, the leg must quickly resist the combined force of weight and impact at the instant the foot touches down.

To make this even more challenging: (1) The knee is somewhat bent at the moment of touchdown and (2) The foot is not directly under the body but is some distance in front of it. This is an awkward position in which to support oneself.

As the runner moves to a higher speed, the muscles must be conditioned to crisply perform this support function. This includes muscles in the foot, the leg and up to and including, the lower back. If the fast twitch muscle fibers do not immediately respond and support the body, the runner will have the sensation of weak legs that could betray their owner and allow a fall. This is not the proper setting for high-speed running.

Exercises in the weight room will not fully prepare the runner for this situation because the weight room accentuates development of the slow twitch strength fibers of the muscles. Hopping on one foot, with the knee somewhat flexed, is a better preparatory exercise. But, there is no substitute that is equal to a run on the track. The ability for fast twitch muscle fibers to perform their required duty can be readily achieved. Work on it if you need to. Your advancement as a sprinter will be curtailed until this capability is achieved.

If it is determined that additional work is required for the fast twitch muscle fibers to properly *take hold* upon touchdown, do not be overly aggressive. If there is any unsteadiness, this is an opportunity for injury to occur. Avoid running the curve for the time being. Take only what the body has to offer right now. Don't lose sight of the fact this is a developmental period. Train intelligently and the body will soon afford you what you need.

If one chooses to include a walk in the weekly routine, this will afford the body a welcome rest and also encourage a plentiful supply of blood for the rebuilding process. It should not, however, provide an exit route for the good form techniques one has preached to the body all week. Ordinary walking can become good-form walking. Keep head erect, shoulders low, a free and easy swing to the arms, path of elbows moved slightly outward, no crossover action of the hands and forearms, stomach in, hips slightly lowered and swung forward, smart knee action as each leg is brought forward, a soft foot plant with a hint of wider stance, pronounced ankle bend and toe bend for the push off. Breathe from the nose to the diaphragm. One's body should be happy with the stride length and walking tempo.

There is no reason many features of this style of walking cannot be implemented as a normal way of life. Practice it every day and eventually it will become your natural walk. This *everyday-logic* should be incorporated into one's daily living as much as is practical. The greater extent that good technique becomes our norm, the fewer errors we will make on race day. If you're serious about running, be serious every day.

Allow the Brain to Assist

The human brain is an amazing machine. It does many things for us; we may not even be cognizant of many. Take, for instance, an afternoon visit to the grocery store at the local shopping plaza. An empty parking stall is found near one end of the parking lot. After leaving the car, one then walks diagonally from the stall and across the driveway that runs in front of the store. For some unknown reason, the eyes fixate on a single point of the curb that separates the driveway from the walkway at the storefront. This point is no different from any other point along the curb, but the eyes have picked out this one point. One walks diagonally toward this point while continuing to look at it. When this point of the curb is arrived at, it is found that one can step up perfectly onto the curb with no change in stride.

Without our even realizing it, the mind has calculated exactly where along the curb one must aim so that the distance to it exactly corresponds with our stride length. This is all taken for granted without a moment's appreciation of what the brain has just done for us. If the author had attempted to calculate this problem mathematically, the store would have closed for the night before the answer was obtained.

The mere acts of walking, sitting down, opening a book, reading the printed words, converting those words to useful knowledge, creating a mental image of yourself performing certain actions, the execution of those motions, all require the application of brain power. The mind is a wonderful thing. Appreciate it. Allow it to work for you in everything you do. Be vitally aware of the working relationship between mind and body. The application of this interrelation can make you a better runner.

A masterful work of art sets itself apart from the ordinary by the artistry incorporated in the smallest of details. And so it also is with running. If one's goal is to be an ordinary runner, then ordinary attention to technique will be quite adequate. But if one wants to become a superior runner, then extraordinary attention to the details of each and every technique is called for.

Even if you are still working on the fundamentals of improving your strength and quickness, close attention can also be devoted to incorporating the many details of good running form. Then, as your physical attributes approach fruition, the proper techniques will be automatically incorporated. Begin now to search for the techniques you will want to retain in your running form. This will give you more time to practice with them. So undertake now the process of *feeling* your form as you train. Become cognizant of what each of your body parts is doing. *Practice visualizing your running form.* Develop a heightened awareness of the many messages going in and out of the brain. No one gets all of them, but we can get some. Allow yourself to *feel* what your limbs are doing. Once you are able to successfully employ this training technique, you will be on the road toward your goal of becoming a better runner.

Put It Together on the Track

Checking the details of one's running form before ever leaving the house can be a major help in finding what may be potential trouble spots when taking to the track. Also, frequent visits to the weight room are a *must* in building muscle strength. But remember, there is no real substitute for going to the track and running.

If you need to practice getting out of the blocks more powerfully, you must repeatedly put your body through that routine in order to hone your form, timing and coordination. If you need to improve your acceleration, you must do many repeats of the quick, driving strides necessary to quickly build up speed. If you are looking to raise the bar of your top speed, you must work on the arm and leg techniques that will bring you that greater speed. Challenge your fast twitch muscle fibers to begin the acceleration of every limb movement.

In short, your muscles must be conditioned to perform the specific functions that are necessary for your particular event. This is done in practice sessions where the muscles are exposed to the rigors of what will be expected of them during competition. In this manner, and *only* in this manner, will the muscles begin to understand how they must perform so that the entire body will operate to the level of your expectations.

To improve your running, practice your running. This is how the required skills are developed to become a better sprinter. So, take to the track and practice. Afterward, think about the results you achieved and prepare a new plan for tomorrow. The next day, take to the track and practice again— smarter!

4

THE WARM UP

In this chapter, the meaning of the term "warm up" is expanded to also include stretching and the final tune up. These latter two topics are treated separately after the section dealing with the jog that is used specifically to warm up.

The Jog

The jog is great for warm ups and cool downs. But the jog can be a good time to practice one's form. While putting in the laps in order to warm up and reach the stretching phase of the workout, the runner can also be thinking ahead to what has been planned for the day. Too often the jog time is relegated to just putting in so many laps, at the end of which we know the body will be sufficiently warmed up to proceed to the next phase of running preparation. Don't just trudge through your laps. You can do better than that.

One's time on the track should be made as profitable as possible. During the jog, it is important to stay relaxed. But this doesn't mean becoming a formless glob of jello. The jogging form should be such that one's speed could be gradually increased all the way to maximum without a major change in form. There are, of course, some differences. In the jog, the heel of the foot strikes the track, but the foot should quickly roll and transfer weight onto the ball of the foot. If this doesn't seem to work well at a slow jog, shorten the stride and increase the turnover rate.

Relaxing while engaged in the jog is best accomplished if the mind is also relaxed. The jog should not be viewed as a challenge that must be overcome. Better to think of it as a pleasant day in the fresh air and sunshine, and you are fortunate enough to be in this place at this time to enjoy it. When the mind is relaxed, a greater relaxation will pervade the rest of the body. This allows one to receive a greater benefit from not only the jog, but also the practice session to follow.

The warm up jog is an excellent occasion to simultaneously practice one's running form. Be cognizant of what the various body parts are doing. Feet are to be kept pointing straight ahead. Do not let the feet land under the body centerline, but keep them spread moderately apart. When the feet move laterally outward, so must the elbows also move outward. The hands should not be allowed to excessively drop; keep the elbows crooked. Hand swing should be predominantly fore-and-aft. Fingers can be slightly curled to assist in avoiding upper body tension, but no slack in the wrists. The hand should have a gentle flare outward at the wrist; fingers that are slightly curled will then remain in alignment with the forearm. Flex the wrist in the direction of the arm swing; this technique improves the usefulness of that arm swing. Shoulders must not be hunched; shoulders, and consequently the elbows, should be low.

Concentrate on the entire movement being smooth. We are practicing those techniques here that we will be using later during high-speed runs. More smoothness here will bring more smoothness at higher speeds. Try to become detached from your body and visualize yourself from an out-of-body perspective. Search for faults in your form so you can concentrate on correcting them. Strive for an effortless fluid motion.

When satisfied with your jogging form, begin thinking about the stretching phase ahead. Mentally note any changes you may want to implement in your training routine today. Think about something other than your jogging form for a few minutes. Then, after a period of time, return your thoughts to the jog and reanalyze your form. See what bad habits you may have slipped into while your mind was distracted by other thoughts. This can highlight areas of one's running form that may need special attention. Also, these same bad tendencies may return near the end of a race when one is tired and holding form is more difficult, but at no time is it more important.

Once we are aware of bad tendencies, we are in a far better position to guard against them. Use your jogging time wisely. Start right here to iron out any wrinkles in your running form by always practicing good running techniques. Develop good habits in the jog and they will serve you well later on.

Some sprinters refrain from the warm up jog because of the numbing effect it appears to have on the quick muscle response needed for high-speed work. The author believes this negative effect of the jog is due, at least in part, to the repeated impact of the foot striking the track. This impact is transmitted through the foot, to the knees, the hips, and subsequently to the spine. This can have long-term negative effects on the skeleton.

But the short-term effects of these impacts include the response required of the leg muscles to immediately support the body. This requirement for the muscles to support the body begins at the moment of the heel strike. The leg and its muscles must instantly transition from a free-swinging state to a supporting member that must also resist the force of impact. The harder and sharper is the heel strike, the more abrupt must be the muscle response to take on the newly invoked responsibility to support the body upon each foot's touchdown. During a jog, the rapid and repeated tensing of the leg muscles, which is occurring in order to assume the load of the body upon each touchdown, takes its toll on the fast twitch muscle fibers. Later, we will be relying on these fast twitch muscle fibers for a good performance in the sprint.

Therefore, when jogging, concentrate on a soft touchdown. Land with a knee that is already slightly flexed. Imagine that your bones are made of glass, and you don't want to fracture one. An additional body-friendly approach to the jog is to slightly drop the hips and sling them somewhat forward. This will engender a softer foot strike that should be immediately noticeable to the runner. This is good practice, for we will want to later incorporate this technique in our sprinting form.

But primarily, a softer touchdown provides a longer time interval for the leg muscles to respond and begin supporting the full load of the body. This, in turn, lessens the drain on our limited supply of fast twitch muscle fibers. Considering the high number of times the episode of a foot strike will occur during a person's jog, this fast twitch saver is worth considering. By employing a softer touchdown, the runner can now proceed with the warm up jog with less fear of the slowing repercussions otherwise incurred during the performance of this activity.

Use your jogging time to best advantage. Think about any mistakes you may have made on your last race day, and reinforce your ideas about how to prevent any recurrence. Think about some technique you may want to try differently today. Think through the training plan for the day. During the jog, mimic as closely as possible the form with which you intend to run. Visualize your jogging form from some vantage point outside your body. Is this the form you want to run with? Work toward improving your running form, even as you jog. Make the most of this opportunity to improve your game. A mild perspiration will be your clue that the jog is performing its primary function; your body temperature is rising.

The Stretch

There have been studies performed to evaluate the effectiveness of the stretch in preventing injury. Studies are good in that they provide insight to the subject topic. But one should be wary when making the jump from providing insight to drawing a conclusion. There are many variables in a study: the sport in which the test persons were involved, associated warm up routines that were or were not engaged in, the ages of the persons in the study and the conditioning their bodies were subjected to in the years leading up to the study. You would be extremely fortunate if the conditions of a reliable study closely matched the conditions of your life. The reader is urged to use his own judgment when deciding how to best utilize the results of a study, especially if it would involve changing an established pattern.

Proper warm up is essential to reducing the risk of injury when preparing to undertake a physically demanding event. What would be considered proper warm up for an athlete engaged in one sport would be different from what would be considered proper warm up for an athlete engaged in a different sport. For the sprinter, proper warm up has three phases: the jog, the stretch and the tune up. Their sum total is what constitutes the warm up. We have just discussed the jog, which we used in order to warm the body's muscles above their resting temperature. Now we will discuss the stretch, which we use in order to stretch the major running muscles beyond their resting length.

We use the stretch to gradually elongate the muscles to a length that is somewhat beyond where they will be taken when we subject them to the rigors of the sprint. The stretching routine is a controlled environment where we slowly condition the muscles to accept these extended lengths. If we feel pain, we can back off. If we feel stiffness, we can hold here until the muscles are comfortable with proceeding further. If we were to engage in the sprint without having gone through this safety zone, the risk of injury quickly escalates. For the performance of our sporting event, we must be aware of not only the degree to which the muscles will be stretched, but also the quickness and intensity with which they will be contracted. The warm up is intended to safely arouse the muscles from their sleep mode. Proper clothing should be worn to reduce the inevitable cooling of the body while performing stretching activities.

The muscles that are being stretched should be totally relaxed. For this reason, stretching should be done in a sitting or lying down position whenever possible. In these positions, the foot, leg and lower back muscles do not have to assist in balancing or supporting the body while they are being stretched. This enables these muscles to fully relax, and in this manner the stretching can be more effective.

There is no such thing as a partially tensed muscle *fiber*. When a *muscle* is merely moderately tensed, only a portion of its fibers are brought into play. Those fibers that are brought into play are fully tensed while the remaining fibers are fully relaxed. Each fiber is similar to a light switch; it is either on or off. Depending on how much strength will be needed from the entire muscle, the brain instructs how many fibers will be tensed. If stretching is performed while in the standing position, a leg muscle being stretched will contain some fibers that are relaxed and other fibers that are tensed in order to support the body. This is not the optimum condition for the stretch. Rather than standing, a sitting or lying down position with all the muscle fibers relaxed provides a more appropriate setting for the stretching phase of the warm up.

A large beach towel can be laid out for the stretching routine. If the ground is wet, a plastic shower curtain can be added under the towel. Perhaps a dry area under the grandstand can be utilized instead. The author failed to do this one drizzly day during training, and skimped on stretching. During a short high-speed run, the plantar fascia in the bottom of the foot was torn. A three-month hiatus from running was then taken while it healed. A thorough long-range effort plus the daily stretching of feet and toes can be helpful in preventing this injury.

Stretching helps condition the muscles for the physical workout to come, whether that be to improve strength, endurance, coordination, quick contraction or the often overlooked quick relaxation of the muscles. Contracting muscles should not have to work against opposing muscles that are slow in relaxing.

Depending upon the athlete's muscular conditioning, stretching can be the single major deterrent to injury. The novice athlete is more prone to injury if stretching is ignored than is the more experienced athlete who has already worked at conditioning the muscles. The emphasis herein is directed toward those runners who are still in the conditioning phase of their training program. Additionally, stretching takes on an even greater importance in older athletes. As one's muscle conditioning improves, each stretch position can be reduced to a hold of 10–15 seconds as compared to a 20–30 second hold in the early stages of training.

When stretching of the body's soft tissues is begun, it should be done with the expectation that the left-side limbs and the right-side limbs will not move to exactly similar positions. For example, the right leg should not be stretched to a particular position solely because the left leg has just been stretched to such a position. Treat each muscle as an individual; learn its capabilities and also its needs. The muscles on one's weaker side may be more pliable than muscles on the stronger side. Tissue at the site of a previous injury will be less supple. Also, if a hard workout was performed on the previous day, expect the muscles to be more resistant to being stretched than they otherwise would. Strive to make left side and right side similar, but don't expect that this will occur naturally.

Remember, the goal here is not the contortion of one's body to the most extreme angles. The goal is to strive for the most sensible stretching of the muscles considering what it is you want them to do. Do not attempt to reach some predetermined arbitrary goal on any given day. A stretching routine that is too aggressive can lead to an injury that running a race would not. Do not tug or rock; this only invites injury. Stretch slowly and steadily. Just take what each part of the body is willing to relinquish on any given day. Do not lose sight of the primary goal—running—running without injury—running better!

Stretching to the point that it causes pain is counterproductive. A muscle's response to pain is to tighten. When stretching, close attention should be paid to how the muscles are responding to the stretch. The author is a proponent of moving each limb to a slightly less extreme position and holding that position for a longer period of time. Approach the stretching phase of the warm up with the understanding that one's muscles need this conditioning. Provide the time in your daily routine to do the job right.

The length of time spent stretching will depend upon the conditioning of the muscles. As the training season progresses and the muscles respond, less time will be needed to stretch out the muscles. On practice days, stretching should be performed to the extent that it takes the limbs well beyond the configurations that will be used in the sprint. While this may not encourage the fastest sprint today, remember this is a practice day. When the muscles are conditioned so they will readily accept this longer stretch on practice day, the stage is now properly set so the runner may perform only a cursory stretch on race day, and still stay out of the realm of a muscle injury.

Be of the mindset that this stretching routine on practice day is just as much a preparation for race day as are the running routines. On practice day, it is not necessary to impress anyone with one's race speed. We can therefore indulge in a more thorough and complete stretching routine. This procedure builds some reserve flexibility into our muscles so that on race day it will be permissible to perform only a brief stretching routine. In this manner, we will have brought a better-prepared body to the starting line on the day that it counts.

Regarding stretching routines, the hamstring, calf, Achilles and bottom of foot can all be stretched at one time by use of a light rope with a loop fastened in one end. Lying on one's back on the ground, the loop is placed over the toe of the shoe. The rope should bite into the tread of the shoe near its front. The leg is raised to a near vertical position, keeping the knee locked straight. Now a steady pull is applied to the rope with both hands.

The leg muscles should be relaxed as much as possible with only the rope holding the leg in the air. Lead the rope in the general direction of the same-side shoulder. One should be able to feel a good stretch in all the areas just mentioned. Depending on the body's needs, leading the rope slightly more horizontally will afford a stronger stretch to the hamstring; leading it slightly more vertically will afford a stronger stretch in the foot area. Do not lead the rope toward one side; always keep it in line with the leg being stretched. Work the other leg similarly.

The quadriceps can be stretched by lying on one's side. The bottom leg will be the passive leg in this stretch. Place it where it is comfortable, but will still provide stability from rolling of the body. Grab the ankle of the other leg with the same-side hand and pull the foot behind the body. More knee bend will stretch the lower quads; less knee bend will stretch the upper quads and lower abdomen.

Pull on the ankle, not the foot. Pulling on the foot will only put an unnecessary strain on the top of the foot. While holding this stretch, the same-side shoulder and the head are leaned backward. This will add stretch to muscles in the abdomen. Progress may be disappointingly slow, but stay with it. As we shall see later, this ability will allow a broader selection of running styles. However, the primary objective of this stretch is the ability to perform a complete kickback motion when running; one that sees the heel of the foot swing upward to the point it contacts the buttock.

If the big toe should rest on the ground to provide stability, that's fine. But do not let the toe become the anchor for the pull of the stretch. The stretch must be maintained by a strong pull on the ankle with the arm. This will avoid putting unnecessary sideways stress on the knee of the lower leg. At the conclusion of each individual stretch, before releasing your grip on the ankle, roll somewhat forward so that you are again lying fully on your side. Now, when you release your grip on the ankle, the foot can swing freely forward without scuffing against the ground. Scuffing the side of the foot against the ground puts a large and unnecessary sideways torque on the knee. Avoid placing lateral forces on the lower leg while the knee joint is being flexed. Your knees will thank you later by continuing to serve you well.

The lower abdominal muscles can also be stretched by going to a squat with a full bend of one knee. The other leg is extended to the rear, with knee locked straight and toes placed on the ground. Now raise the trunk, by bending at the waist, to as nearly a vertical position as possible. This will improve the ability of the leg to push off from a position well behind the runner. Take the time to perform adequate stretching of both sides of the body.

The groin can be stretched by sitting on the ground with the legs extended forward and spread apart. Now, with the hands, push on the ground from behind. Slowly, inch the entire body forward. This motion will force the heels (and legs) outward. Take it slowly and do not hesitate to back off if this causes pain. We want to stay clear of an injury.

The lower back can be worked by assuming a sitting position on the ground and bringing one foot in close to the buttocks which will cause that knee to point upward. Twist the upper body in the direction of the raised knee by applying pressure to that knee with the opposite elbow, and at the same time push sideways on the ground with the free hand. Reverse the actions to twist the upper body in the opposite direction.

The shoulder muscles can be stretched by lying on the ground in a partially reclining position with the knees only slightly bent. The upper body being supported by the elbows placed on the ground behind. In this position, only the heels, buttocks and forearms are touching the ground. By slowly moving the buttocks toward the heels, the muscles at the front of the shoulders will be stretched. Do not let the elbows splay outward but keep them in close to the body. If the elbows were to be placed outward from the body, an additional strain would be placed on the rotator cuff and no additional benefit would be derived in return. Shoulder flexibility will enable the runner to employ a full-amplitude swing of the upper arm to the rear with less inhibition.

While sitting on the ground with both legs extended in front, grab the toes and gently pull the upper body forward. The head is dropped down toward the knees. The knees can be slightly bent if necessary. Do not allow the feet to point sideways. They should be pointing upward; this is the orientation we want for them when we run. Now relax as much as possible. This position will add the stretching of the lower back to all the previously stretched muscles on the backside of the leg. Eventually, the wrists should reach the toes and the hands will drop over them to grasp the underside of the foot. The toes are then bent upward with the heel of the hand, while the fingers pull on the ball of the foot to stretch the Achilles. This configuration is somewhat dependent on the shape of one's torso and the relative lengths of the limbs. Proper stretching of the feet and toes can only be done while not wearing shoes. Shoes will prevent the necessary bending upward of the toes. Best to remove the shoes for this portion of the stretching.

It is good to occasionally grab two fistfuls of toes and bend them downward. This, to ensure there is sufficient flexibility here so the takeoff mechanism is not impeded in any way.

While using each hand to pull on the foot and toes is good, the takeoff mechanism of the foot is just too strong to receive a good stretch in this manner. So, as is with most rules, we must have an exception to the rule of sitting down while stretching. We must stand up to impress a good stretch on the underside of the foot. While standing with the ball of the foot at the edge of a step or curb, hold onto something stationary to ensure steadiness, and slowly lower yourself so the heel is below the level of the step or curb. This will stretch the takeoff mechanism. Do not be so aggressive as to cause irritation. We are doing this to prevent an injury, not cause one.

In a standing position on level ground, outstretch the arms to the sides to reach their maximum span. Repeatedly swing the upper body 90° to the left and 90° to the right to further loosen up the midsection. Keep the feet spread apart during these motions to reduce twisting on the knees.

Regarding long-range goals of stretching, two areas commonly overlooked are the rearward swings of the upper arm and of the lower leg. Men, generally speaking, are less flexible than women. Therefore, men may need to work harder toward improving this aspect of their game. But do not be overly aggressive and irritate the body or aggravate an old injury. Do not set any predetermined goals or time schedules. Take only what the body is willing to give on any particular day. Treat the body firmly, but sensibly. Progress in some areas may take a year or more to become noticeable. That's why they're termed long-range goals.

For the long term, the plantar fascia on the bottom of the foot can be kept limber with the use of a golf ball. When in bare feet, hold onto something solid in order to maintain full control of your weight, stand on only one leg. Place the arch of the free foot on a golf ball. Roll the golf ball around with the foot while pressing down on it with measured weight. This will give a good stretch to the plantar. The proverb "a stitch in time saves nine" comes to mind. There is no substitute for well thought-through preventive maintenance. Take care of your body if you expect it to serve you well.

If you have had a previous muscle or tendon injury, pay particular attention to this area. The healing process may have resulted in a shortening of the tissue. You know how quickly and how unexpectedly an injury can strike you down and how debilitating it can be. Time spent stretching is well worth the investment. Of course, the good effects of stretching have their limitations. Always use common sense and do not attempt anything for which the body is not prepared.

An attempt has not been made to outline all the stretching routines; they are not the thrust of this book. But the sprinter may want to supplement one's current stretching routine with some of what has been outlined here. One additional point, though. Stretching is not something that is done only once near the beginning of each training session and then forgotten about. The muscles do not remain stretched and limber all by themselves for the remainder of the workout.

Periodically throughout the workout, take the time for some additional stretching to ensure that the muscles are ready for the next strenuous trial to which they will be put. This may seem like an unnecessary waste of time, but it helps ward off injury. Recuperation from injury is the slowest form of running imaginable. Avoid it as you would the plague. Every effort toward injury-free running is well worth the time expended in this direction.

Unfortunately, along with the advantage of stretching, we also get a disadvantage. Compared to a muscle that has not been stretched, when a recently stretched muscle is called upon to contract, it must first overcome the newly stretched distance before it can begin to move its attached limb. This additional work by the muscle will consume more energy and also delay the commencement of the limb swing. For the sprinter, these should not be problems on a practice day, but would present big problems on race day.

On race day, it is appropriate to modify the stretching routine. An abbreviated stretching routine on race day will afford a crisper response from the muscles/limbs involved. A thorough stretching was done on practice days in order to provide our best defense against injury. On race day, however, our priorities change. Here, we are looking for performance.

Race-day performance is why we practiced so diligently. If we were not going to compete to the best of our ability, we didn't need to train so intensely. But we did train. We trained hard. We trained well. Now, in order to reap the greatest benefit from that training, we are willing to encroach *some* into that safety zone created by stretching. Thorough stretching during training is what will allow us to now reduce, or even forgo, our stretching and bring our fastest body to the starting line on race day.

The Tune Up

Just as one began the static stretching routine easily and became more aggressive as the muscles responded, so should the running, or tune up, phase of the warm up begin. This again warms the body that will have begun to cool down during the stretching phase. Start with a 30-meter medium speed run, and then drop back to a walk. Then another run, a little faster, a little longer. The length of runs and walks to be determined by the individual as makes him feel comfortable to begin the next higher speed run. The intention here is to have the body become accustomed to, not resentful to, running faster.

Do not rush through this phase in order to reach its completion. Allow ample time for modest recuperation between each run. The number of these runs required to become race ready will vary with the individual and with the degree of conditioning that individual has reached. Perhaps 4 or 5 runs would be considered a median number. They should be conducted in a manner so that, when completed, the body feels energized, not depleted. At this point, the body will have demonstrated to itself, and to your psyche, that it is ready to take on the next challenge, whatever that may be for this day.

Exaggerated leg movements such as high knee lifts and butt kicks should be interspersed between short bursts of speed, to turn on and tune up the body. Don't forget the arms. Large overlapping windmill-like circles in front of the body will loosen up the shoulders. Strive for large circles. Do some windmilling in both directions and finish up with large amplitude fore-and-aft swings. If desired, brief plyometrics such as skipping and bounding to improve muscle quickness can round out the tune up session. At the end of the tune up session, one will be ready for the serious work of the day.

Some runners like to occasionally shake out the legs, making the bones appear flexible. If this is one of your routines, hold onto a stationary object for balance. This will remove from the supporting leg, the responsibility to maintain the body in balance. If the supporting leg does not have to balance the body, these leg muscles can remain more relaxed as you shake out the other leg. Leg muscles would be severely tensed if they had to maintain the body in balance on just one leg. This could undo whatever muscle relaxing had been accomplished by previously shaking it.

A relaxed muscle admits more reinvigorating blood to itself than does a tense muscle. Before making a speed run or just before stepping to the starting area in a competition, it is helpful to get the maximum amount of oxygen-rich blood to those muscle cells that will soon be using up oxygen at an extraordinary rate.

The mere act of maintaining the body in an upright position requires a certain amount of muscle tension in the legs and body. The quadriceps muscles can be relaxed by observing the following simple routine. Keeping the feet pointed straight ahead, spread the feet apart so there is perhaps 15" clear between them. (The feet should be slightly further apart than are the hip joints.) Keeping the knees straight, but not locked, bend forward at the waist. With the hands, firmly grasp the legs just above the knees. Elbows are locked straight. This position forms a triangle (the most stable of geometric shapes) of the body above the knees.

Keep body weight on the heels with just the slightest weight on the balls of the feet (not on the toes) to maintain balance. One can avoid a downward stretching of the skin by initially grasping the legs about 1" lower and then, while pressing the hands against the legs, slide the hands that 1" back up the legs. This action will develop a small roll of skin immediately above each hand and in this manner avoid stretching the skin of the legs.

As the hands grasp the legs, one should feel the quads go slack, as it is no longer necessary for these muscles to provide balance for the upper body. Of course, the leg muscles could be tensed while in this position if one desires, but the objective here is to relax the muscles. Only the triangular shape should now support the body. Round the shoulders so that the effective length of the arms is as long as possible. While in this position, do not allow the head to hang down. The brain would feel the increased blood pressure and begin slowing down the volume of blood being pumped. Keep the head erect and be looking straight ahead. We want the body to be primed for an upcoming speed run.

Holding this position for perhaps 15 seconds allows an increased blood flow into those muscles, now relaxed. When releasing the support that had been provided by the arms, one will feel the muscles and tendons again tense as they provide the required support for the upper legs and torso. Upon returning the body to the vertical position, the legs will feel refreshed, ready for the next challenge.

Gentle motions of the joints will release synovial fluid that is important to their lubrication. A thorough dynamic tune up is essential after the static stretching has been completed. Each time one takes to the track, give the body the opportunity to adjust to, and thereby improve, one's upcoming speed runs. Begin moderately and gradually increase the speed of several short runs. Maintain your best form as the speed of the runs is increased. Proper techniques should be incorporated into runs of *all* speeds. Good form will then occur more naturally and serve you better when at high speed—and on race days when it is needed most. The better the warm ups, the better will be the practice days. The better the practice days, the better will be the performances on race days.

5

PRE-RACE

Be ready for race day. The author believes in diligent preparation for a race—complete and total preparation. This means completing every aspect of achieving readiness for the starting gun. One must attain the highest degree of physical fitness that the body can reach. All running techniques must be established and firmly placed in the racing playbook. Running paraphernalia must be checked and assembled. Sufficient time should be allowed for rest and organization of race-day incidentals. Adequate opportunity must be provided for race-day warm up and psychological readiness. Give yourself every opportunity to do your best. Race day will demonstrate how well you have completed your preparations.

Prior to race day, equipment must be inspected. The racing shoes need to be checked. Do the spikes need replacing? Is each spike tight and secure? The author is appalled at the number of errant spikes seen about the track. Foreign matter that may have gotten jammed between spikes should be cleaned off. The spikes must conform to instructions for the meet. The soles of the shoes should be checked to determine if they have begun to delaminate and come loose from the shoe. If so, good contact cement can remedy this (read the instructions). But this should be considered as only a temporary fix. By the time the shoes begin to come apart, they will in all probability have lost their support value, and should have been replaced before now anyway.

The laces should be checked to see if they have begun to wear and weaken. If the shoe is zippered, the zipper should be checked for trouble-free operation. The shoes must fit the feet snugly, but comfortably, with no chafing. Self-adhering cushioned pads placed at any trouble spots can provide a welcome improvement in this regard. The toenails should be trimmed so they cause no discomfort when snugly fitting shoes are laced up. Properly trimmed toenails are less apt to chafe through footwear from the inside.

The author does not like shoelaces that are too long. Neat and tidy is the order of the day, especially around the feet. If the lace is too long, a shorter lace should be used if the correct length is commercially available. If the ideal length of lace cannot be purchased, a long lace can be shortened by removing the appropriate amount from its center and tying a knot to join the two halves. If done correctly, the lace will now be a convenient length, not flapping around, but still long enough to allow the shoe to be put on or off without unlacing the top hole. If one is pressed for time, having to lace the top hole will only add to the pressure one is feeling.

The runner should also check that personal support clothing is doing its job. There comes a time when even that needs to be replaced. While on this subject, it seems that men's supporters are traditionally made of the coarsest material available to the garment industry. For those who have a chafing problem, you may want to try this alternative. First, don a pair of cotton jockey shorts, and then put on the supporter. This may seem strange at first, but works just as well, and eliminates the vexing problem of chafe and its consequential itch.

All race-day paraphernalia should be together and the runner must make certain it all gets taken to the track. Include clothing for a change in the weather (including rain), warm up clothing, towel, a small bottle of contact cement for emergency repair of shoes, extra safety pins for the competitor bib number in case the registration table runs short (these can also be used for other apparel crises), hat, sun block, insect repellent, medicine to normalize one's digestive tract, beach towel and plastic underlay upon which to do stretching, a pocket-size measuring tape to accurately set the location of the starting blocks, your personal audio device, energy snack and drink, etc. Take a padlock if a locker might be available to store street clothes, a watch so you can pace your race preparations to meet the scheduled race time, and pen and paper to record race results and the evaluations of your performance. Always be prepared to preserve on paper the fleeting thoughts that cross your mind. The cell phone (turned off) is for emergencies only. Concentration on your upcoming event should not be disrupted. Today, your connection to the outside world should be made on your timetable, not someone else's.

Don't forget the shoes. Take both your spikes and your racing flats in case the track surface has been changed since your last visit to the venue; also, training shoes for warm up. If there is a possibility that starting blocks may not be available, take your own with you. Mark them with your ID. Bring along a suitable drop-bolt in case the starting area of a bituminous track is equipped with a recessed tube to provide anchorage. Of course, the racing singlet (or lightweight alternative) and undergarments should be with you.

On really hot days, stay out of the sun as much as possible. It is amazing how quickly that brilliant source of energy can drain us of ours. If the facility has minimal sun protection, a broad-brimmed hat is invaluable. The author has a well-ventilated straw hat with wide brim to which a chinstrap has been added that allows it to also be worn during warm up runs. If it appears a good part of the day is going to be spent on the field in the hot sun, consider bringing your personal shade such as a collapsible hut or beach umbrella. If the weather is cool at the site of the track meet, it is not a good idea to depend upon direct sunlight for warmth. Instead, appropriate clothing should be worn to sustain proper body temperature.

An adequate intake of liquids must be maintained; liquids are essential to proper functioning of the body's systems. Don't wait to feel thirsty. The feeling of thirst tells you the body is already becoming depleted. Stay abreast of the body's liquid requirement, but avoid excessive fluid intake that would dilute the body's chemical balance. If one has been sweating heavily, fluid replacement in the form of a sports drink should be considered. These more closely mimic the body's fluid lost in perspiration than does plain water.

Of course, anything is possible and freakish things can happen, but an equipment failure for a runner should just not happen. We rely on only a minimal amount of very basic equipment and all of it can be readily examined if we take the time. It should be inspected closely, looking critically for impending trouble.

The author prefers to be completely organized and do as much as possible ahead of time. This includes becoming familiar with the track and the stadium facilities (preferably before the day of the meet), knowing how to get to the stadium, determining how much time to allow for the trip and laying out everything that will be needed before going to sleep the night before the meet. Complete preparation is more conducive to better rest; there are fewer things on one's mind.

It is best to arrive at the stadium early. Then one knows that no transportation foul-ups will interfere with being ready for the competition. This allows a better selection of locations to put down one's running bag and establish *squatter's rights* to the place that might be preferred. This preference might be for the expectation of shade later in the day (being cognizant of the sun's motion: rising in the east, passing through the south [for those of us in the northern hemisphere] and setting in the west), or a place out of the rain, or away from foot traffic, or whatever will be important to the runner on that day.

One should not try something new on race day. Smoothing out any quirks and glitches should be done during training. There's no time or place for that on race day. Show up prepared for your event. If there is an exceptionally important meet coming up, and if a facility will be available for training, relocate to the vicinity of that meet as much in advance of race day as is practicable. If one becomes familiar with the facility ahead of time, it will feel more comfortable on race day.

Train on the track. Stretching should be done on the infield or head of the track as will be available on race day. Note any areas prone to wetness so they can be avoided. Survey the entire facility from the grandstand. Is it advisable to have insect repellent? Locate the rest room (and a backup restroom to make sure the bases are fully covered). Adjust to any altitude, time zone or climate changes if these are applicable.

Learn to feel comfortable with whatever the facility has to afford. Do not dwell on its shortcomings; this is what the facility can offer at this time. If you feel it is less than what you would have liked, prepare yourself to deal with any of the differences. This will minimize any detrimental effects those shortcomings might otherwise have upon your performance. The ability to overcome obstacles and still perform reliably is one of the hallmarks of a champion.

After entering the track, locate the finish line. Form a clear picture in your mind of how it will look as you approach it from ten meters out, five meters out. Note any permanent visible marks that will help pinpoint where you will want to employ a final burst of speed or your lean for the line. If you plan to run the 200m, locate exactly where the straightaway begins. Then determine where you will begin your *float* as you come off the curve. This will allow you to derive maximum advantage from the maneuver. Also, look for an official bulletin board to see where any announcements would be posted that could affect your event. Make certain that no throwing events will be taking place near where you intend to warm up.

The pre-race rush on toilet facilities, with its consequent increased consumption of toilet paper, can deplete the supply of that suddenly-precious commodity. This happened to the author on one occasion. But once was once too often. Preparation is now made for this situation should it happen again. A full roll of toilet paper can take up an excessive amount of space in a runner's bag. But one can take a mostly-depleted roll, flatten it and place it in a plastic zip-top bag. In this way, very little space is taken up and one is prepared to deal with that otherwise disastrous emergency.

As soon as practical after arriving at the track, check in at the registration table. Here, the runner will pick up the bib number to be worn during the race. There may be some additional information disseminated that could be different from preliminary information distributed on an earlier date. Be sure to read over any written material that may be distributed at this time.

It is your responsibility to stay current with what is going on. Do not become so engrossed in your own routine that you are oblivious to the world around you.

Later, it will also be necessary to check in with the official in charge of your event to receive more detailed information including the flight to which you are assigned and the lane number in which you will be competing. It is suggested this information be written down to ensure it is retained correctly. Don't let an administrative glitch ruin all the effort you have put into the preparation for this day.

Attune your ear to the sound of the starting signal in earlier events so your brain will not have to analyze and interpret an unfamiliar sound when it's your turn to come out of the blocks. Pay attention to any instructions given by the starter official. They are intended to be of help to the field of runners. Observe the starter official as earlier races are being started. Is this a good starter? Is a fair start ensured for each runner or are ready-or-not starts given when the starter feels the runners have been given ample time to be ready? If the latter, don't be caught unprepared. Get into the blocks quickly and be ready. Complaining later will get you nothing but increased frustration.

In short, try to anticipate any problem areas and do what is necessary to avoid or minimize their negative effect. Know what races precede yours so that you can gauge when it will be time for your event. Also, stay within earshot of the public address system (at a location where it is understandable) so you will be aware of any changes. Nowhere is the adage more true than in the arena of sport: Failing to prepare is preparing to fail!

To achieve optimum results, race preparation must be conducted with the goal of delivering the body to the starting line in condition to perform its best. To accomplish this on a consistent basis will require the sprinter to have a good feel for how well the warm up is progressing. The warm up must be performed in a manner that assures the sprinter will be prepared to perform at maximum capability for those few seconds that comprise the short sprint. This is an unforgiving event. It affords no opportunity to recover from a misstep. Be ready. Do it right the first time. It is the only time you will get.

The author prefers thorough preparation rather than an episode of Freddie Fuddle who, as the last call for his event is being announced over the public address system, is frantically asking for directions to the rest room. Anything that detracts from one's concentration on an event can detract from one's performance in that event.

Be warmed up. Be stretched out. Be tuned up. But remember, the routines you followed on practice days were just a preparation for race day. One would not perform on a race day all those routines done on a practice day. Those routines were all designed to prepare the body for race day. Now, race day is here. Don't do practice day routines on race day. The thorough jogging and stretching performed on practice days have done their job. They have brought you here to race day without any major muscle injury and they have also brought you here with a more limber body.

Now, on race day, one's perspective changes. Because you have come to race day with a more limber body, it will now not be necessary to perform as much stretching. A thorough jogging and stretching of muscles on race day would not promote the desired quickness of motion. Therefore, for maximum quickness on race day, those jogging and stretching routines can be abbreviated.

On race day, it is still important to perform a light jog in order to raise the body's temperature; while doing so, utilize a soft touchdown. The body beginning to perspire will be evidence of the raised temperature. Excessive perspiration beyond this degree will provide no positive effect. It is more apt to disrupt one's chemical balance and cause an unnecessary tiring. It's too late to now attempt to lose that excess weight. Having attained a light perspiration, the runner can now engage in a modest stretching routine if so desired.

A brief tune up session will complete one's preparation of the body. During the dynamic tune up, concentrate on being light on your feet. In the upcoming race, you will want quickness of motion. Rehearse it now. Sharpen all the technical skills you have trained so hard to master. This must include some practice starts off the blocks. It doesn't hurt to have your own starting blocks available as backup in case all those furnished by the facility are in use. Get the mind and the body fully primed so you will be at your peak when race time arrives.

Your bib number should be securely fastened in all four corners. Take care of details earlier rather than later. Leave time for a final trip to the rest room without being hurried. As race time approaches, racing shoes should be donned. By observing good hygiene, which includes keeping both the feet and the shoes clean, the weight of socks can be eliminated from the feet for the race. When donning racing shoes, brush off the feet with the hands to be certain no debris is adhered to their bottoms or crevices between toes. Foreign matter would suddenly become more noticeable when wearing your snug-fitting racing shoes. An annoyance here, no one needs.

Once you have put on your racing shoes, stay out of the grass if it is damp from rain, dew or sprinklers. The shoes would quickly soak up this water. We receive no bonus points for carrying this additional weight on our feet all the way to the finish line. Lighter shoes are quicker shoes.

Shoes should be laced up so they fit snugly. One cannot tolerate any loose motion between foot and shoe. The shoe should fit as if it is part of the foot. Shoes should be sufficiently snug so they maintain the shape of the foot. The foot should not be allowed to deform under load. The elastic spring-back of the foot, from the loaded condition, is too slow to supply any springing action to the running motion.

It is better to not let the foot deform upon impact in the first place. Running on a soft foot is somewhat akin to running on a soft surface where energy is lost into the surface as it deforms, with a consequent loss of speed from the runner. Firm support from the sides of the shoe helps maintain proper foot shape. However, do not lace the shoe so tightly that the lace depresses the instep and causes pain when you walk. If you feel pain, back off the lace. Snug is good, but don't change the shape of the foot. Afford the foot bones the space they need in order to do their job.

It is not necessary for the runner to dwell on the importance of the race, in what place he expects to finish (except for qualifying heats), medals at stake and that sort of thing. All the runner has to do is focus on the race and thereby turn in one's best performance. The fluff stuff such as places, medals, titles and such will all fall into place by themselves, just where they belong. The runner's personal guidance of them is not needed at this time. Worrying about extraneous items does not help. All one needs to think about is running the race.

Don't let pre-race pressure or self-doubt drain the energy from you. As race time approaches, start revving up the engine. Some short practice runs, running in place and muttering inspirational phraseology (such as "yeah" or "go") all may help. If race time is approaching and you are having difficulty getting *up*, you might try jumping jacks with good arm swing to elevate the heart rate without seriously tiring the running muscles. Listening to the theme song from "Rocky" can also elevate the emotions.

Circling the arms in front of the body in overlapping windmill style works well and loosens up the shoulder muscles. These muscles may have gotten overlooked in the pre-race warm up. Strive for large circles. The larger the circle, the more relaxed are the shoulder muscles. Scribe circles in both directions. Finish up with full swing fore-and-aft movements. This will act to prime the arms for the upcoming running motion. A drag racer wouldn't pop the clutch without first revving up the engine; neither should you. Before the command "On your marks" is given, your alertness level should be running off the chart.

It would be contrary to the ethics of good sportsmanship to enter a competition with anything that would provide you with an unfair advantage over your opponents. However, the author also believes it is equally imperative to not allow yourself to enter a competition under any handicap or *dis*advantage. Do *not* enter a competition with anything *less* than your best. It is *your* responsibility to provide yourself with every opportunity to do the very best of which you are capable. Proper preparation can readily translate to peak performance. You trained hard for your race. Now's the time to say *why* you trained so hard. Say it with your best performance.

6

THE START

Choosing the Type of Start

Theoretically, the start of a race is that moment when the starter official fires the gun. This chapter is devoted to discussing those things a runner should do just before and just after that signal. We therefore need to talk about an *interval* of time during which a runner begins the race.

For this discussion, we will begin this interval when the starter official gives the command, "On your marks." We begin the interval here because properly placing the feet into the blocks is the physical commencement of obtaining a good start. Let us also establish a conclusion for this interval. An arbitrary number of ticks of the clock is not used here to define its conclusion. This, because all runners are not the same. They will, therefore, not all be at the same stage of their race at some predetermined time after the gun. For this discussion, we will establish the conclusion of this interval as the action of the runner coming fully erect and now moving down the track in good running form. The word *fully* is emphasized. This portion of the race immediately after the start signal is often referred to as the *drive phase*.

It is during this critical starting interval that the runner establishes his speed and position that could very well determine the ultimate outcome of the race. Occasionally, we witness a race wherein one runner demonstrates a substantially greater speed than do the others. But more often, we see a field of eight runners moving at quite a uniform speed between the 30-meter and 90-meter marks. The order of their finishes having already been determined by some previous event—the start.

But, a word of caution. All too often, a runner's performance at the start is judged by his position in the field at about the 5-meter mark. This frame of reference is used because it is easy. If we watch one particular runner, our eyesight can readily tell us that runner's position relative to the other runners in the field. What our eyesight does not tell us, however, is the runner's speed at this instant. This is unfortunate because a runner's position in the field at this moment is not the full story. The runner's speed is the real story and is the true indicator of how well or how poorly his start was performed.

If the runner in the lead is also the runner who has attained the best speed, then this is a moot point. But on occasion, a runner who is in the middle of the group at the 10-meter mark will, seemingly from nowhere, emerge to the front at the 30-meter mark. How can this happen? Our eyesight tells us this runner did not have a good start because of not being near the front as the group came out of the blocks. What our eyesight does not tell us is that this runner, through good starting technique, was building up the best speed. This speed was then used to pass rivals who *appeared* to have a better start.

The message here is that the runner should not panic if not with the leaders as the field comes out of the blocks. Position in the field at this point is less important than is the ability to build speed. The runner who does the best job of building speed during the start is the one who truly has the best start. If you develop better speed at the start, while you may not be known as the best starter, you may instead be known as the fastest runner.

A race may be considered as being made up of three segments: the *start*, the *run* (or central portion) and the *finish*. The longer the race, the more significant is the run segment. Conversely, the shorter the race, the less significant is the run segment. Therefore, as the run segment becomes less significant in the shorter races, the other segments of start and finish become relatively more significant than they otherwise would. The finish of a race is, generally speaking, not under the runner's complete control. It, more or less, just happens. At that stage of the race, there is little planning or strategy; we play out our hand as best we can. We will look at the run and finish segments in later chapters.

That now leaves us with the start. Here, there is much under our control. Here, there is much we can do to improve our situation. Since we can be assured that the start will continue to be a part of all our races, it is obvious we should spend some time to learn as much as possible about this portion of the race. The more we know about it and the better we plan it, the better job we will do of controlling and executing it. In this chapter, the start is dissected and laid open so that each of its elements can be studied. An attempt is made to take the mystery and guesswork out of this most critical segment of the race. A better understanding of exactly what is happening here will allow the sprinter to develop an improved start. The start is perhaps the most complex segment of the short sprint, and in no other race is it more important. So let us begin with the fundamentals and build from there.

There are three basic elements or measurements that could be used to chart a runner's progress through a race. These three elements are distance, speed and acceleration. If you're not technically inclined, please don't close your mind; it won't get that complicated. If the proper data were taken, each of these separate elements could be plotted on a chart, and these charts would show the following information:

Distance Chart—shows at each specific second into the race, the *distance* the runner has traveled from the starting line.

Speed Chart—shows at each specific second into the race, the *speed* at which the runner is traveling.

Acceleration Chart—shows at each specific second into the race, how *quickly* the runner's speed is *changing*. If the runner's acceleration is zero, this means a constant speed is being held. (Even if a runner is moving very fast, if the speed is constant, then the *acceleration,* or *change-in-speed,* is zero).

We don't need to get into charts and formulas. We should just recognize that these three separate elements exist and that they each contribute different information to the total picture of how well a runner starts the race. These terms will be used later in this chapter so their definitions are provided up front. Let us put this aside for now and see what makes a good start by looking at three different types of starts.

Type I: The jump start—Springing forward utilizing both legs simultaneously, the runner leaps out of the blocks. Because good power is obtained from both legs, the initial distance is covered quickly and this runner leads the race at the 1-meter mark. However, this person is in a poor position to accelerate and further build up speed because, upon landing, both feet are more directly under the body. When the legs are in this position, they are not well placed to drive the runner forward and attain more speed. This runner is immediately passed by the other runners. Marion Jones (not known for obtaining good starts) appeared to use a variation of this type of start, but had the high-end speed to overtake her rivals during the run segment, or fly phase, of the race.

Type II: The "this is a running race so get up and run" type of start— This runner completes the start segment of the race quickly and begins the run segment as soon as possible. This runner will probably be looking good at the 5-meter and 10-meter marks because initial acceleration was good as the body came erect. However, the building of speed after this point will be difficult because the feet are more directly under the body and no longer in good position to accelerate it forward.

The author has a problem with the "get up and run" philosophy associated with the type II starter. It is believed that at this stage of the race we have not truly begun to run. It is believed a more accurate description of what we are doing during the first several strides of the sprint is accelerating. Therefore, a philosophy that promotes running at this stage of the race appears to be flawed.

Type III: The power start—This runner stays low coming out of the blocks and keeps the legs driving from behind. This provides good acceleration over a longer period of time. Very basically, to accelerate to a higher speed, a runner must utilize the legs to push the body forward. This can be done most powerfully when the legs are positioned behind the body in a pushing mode. Since this runner is accelerating in this manner over a longer time interval, he is continuing to build speed and will look good at the 30-meter mark.

Accelerating is the key word here! We are accelerating from zero speed up to running-form speed. Don't think *running* here; think *accelerating*. Coming out of the blocks with the best possible acceleration to build up to the highest speed is the essence of the start.

One might say that if a particular runner covers the greatest distance at the start, that runner must logically have attained the greatest speed. This is often true, but is an oversimplification, and with oversimplification comes inaccuracies. It presupposes that all other things are equal, and in the real world this is seldom the case. For instance, one runner may have very good acceleration during the first second after the start signal. In contrast, another runner may have better acceleration during the next second, after the legs are unwound and the body is moving. To determine which runner is now at the greater speed, we must look deeper than just looking at who is now ahead. We are *not* all alike. But let us return to our previous thought, acceleration out of the blocks.

If we accept the premise that we are in the acceleration mode immediately after the starting signal, then we must also accept that we need to be in that posture and perform those actions that best befit this acceleration. If, for example, a person were shown a large crate and told to slide it across the floor, that person would crouch behind it, and with the power of the legs from behind, push the crate forward. This is the same technique one uses to push a stalled automobile.

Similarly, at the start of a race, we have our body weight that we must get moving down the track. In order to accelerate the body forward, one must apply backward force to the track. One cannot apply backward force to the track when the feet are in front of the runner, or while floating through the air between foot plants. One can only accelerate forward when the foot is on the track applying backward force to it. Applying this backward force to the track as strongly as possible, and as many times as possible, during the first few seconds of a race will provide the greatest acceleration to the highest speed.

Remember, power implies the element of time. Applying the same total force in half the time interval requires twice the power. We are running against the clock. We must apply the greatest force, as fast as possible, to get moving forward the quickest.

This certainly sounds like all we need to know in order to arrive at the conclusion that we must make the greatest number of steps during the first few seconds of a race in order to get the best start. Unfortunately, this is another oversimplification, which assumes that as we increase the rapidity of the steps, we are able to maintain the same forward thrust from each of those steps. This is not the case. As we continue to increase the rapidity of our steps, the forward force from each of those steps begins to decline. Carrying foot rapidity to its extreme, the body would barely move forward while the feet are just a blur of high-speed action.

What we need for good acceleration, then, is the best tradeoff between rapid leg turnover and a long powerful push from each leg. When coming out of the blocks, we can get a long strong push from the leg whose foot is against the forward block. We sacrifice much of the push against the rear block in order to quickly bring the rear leg forward and replant that foot. We then get the first full push from that leg after it has performed its first touchdown.

We should not be too quick to bring the forward foot off its pedal. This push from the front pedal is the strongest forward thrust the runner's body will receive during the entire race. One should not cut it short. Push hard on that front pedal to get a strong leg extension. The length of time the forward foot is in contact with its pedal is key to setting the proper leg turnover rate at this critical time. The objective is to put as much rearward pressure onto the blocks as possible. This is what pushes the body forward. The runner must *not* run away from the blocks. The runner must *push* from the blocks. We only get to use them once; make the most of it.

The runner should not raise the head in order to see where he will be later on. Raising the head creates the tendency to raise the entire torso. The runner should keep the head down and look at where he is now. One must concentrate on the job at hand, which is accelerating to a higher speed.

As a runner gets closer to top speed, it becomes increasingly difficult to add still more speed. The acceleration therefore diminishes. As the acceleration diminishes, and a more constant speed is reached, the supporting feet must come more directly under the center of weight. As a result, the forward lean diminishes and the body becomes more vertical. As the runner completes the acceleration of the start segment and begins the run segment of the race, the body is now in an erect posture.

As the runner comes out of the blocks, there are three aspects that are so closely intertwined that they cannot be separated: how low the runner remains when emerging from the blocks, how far in front of the supporting feet the center of gravity is extended and the acceleration the runner is experiencing.

The relationship between the first and the second is obvious when we consider the attitude of a runner's body and note the location of the feet and the location of the center of gravity, which is located just above the hips. The relationship between the second and third is a fundamental requirement of basic dynamics; the further in front of the feet that the center of gravity is projected, and the longer it is maintained in that position, the greater the acceleration must be in order to maintain rotational balance. Without this acceleration, and the rotational stability it maintains, the runner would fall forward. In short, running low when exiting the blocks provides the runner with greater acceleration toward a higher speed.

As an aid toward staying low, instead of thinking of staying low it may be helpful to think of projecting the torso further forward. After all, that is what the thought of staying low had intended to accomplish anyway. Either thought, if successful, will incur greater acceleration. Remember, the start is not about running away from the blocks; the start is not about staying low; the start is about accelerating to a higher speed. More speed wins more races.

It is difficult to analyze one's own form during the start segment of a race because things are changing so rapidly. The speed is changing, the acceleration is changing, the stride is changing and the body lean is changing. A friend with a video camera can be of great assistance here. Footage taken from the front, from the oblique and from the side can show a great deal when replayed at different speeds.

In a different setting, a steep hill can provide valuable information directly to the sprinter. During one period, the author used a steep hill near his home, which rose approximately 15" for every 10' horizontal (a 7° slope). The hill maintained this constant slope for 130'; it then continued at half that slope for another 100'. When running, this would be considered to be a steep hill. In running up a hill at full speed, one replicates a thin slice of the drive phase.

But, when running as fast as possible up a hill, instead of everything rapidly changing as normally occurs when accelerating on level ground, now everything is constant as long as the slope of the hill is constant. This routine, in effect, freezes a frame of the start picture and permits the runner to analyze oneself by making adjustments and evaluating their effects while on the fly; a truly valuable training opportunity. For instance, while running up a hill at full speed, the runner can make an adjustment to the width of the foot plant and immediately feel what difference it makes in the strength of the push off. Different styles of arm swing can be experimented with. The author was astonished at the marked differences in performance that were attributable to even slight adjustments in techniques that were made while on the hill. It is recommended, in the strongest terms, you take a day from your normal training regimen; travel to the location of a hill and do your own experimentation. This will afford valuable information, specific to you personally, not available in any other way.

Utilize this opportunity to check out specifics of your foot plant, knee control, shoulder hunch and arm swing. Each of these may be fine while at a jogging pace, and even at top speed, but may betray the runner under the duress of the power drive necessary at the start. They should be checked out under the most severe conditions.

Some conscientious time spent *on the hill* will provide an unparalleled insight to the form you will want to utilize during the drive phase of a race. When you determine exactly how you want to perform particular techniques, be sufficiently introspective to learn how they feel to you. Your mind will be able to virtually see your performance of these techniques if you permit yourself to feel what your body is doing. This feeling of doing it right will be your most valuable tool in being able to accurately replicate what you have learned when you again take to the track. Now comes the practice. It will take many repetitions on the track to enable one to precisely perform these techniques under the pressure of the racing scene. As Yogi would say, "If you can't do it when it counts, it doesn't count."

The start is a balancing act with the body literally hanging in the balance. On the one hand, there is the stride length as we leave the blocks, the rapidity of the foot plants and the forward thrust of each leg. On the other hand, those elements are balanced against one's inertia and the downward force of gravity acting on the outstretched torso, which is at some distance in front of the feet. The former set of elements must slightly outweigh the latter in order to obtain a smooth raising of the torso as the legs, driving from behind, deliver the power that is needed to force their way under the torso and raise it to the vertical.

One should not attempt to cut this balancing act too fine. If there should be a slight falter in the driving force from the legs, that first set of elements would not deliver the required power, and the outstretched torso would begin to fall. To prevent this fall, the runner would be forced to take a long stride in order to place one of the feet further forward to gain additional support. This long stride would suddenly pop the runner up to the vertical, and a poor start would be the result.

The true determinant of acceleration a runner will achieve is not the angle of lean, but the distance in front of the feet that the runner carries the center of weight. To displace the weight a certain distance forward, the shorter runner will utilize a lower angle of lean, while the taller runner will accomplish the same thing with a higher angle of lean.

If you are having difficulty finding the right turnover rate as you come out of the blocks, you may want to experiment with making the arm swing set the turnover rate, and let the legs just follow suit. Find your groove and then practice so it becomes reliable. Stay low as long as possible and keep the legs driving from behind in order to accelerate to the highest speed before coming erect. Do not think *arms* and *legs* when driving from the blocks. Instead, think *elbows* and *knees*. Drive the elbows backward and the knees forward to get the power you're looking for.

The object of the start is not to see who can travel the first few meters the quickest, but rather, to achieve the highest running speed during this critical part of the race. Acceleration to a higher running speed during the first few seconds of a race produces greater long-term dividends than does covering the greater distance. Think pushing. Think *acceleration*.

How much to accelerate is a function of how soon you know you will begin to fade. No one can run at top speed for 26 miles, and no one can run at top speed for 100 meters. Even in this short sprint, the runner must learn to pace oneself. The act of acceleration requires the expenditure of more power than does the act of maintaining a constant speed. The longer you accelerate, the sooner the pressure in your tank will begin to drop. Experience in running the event will let you know how much effort to put into the final portion of your acceleration. Knowing when to level off will let you reach the finish line in the shortest total time.

Do not reduce your rate of acceleration before this point. Accelerate fully and then level off without struggling for that ultimate ounce of speed. In this manner, you will have run your best speed over the longest distance, and will slow down less in the second half of the race. When you've got the finish line in your sights, pull out all the stops. Plan your race. Then, have the determination to stick with the plan. Only then will you know whether or not it's the right plan.

Strive to get the most efficient push from each leg during the early strides. A subtle oscillation of the hips will develop more power. But this will disappear when higher speed is reached and minimum ground contact time is sought. After approximately ten strides, one will have completed the start segment of the race where acceleration has been the main focus. At this point, the run segment of the race begins, where other factors will demand the runner's attention.

Setting the Starting Blocks

Since we now know what we want to do after the start signal, let us take a look behind the starting line to see how we can best achieve that start.

In the mind of the author, nothing epitomizes the sprint more than the sight of the runners' feet stepping into the starting blocks. This one action symbolizes speed. It is at this moment that the anticipation of the sprint begins to mount. Everyone knows the race is about to begin.

The setup of the starting blocks is critical. There is no one location of the starting blocks that is right for all sprinters but there is a location that is right for each sprinter. Always check that the anchorage for the starting blocks is secure and that each pedal is locked in its proper place. Where is this proper place? The answer to that question can be quite elusive, but let us begin our search for it.

Generally speaking, one of our legs will be stronger than the other. This should be the leg that utilizes the forward pedal. This leg will soon be performing an action similar to standing up from a deep knee bend using only one leg. So let it be the stronger leg.

Do *not* determine the location of the pedal for the rear foot by measuring a particular distance back from the starting line. Instead, measure back from the starting line to set the location of the front pedal only. Then, to set the rear pedal, measure the distance between pedals. This is the logic we will use when setting the location of each pedal. So, we should begin using this thought process right from the beginning.

If the runner wants to go for the type III start described earlier, the pedals should be set at locations that will permit driving out of the blocks with the maximum number of strong steps before coming erect. If the pair of pedals is too near the line, the runner's feet will be more nearly under the center of weight. In this location, the legs will drive under the torso too easily and too quickly. The runner will become erect too soon.

On the other hand, if the pair of pedals is too far behind the line, the legs will be unable to drive themselves under the outstretched torso. In this predicament, the runner will begin to fall forward and will automatically take one long stride to prevent a forward fall. This long stride will *abruptly* pop the runner up into a vertical position. In both cases (pedals too far forward, pedals too far back), the torso will become vertical prematurely.

The runner is urged to analyze one's own start to determine if one of these conditions is causing a premature raising of the torso. Pay close attention to the power the quads are expending. Are they handling it with ease, or are they struggling? The *feel* in the legs will tell you if the pair of pedals is too close or too far from the line. Then adjust the pedals backward or forward to minimize the fault. If you move the pedals too far, you will find yourself coming up too quickly because you are now in the other fault zone.

Have patience. Get the feel of your foot-plant location as you dig your way from the blocks to determine which fault zone you are in. Then adjust the pedals accordingly. Find the location that permits you to reliably deliver the maximum number of strong thrusts to the track before becoming erect. The optimal setting for the pair of pedals will allow the runner to achieve a slow steady rise from crouch to vertical. If in doubt, opt for pedals slightly more forward than rearward. This will result in a start that is somewhat more conservative but will avoid the disaster that would ensue if the pedals were too far back.

The spacing *between* the pedals should be set using the same course of logic as was just used when shifting the pedals as a pair. Only here, we are looking to achieve an equal and balanced feel *between* the two legs. Now, one pedal will be shifted to increase or decrease the distance between them. Determine which leg is causing you to pop up too early. If you find you are taking a long stride with one leg upon the occasion of its first foot plant in order to maintain balance, move the other pedal forward. If one leg does not seem to be working sufficiently hard and may be coming under you too easily, move that pedal back. Strive to attain an equal contribution from each leg. Once this correct spacing between pedals is achieved, again shift them forward or backward as a unit, as described earlier, in order to fine-tune their distance behind the line.

The runner can also use the sense of hearing to determine if the foot cadence is equal or unequal. Obviously, this would be done when there are no other footsteps or similar distractions nearby. One should experiment with pedal locations until the desired result can be consistently achieved. When both pedals are correctly located, one will be able to achieve a powerful exit from the blocks with both legs contributing with equal power. When both legs are driving their hardest, the runner then wants to maintain the torso in front of the feet for the longest time.

It is noted that the position of the pedals directly affects only the first stride taken with each leg. But one must be aware that the stride length and stride tempo utilized in the first stride, will then affect the stride length and stride tempo utilized in the following stride, which will affect the stride after that, and so on. In this manner, the positioning of the pedals can be a contributing factor to the runner's stride for the entire period of acceleration. It is not outside the realm of possibility that inefficient stride characteristics could be carried all the way to the finish line. The runner should be alert for this tendency. Once identified, it can be dealt with.

I am reluctant to suggest any figures for the placement of starting blocks because there is such a wide variation in the setting of them. But, if you are a novice sprinter, you need some place to start. You may want to place the forward block 16" behind the starting line and use an 18" spacing to set the rear block. Taller runners will be more comfortable with larger numbers as compared to shorter runners. Don't put too much weight on the suitability of these numbers for your particular instance. It's not wrong to vary from these numbers. If you are a novice sprinter, I strongly recommend NOT measuring the settings of starting blocks used by other runners. Chances are, those settings will not work for you; it's better to take the time to develop what works for your own body size and leg strength.

The novice sprinter will initially have to spend a considerable amount of time in the blocks practicing the raise to the set position. It will take time to achieve a comfortable feeling of weight distribution between arms and legs. It will take time, but it will be time well spent.

Theoretically, a runner could improve his race time by moving the starting blocks closer to the starting line and thereby shorten the race. In a perfect world a runner would, in this manner, start the race and already be closer to the finish line. This tactic would require that the runner maintain the same body form except that the arms would now angle backward more sharply from the shoulders. Everything would move forward except the hands, which would remain at the line. In the *set* position, greater weight would now be placed on the hands, which are now closer to the center of weight.

Moving the starting blocks forward in an attempt to gain this slight advantage is not a good idea. The risk of introducing a false start, because of the increased stress placed upon the arms due to their angled orientation, far outweighs any advantage that one is seeking. Additionally, this greater stress on the arms would have a tendency to tense the entire body and thereby slow one's reaction time. It is more probable that one would compromise an otherwise good starting posture in search of this very small gain. The start is, by its nature, exceedingly difficult to master. One should not make it more complicated than necessary. The runner should set the blocks in a location that will provide a comfortable forward lean. This will allow good reaction time for that very first motion.

During the process of arriving at the proper setting of the starting blocks, one must have a plan. The runner must know specifically what needs to be achieved and must also know how to reach this objective. Much practice, utilizing correctly set blocks, will then provide the framework for obtaining a good start. It will take the drill of many repetitions, on fresh legs, to be able to reliably accomplish this. Ample time must be placed in the training schedule to master the techniques for accomplishing the best start of which one is capable.

Techniques for the Start

But, there is much more to obtaining a good start than just the proper setting of the starting blocks. How the runner performs after having set the blocks is of even greater importance. What follows is a look at several starting techniques. Please note that if the runner changes any of the starting techniques being used, it would be appropriate to again go through the previous procedures to set the pedals to their optimum locations.

When the command "On your marks" is given, step over the blocks to a position in front of them. Walking around the blocks only invites the possibility of contact with the runner in the adjacent lane. No one needs this. To promote relaxation, the runner should now take a huge inhalation, then a maximum exhale. Follow this with a slow generous inhalation. Then, let the body's normal breathing pattern resume.

From a position in front of the blocks, the runner backs into them and carefully places the rear foot against its pedal, then the forward foot against its pedal. The sequence of this foot placing is not critical. Some runners prefer to give the leg one final shake before setting the foot in its place. This shake is of questionable value. Most runners prefer to place the toes of each foot flat against the pedal with only the point of the shoe touching the track. However, some runners place the toes flat on the track with the ball of the foot against the pedal.

The author's preference is for a combination of these positions. The main requirement for the rear leg is quickness for its forward movement. Here, the toes are placed flat against the pedal. At the gun, the forefoot should deliver a quick impulse to the block. This will allow a quick clearance of the block and enhance an early commencement of the forward movement of the lower leg.

On the other hand, the main requirement for the forward leg is a more sustained powerful push from the block. Here, the toes are placed flat on the track. This leg will be supporting the runner for a longer period of time until it reaches its optimum extension. Because this leg will be supporting the runner for an extended period, the toes placed flat on the track will better support the runner than if the point of the toes were utilized. The strength and duration of this push is what's important, not whether that push comes from the pedal or from the track. Toes flat on the track are more conducive to obtaining a strong drive with this leg. There exists only a split second before the foot from the rear pedal touches down. Make every effort to obtain the best drive possible from the forward leg before the leg from the rear pedal touches down again.

After the feet are placed, the runner kneels to the ground on one knee and wipes any debris from the hands. The hands should be kept free of foreign matter. One may want to give a final look down the track to be assured that it is clear. In placing the hands to the starting line, it is not necessary to extend them outward to the full width of the lane. Swing the hands forward in a straight line from the hips and place them at the line. This is as far apart as they need to be. This location will provide more than enough lateral stability so one doesn't fall over sideways. In this location, the arms will raise the shoulders higher than if the hands were placed outward near the lane lines. Also, at the gun, the arms will be able to move directly fore-and-aft and already be in the vertical planes in which they are to work. Their motions can be more accurately controlled when in close to the sides of the body as compared to being somewhere further outward.

The runner should set the fingertips onto the track at the starting line. The fingers must be placed behind the line, not touching it. Then, momentarily lean far forward putting additional weight on them. This is to make certain the fingers are comfortable and have not been placed on a sharp protrusion of the track surface. In this way, when the starter gives the *set* command and additional weight is placed on the fingers, there will not be an unpleasant surprise by any distracting discomfort. The runner will have already been there and is comfortable with the finger placement. After this testing of the finger placement, the runner should return to only a moderate forward lean that can be comfortably held for as long as is necessary. Arms should be virtually straight but the elbows unlocked. Unlocked elbows will allow the arms to be swung more quickly and powerfully.

The runner may want to experiment with hanging the head and shoulders down, and continue this through the set command so that the eyes are staring backward toward the legs. If the eyes were to focus on anything, they would see what is behind the runner. But, one must not allow the eyes to see anything. The runner's mind should not be concerned with what the eyes are seeing. The mind should be concentrating on only one thought. And that single thought is the first motion that will be made at the sound of the gun. However, if there is one motion of the start that has been giving the runner difficulty, then the correct execution of *that* motion could possibly be uppermost in one's mind. But one should think of only one motion; most preferably, the first one. Get it right! Get a good start!

Once settled into the blocks and that first important motion firmly implanted in the mind's eye, the author closes the eyelids so that just a squint of vision remains. This has been found helpful in reducing the tendency to raise the head when the gun sounds in order to look at the area of the finish line. With the vision thus reduced, it is easier to remain looking down and avoid the tendency to raise up prematurely. Also, with no extraneous sights to contend with, total concentration on the task at hand (acceleration) is easier. By the time running speed is reached, the eyelids are fully open so that peripheral vision is optimized.

As we know, when the forward leg is used to drive the runner from the blocks, the leg begins its action in a bent position. As the knee is straightened, the distance between the hip joint and the foot is forced to increase. If the foot is braced against the starting block, the only possible result from straightening the knee is for the body to be driven forward.

This is quite basic, but it is desired to point out that we don't have to rely solely upon the leg for this type of action. The hip joint can do the same thing as is asked of the knee joint. When in the set position, the hip joint is in the bent position. At the starting signal, one can begin straightening the hip joint while the feet are still braced against the starting blocks. One should think shoulders here; drive the shoulders forward. The reader will recall that it was indicated earlier that the runner might want the head and shoulders to be hanging down. This is the reason one may want to take that position. The action of quickly straightening the waist and raising the head and torso to the horizontal has a powerful effect upon putting additional pressure against the pedals.

Additional pressure against the pedals, no matter from what cause, aids in pushing the body forward. If the runner has opted to keep the head and shoulders low when in the set position, when the gun is fired a violent swing of the head and upper torso is performed. The runner makes a lunge that will project the top of the head as far as possible toward the finish line. This motion will put good rearward pressure onto the pedals and propel the weight of the upper body forward. This will assist the runner in obtaining good initial speed out of the blocks. It is simply basic physics that any movement of the runner's body that causes the feet to exert additional pressure onto the pedals, can only result in providing the runner with additional push forward.

Do not swing the torso any higher than necessary. Raising the torso above the horizontal position begins to detract from the advantage initially realized by its forward swing. This action of swinging the upper body can be responsible for initiating the forward movement of a substantial amount of body weight. Consider using it to your advantage.

In addition to the position of the starting blocks, there is another factor that will affect how quickly a runner raises up after the start signal. The height to which the buttocks are raised, when in the set position, will influence how quickly the runner will raise up to the run position, or in the alternative, remain low in the acceleration posture. Think of the forward leg as being the main driving force that, at the gun, pushes the body forward and upward. This force operates between two points. One point is the ball of the foot against the forward pedal, and the other point is the hip joint of that forward leg. Regardless that the leg is bent at the ankle and at the knee, this force can be considered as pushing in a straight line between these two end points. From this, it can be seen that if the buttocks were to be raised higher at the set command, the angle of the pushing force from the pedal to the hip joint would point higher. The leg would now push the hip (and the rest of the body) more upward than forward. Conversely, a lower buttocks position would permit the leg to drive the body more forward than upward.

Each runner must assume a posture that is compatible with that individual's body dimensions, leg strength, stride length and turnover rate. The runner should experiment with different heights of buttocks for the start until the proportion of forward thrust and upward lift that works best is obtained. Then, this must be practiced often enough so that it can be reliably duplicated on race day.

There is also the school of thought that, at the set command, the buttocks should be raised to the height that they will have when the runner is performing the first stride. The reasoning is that if the buttocks are placed at this height at the set command, then at the gun, time and energy will not have to be consumed in changing them to this height after the race has begun.

The author has a differing opinion on this subject. The author contends that the foot utilizing the forward pedal should be in charge of the scene just as long as that foot is pushing the runner forward from that pedal. This one action is the strongest contributor to obtaining a good start. All other actions should support this push from the forward pedal.

We must remember that the starting blocks are at ground level. The runner's leg that is pushing on the front pedal is attached to the runner at a much greater height. When the runner pushes against the pedal, that action forces the runner both forward and upward. One cannot get a forward push from the pedal without the accompanying upward push.

If one were to place the buttocks at running height before the push were to begin, there would be no place remaining for the leg to push to. The ability to push up would no longer be available, and the accompanying push forward would also be lost. The advantageous push from the front pedal would now be gone.

Raising the buttocks to the running height at the set command defeats the ability to get a proper push from the starting blocks. The author believes it is better to set the buttocks at a lower height; one that will engender a strong push from the front pedal. The runner should take whatever assistance can be gotten from the starting blocks during that very brief interval in which they are available.

When looking at the issue of what height one should place the buttocks when in the set position, there is much to think about. While it is always important to see how someone else does it, in the final analysis you must do what works for you, not what works for someone else. The length and the strength of one's leg are major factors in forming this decision. During the process of establishing the buttocks height to be used, a series of compromising tradeoffs is inevitable. But the runner knows what leg strength is available and always gets the final vote.

One should repeatedly practice the first motion that will be performed at the sound of the gun. Concentrate on responding quickly to an external sound. With practice, reaction time can be improved. It is noted in passing, that the pathways of the motor nerves (the nerves that control the muscles) from the brain to the neck muscles and to the back muscles, are shorter than are the pathways from the brain to the leg muscles. *Theoretically*, if a runner utilizes a forward-swinging torso at the gun, these shorter pathways should provide the runner with quicker reaction time at the sound of the gun, and thereby allow forward motion to begin an instant sooner. *Theoretically!*

All this body action will require that the feet stay in contact with the pedals slightly longer than they otherwise would. This is okay. In fact, it's good. The runner will have pushed the upper body to a greater forward speed by getting more assist from the pedals. Since we only get to use the starting blocks during this brief instant, it is imperative that the maximum push be achieved at this time. This maximum push is obtained by lunging the shoulders forward, not upward.

When the set command is given, the buttocks are raised. At this time, one should take a generous inhalation, not maximum, just generous. The runner will want to hold this breath until after the starting signal. The breath is held to ensure all is quiet and so one can better hear the starting signal and respond immediately to that sound. More importantly, the runner does not want to be caught in the middle of an inhalation or exhalation when the gun sounds.

In addition to preparing the athlete to respond to the sound of the gun, a generous inhalation will also inflate the lungs to the correct amount that will enable the runner to take the first several steps of the race without the necessity of taking another breath. The runner cannot develop maximum power while an inhalation or exhalation is being made.

While calling upon the legs to expend maximum power, the diaphragm muscles must temporarily be held rigid. At this time, one cannot permit the relaxation necessary to breathe. One must have a sufficient amount of reserve air in the lungs to enable one to wait for the starting signal, and then to extract maximum power from the legs by maintaining pressure within the lungs for the first several steps before again resuming breathing.

Having more than a neutral amount of air in the lungs will assist in developing the internal body pressure, upon which we rely so heavily, when it is necessary to momentarily develop maximum strength. This short-lived internal body pressure is developed by contracting the breathing muscles and compressing the air that is within the lungs to provide the body with maximum power for those first few strides.

This technique can also be used in another highly useful manner. When in the set position, instead of passively waiting for the starting signal to begin the race, the starting signal should be anticipated and this increased internal pressure established *before* the starting signal is given. This self-induced high pressure in the body will now set the stage for one to explode from the blocks. This affords the runner the ability to immediately make the strongest possible drive off the starting line.

If one would like, this buildup of internal body pressure can be checked at home. Take a generous inhalation, trap the air within your lungs, contract the diaphragm and build up body pressure. As you will notice, this buildup of body pressure does not occur instantaneously. It develops over a period of time—perhaps half a second. For an athlete who is about to perform a maximum-exertion effort (the first few strides of the sprint) and be timed to $\frac{1}{100}$ of a second, this time required to build up maximum body strength is of major importance.

The buildup of internal body pressure when called to the set position (and before the firing of the gun) will provide the runner with the maximum strength and power needed to immediately drive forward and accelerate from the blocks. Do not overlook this opportunity to have a fully-primed body that is ready to race when the starting gun is fired. The buildup of internal pressure is how one normally prepares the body for any maximum-strength feat. After all the years of training, this is now your last chance to ensure you are fully prepared for the starting gun. Take this opportunity. Prime your body with its maximum strength. At the gun—*GO!*

The forward lunge from the blocks should be practiced. Initially, the runner should practice lunging without regard for what steps are to be taken later. One should try to avoid falling on the face, but should practice lunging with such abandon that falling is a possibility. The runner must be wearing lightweight footgear for this exercise. The heavily padded soles of training shoes won't work here. When a good lunge is obtained, the pressure that is exerted on the balls of the feet should be noted. This should be practiced repeatedly in order to get the feel of a powerful lunge. If desired, this can be done on the infield or other grassy surface. The thought of a softer fall can do much to lessen one's inhibitions. Once the runner has felt what a good lunge is like, and the pressure that it generates on the balls of the feet, it is time to proceed to the next phase.

Now the runner lunges from the blocks, as just practiced, and takes several steps just as he would at the start of a race. Continue to stay low. The purpose of this exercise is to achieve a race start that incorporates, as closely as possible, the practice lunges done earlier. The runner can use the pressure felt on the balls of the feet as a yardstick to measure how good a lunge is being performed. The more pressure exerted on the pedals, the more speed will be imparted to the body. A cautionary note: During these practice lunges, one should not resort to the Type I start. The primary push must still come from the foot that is against the forward pedal. After pushing from the pedals, a strong push from each of the first several strides will then accelerate the runner the fullest.

Also, at the sound of the gun there should be a decisive swing of both arms. The arm on the same side as the rear foot will swing backward; the arm associated with the forward foot will swing forward. The swings can be made more powerful if the elbows maintain a noticeable bend and the actions of the upper arms are exaggerated.

When the hands are lifted from the track, the body will immediately begin to fall forward; gravity has zero *reaction time.* To counter this, the runner delivers a sharp push against the rear pedal using the quick powerful muscle system that is also used in the runner's takeoff portion of the normal stride.

A short flicking type push with the rear foot helps maintain initial balance and propels the rear leg forward. This additional support provided the body will allow that leg to travel further forward before it again feels the necessity to touch down. This touchdown is now slightly delayed from what it otherwise would have been if the rear foot had not provided this push. This affords the foot that is on the forward pedal the opportunity to push over a longer interval of time and attain a greater leg extension. In this manner, the power of the quadriceps is allowed to produce a greater forward acceleration of the body.

After what had initially been the rear foot touches down again, the leg on the forward pedal terminates its push and then begins to come forward. Its accompanying arm is driven backward. The other arm comes forward at this time and the alternating action has begun. Each step forces the torso just a little bit higher and pushes the runner to a higher speed.

Remember, the objective during the first seconds of the race is not to see how far we can travel from the blocks, but rather to accelerate to the highest speed. We are not looking to begin the running action immediately. The first action is to push on those pedals to accelerate the body from speed zero, and to thereafter push rearward on the track.

Elbows are to be kept in close to the body and bent. The arms are in sharp fore-and-aft movement. No sideways flailing allowed. One should not look up; this encourages the torso to raise up too quickly. Trust me. The finish line is right where it's supposed to be; no need to check it now.

Quads of insufficient strength will not properly support the runner in the drive phase coming out of the blocks. This runner would then be left with no other option but to prematurely come vertical and begin the fly phase before obtaining good forward speed. The ability to perform one-legged deep knee bends is an absolute prerequisite to obtaining good starts. Quickly straightening the leg with full weight on a flexed knee is the runner's position in the early stages of the drive phase. Deep knee bends can easily be practiced at home. The superbly developed leg muscles of Gail Devers undoubtedly contributed to her consistently good starts.

You should not allow yourself to veer off the center of the lane. A course correction during the start would affect the turnover rhythm with a consequent momentary easing back on the throttle. Also, should your peripheral vision pick up someone crowding close to your lane, predispose yourself to have the concentration to ignore what is outside your lane. As a sprinter, you must ignore not only the sights, but also those forceful sounds that originate outside your own lane stripes. Total concentration on *your* race is a must.

While shorter strides (not quicker) are required when exiting the blocks, this too can be overdone. The stride must be long enough to permit the power of the upper leg to be the primary contributor to one's acceleration. If the stride is too short, the use of the quad muscles is reduced. In this circumstance, only the foot remains as the major contributor to gaining forward speed. The turnover rate must be melded with a stride length that will allow your leg strength to deliver the maximum power to the track.

Most sprinters spend an appreciable amount of time experimenting with the fore-and-aft positions of the pedals until they arrive at a combination they are satisfied with. Surprisingly though, very little attention is given to the lateral foot placement on the pedals. The company that manufactured your starting blocks had absolutely no knowledge of which person would be using them. The distance from the center of one pedal measured across the rail to the center of the other pedal was, therefore, *not* established with *you* in mind. Consequently, do not feel you must place your feet directly in the center of each pedal. The lateral spacing of your feet should be given due consideration. Those with wider hips may need a wider spacing of the feet.

The correct lateral spacing, however, is in large part dependent upon the relative amount of push the runner gets from each foot against its pedal. If you are one who gets almost entirely all your push from the forward foot, that foot will have to be more in line with your center of weight in order to maintain lateral balance. On the other hand, if you get an appreciable push from the rear foot also, and it shares in the initial push off, the feet can be spaced laterally further apart. In addition to forward balance, one must be in complete control of lateral balance when driving out of the blocks.

Do not attempt to put the center of weight directly in front of the forward foot. It is necessary to maintain some eccentricity here so that when this leg has completed its push forward from the front pedal, there will be some tendency for the body to fall to the opposite side. This is good. When the rear foot has come forward from its pedal and makes its first touchdown, this leg is then positioned so that its push will produce a tendency to force the body laterally again to the opposite side.

This sideways tendency is controlled by the lateral foot placement that one uses for the first few strides. The correct amount of lateral distance between these foot plants for one to use is, in turn, dependent upon one's turnover rate. A higher turnover rate should be accompanied by a wider foot placement. A slower, more powerful, turnover rate would utilize a foot placement more in line with one's body. In all cases, because the turnover rate is quite high, no visible side-to-side movement of the body will have the opportunity to take place. However, the tendency to produce this motion is deliberately introduced to the runner's form for these first few strides of the acceleration.

When done properly, one's *lateral* inertia is utilized as a firm resistance for the leg action to push against. This permits a more powerful push by the leg. The body's inertia against increased forward motion must be overcome, but a wide foot plant uses the body's inertia against lateral motion as an aid toward obtaining a stronger push against the track. The lateral components of successive leg thrusts (being in opposite directions) cancel each other out. But the forward components are additive to each other and combine to provide a strong forward push. The overall result of this action is a quicker acceleration off the starting line.

If, however, the body were allowed to move laterally, the body would have lost its ability to provide a firm base for the leg motion to push against. In this case, a portion of the leg extension would be wasted in a sideways motion of the body, and the total push would be diminished. The lateral spacing of foot plants must be melded with the turnover rate so that the proper tendency to displace the body sideways is produced: enough to permit a strong push by each leg, but not so much as to overcome one's lateral inertia and actually produce a sideways motion. If the lateral distance used for the foot plants is so great that the upper body visibly rocks from side to side, this motion would detract from the energy of forward motion and the start would suffer. Wide is good; too wide is bad.

This concept of using a wide foot plant at this stage of the race, and allowing a portion of the leg thrust to push against one's lateral inertia is quite similar to the action of a speed skater on ice skates. In the case of the ice skater, the skater achieves a forward speed that is significantly greater than the speed of the leg extension that is used to propel the athlete forward. This is made possible by the skater pressing partially sideways with each propelling leg extension. The other skate blade prevents the skater from being moved sideways. The result, then, is the skater is squirted forward at a high speed, which is the only way the force from the diagonally pushing leg can be relieved.

In the case of the runner, the athlete also pushes diagonally backward with the driving leg, but relies on the lateral inertia of one's own body to resist being moved sideways. Again, the result is the athlete is forced forward at a speed that is greater than is the speed at which the leg extension is occurring. The squeezing of the fingers while holding a tapered icicle will produce a similar motion. Although the fingers may close only ¼", the icicle will squirt forward several inches. Sailboats and iceboats utilize this same concept to gain forward motion from a wind that is blowing from the side.

The conscious use of this wide lateral foot plant should normally be made for the first three strides of each leg. After this initial acceleration is completed, the lateral spacing of foot plants should be allowed to decrease. This will permit the foot plant to move inward to a location under the hip joint.

Do not try to curtail this sideways motion of the leg as it drives you from the blocks. This is a natural and very advantageous action that the body is utilizing. Encourage it to develop to its maximum. Knowing just what this sideways push can do for you will enable you to use it to your best advantage. This can encourage the power of the hips to add to the leg power.

When coming out of the blocks, the timing of the shift from one supporting leg to the other is absolutely critical. The runner must make three things happen with exactly the right timing in order to achieve a really good start.

First, the forward distance of each foot plant, in conjunction with its timing, must provide for a steady raising of the torso as the legs drive their way under it. Too great or too little forward distance with a foot plant would disturb this steady raising of the torso.

Second, the lateral spacing of each foot plant, in conjunction with its timing, must provide the proper tendency to shift the body's weight from one side to the other. Too small a lateral spacing does not allow the driving leg to develop its maximum power. Too great a lateral spacing causes the body to rock from side to side. Either extreme will detract from one's acceleration.

Third, the timing of each stride must coincide with the time it takes each leg to touch down and then reach the degree of extension it needs in order to deliver maximum power to the track. Insufficient leg extension would preclude the quads from delivering their optimum power. Too great an extension would cause the leg to include that inefficient portion of the extension that occurs when the leg is nearly straight. This latter condition would also slow the turnover rate so that less total power would be delivered to the track. In addition, it runs the risk of producing airborne time during which no forward push is produced.

For the best start, each component must be executed perfectly, and the foot placement and the timing of all three must be made to coincide. To make this happen on a consistent basis will require a great deal of highly focused practice. An obvious requirement for the development of a good start is the allotment of sufficient time in the training program to properly evaluate and develop one's own starting techniques. It may be that the best tool one can have while sorting through the variables, experimenting with different techniques, pinpointing what needs improvement, and then incorporating the appropriate adjustment into the mix, is the runner's own sense of feel.

Only the runner can feel the stress placed upon the quadriceps and the pressure of each driving stride on the under side of the foot. If that pressure is too light or is not equal on both feet, the start will suffer. One must strive for the maximum pressure on the feet for the first several strides of each leg. That is what drives the runner forward. A runner's feel of what is happening inwardly coupled with a coach's keen eye on what is happening outwardly, will afford the best setting to improve this segment of the race.

Before taking position in the starting blocks, the runner should also have a mental picture of what he wants to look like when driving from the blocks. You may want to think of a picture of a runner coming out of the blocks that you want to emulate. This is the form you want to have after the first motion is performed. Give your body an image it should strive to duplicate. Once the body knows what it is supposed to do, it will do a better job of performing as you want. Take to the line with confidence and concentrate on your own race. This is the only one that matters.

A precise execution of the start will be critical to the outcome of the race. It is important to take several practice starts the day of the race, and then again immediately preceding the race start in order to sharpen the mind and the body. If it appears there will not be adequate time to take that final practice start, the author goes through a routine of closing the eyes and envisioning the body raising to the set position. A deep breath is taken and internal pressure is raised. An image of the form the author will have at that moment is now in the mind. Upon imagining the firing of the starting gun, the first motion that will be taken is visualized. That image is then retained until it is really performed in the actual start.

This total concentration on the start helps keep the initiation of the body's first motion firmly fixed at the forefront of the mind. Additionally, the process of increasing the air pressure within the lungs clears the lungs of excess fluid by forcing it from the lungs into the bloodstream. This will enhance the exchange of oxygen and carbon dioxide within the lungs in the upcoming race.

At this point, it seems appropriate to take a more in-depth look at what is happening when one runner exits the starting blocks quicker than does another. Consider two runners who run identical races *except* that runner "A" responds to the gun 0.1 seconds faster than does runner "B." Since, in this example, the two competitors run otherwise equal races, runner "A" will then reach the finish line 0.1 seconds before runner "B." But in real life, there is the fluster factor to contend with that could expand the difference in finish times to more than the 0.1 seconds that occurred at the start.

For simplicity, let us say that runner "A" starts to race at time 0.0 on the clock, and that runner "B" (because of not responding as quickly) starts to race when the clock reads 0.1 seconds. When runner "B" starts to race at time 0.1, runner "A" will already be some inches ahead. Now the bad news begins. Not only is runner "A" a few inches ahead of runner "B" at this instant, but also runner "A" because of starting earlier has had time to begin building up speed. (Please note that this simplified starting scenario is not associated with the minimum allowed reaction time of 0.100 seconds measured on the starting pedals.)

Later, when the clock reads 1.0 seconds, runner "B" will have been running for only 0.9 seconds and will gave gained speed appropriate for that time interval. However, at this same time (1.0 seconds on the clock), runner "A" will have been running for a full 1.0 seconds and will have gained even greater speed than runner "B." At this time, runner "A" will not only be ahead of runner "B," but will also be running faster and opening the spread between the two runners.

At time 2.0 seconds on the clock, a similar situation will exist. At this point, runner "B" will have been running for 1.9 seconds and will have reached a speed commensurate with that running time. However, runner "A" will have been running for a full 2.0 seconds and will have reached an even higher speed. Runner "A" has now been running faster than runner "B" for the entire 2.0 seconds of the race. Runner "B" is now not only behind runner "A," but worse, is aware of falling still further behind at every step of the race. (Remember, that up to this point, except for the 0.1 seconds difference in their reaction times, the two runners have otherwise been running identical races despite the ever-increasing distance between them.)

All too often, what happens now is that runner "B" punches the panic button. Although the race has barely begun, runner "B" is already aware of being left behind. With disaster threatening, the game plan is thrust aside. "B" begins to press harder, resorts to instinct running, and thereby loses still more time and ground against runner "A." If this were allowed to happen, the two runners would no longer be running identical races.

On the other hand, with a full understanding of what is happening, runner "B" will be able to maintain a cool head and run the race as planned. When both runners finally reach their top speed, the distance gap between them will then remain constant. Runner "B" will lose no further ground to runner "A" and will finish 0.1 seconds behind. The distance between the two runners at the finish line will be the distance they cover during 0.1 seconds while running at their identical full speeds.

In summary, the time interval between the two runners remains constant at 0.1 seconds throughout the entire race. However, the distance interval between the two runners grows progressively greater as the two runners increase their speed. The 0.1 seconds delay at the start, which begins as a barely discernable difference at the 1-meter mark, may grow to a 3' difference by the 60-meter mark. It's still a 0.1 seconds difference, but the physical difference of that 0.1 seconds is much more evident at the higher speeds. What starts out as a very small distance handicap for runner "B," soon turns into a large distance handicap as the two runners increase their speed. If this should happen to you, knowing *why* you are losing distance right after the start, will better enable you to continue running the best race you can. However, if this happens repeatedly, you will understand you must improve your start out of the blocks so you don't give away an insurmountable lead.

Don't allow others to distract you from your purpose. You must retain total control over all that happens in your lane. Know from the depths of your bones that your assigned lane is completely yours, no one else's. Take full command over the execution of your start. Do not let activity in some other lane affect your performance. Run your race as you trained for it.

Alternative Techniques for the Start

We must remain cognizant that we are each an individual and as such have our unique body size, strengths, weaknesses, talents and limitations. This chapter, which addresses the start, would therefore not be complete without looking at some alternative techniques that may be useful to different individuals.

The positions of the toes when in the starting blocks as previously suggested were for the use of blocks with a flat surface. Alternatively, some blocks offer a curved surface for placement of the feet. The most natural placement here is for the point of the toes to be at the bottom of the pedal where it meets the track.

The ball of the foot, the ankle, the knee and the hip joint should all stay in alignment. If the knee of the leg on the forward pedal has a tendency to bow outward during its push, much of that leg power will be lost. If you have this problem, try moving that foot outward on the pedal. If the portion of the foot at the little toe hangs off the outside of the pedal, no great loss; it wasn't going to do much pushing anyway. Keep the knee of that leg close in to your body. Remember to keep that knee tucked in when you come to the set position. This may help keep that leg in alignment, which is imperative in order to get maximum drive from the leg. More stadium steps (two at a time) and weight training may also help.

As we drive from the blocks, we support our weight and drive it forward with just one leg at a time. If difficulty is being experienced in getting good drive from the forward leg against its pedal, it may be that the rear leg is completing its stride and touching down too soon. Once that foot touches down, the pressure is relieved from the other foot that is against the forward pedal. When this happens, the usefulness of the forward pedal is lost because the other foot will now be doing the supporting and driving. Additionally, this first short step by the rear leg may possibly set the stage for ensuing steps to be quick steps rather than powerful steps.

The reason the trailing foot is making its first touchdown too early may lie with the other foot and its action on the forward pedal. If the foot associated with the forward pedal is providing insufficient forward push, the outstretched torso will tend to fall. To prevent this fall, the foot from the rear pedal must now touch down prematurely in order to prevent such a fall. The best corrective action here is more dedicated time building one's leg strength.

Although other possibilities are noted, and remedies offered, inadequate push by the leg associated with the front pedal is almost always caused by inadequate strength of leg. Exercises dedicated to building a more powerful leg extension are the obvious solution. Not just strength, quick strength is what is needed here. The closer your exercise mimics your start, the faster your start will improve.

Another possibility is relatively remote but is also related to the foot on the forward pedal. It may be that the foot on the forward pedal is pushing with too great an eccentricity. In this case, the body will be thrust to the opposite side, and again, the foot from the rear pedal will be forced to touch down sooner than it otherwise would in order to maintain lateral balance. The remedy here is to keep the forward foot in closer to the rail. If the body's weight is more directly in line with the driving leg, that leg will push the body straight forward and a fuller extension of that leg can be achieved before the opposite foot has to touch down.

On the other hand, if you have difficulty in getting the first foot plants far enough to each side, you may want to try the following technique. When placing the feet against the pedals, place each foot as close to the center rail as possible. Then place the knee that is associated with the rear foot, onto the track with about 6" clear between the inside of the knee and the center rail. Angle the forward knee outward also, but perhaps only half this amount. The placement of the hands at the starting line will have to be adjusted outward in order to accommodate this spread-knee position. When coming to the set position, keep the knees angled outward as they had been previously set.

The objective here is that when the foot pushes off from the pedal, it will push the leg somewhat in the direction the lower leg is already pointing, off to the side. The resulting wider foot plant should then allow the runner to get a strong push off from that first plant of each foot. Push powerfully (not quickly) from these wide foot plants.

If you feel you should be getting still more push from the forward leg, you might try moving the hips sideways so that more weight is placed on that forward foot. Another technique that can be experimented with is to walk the hand, which is associated with the forward foot, approximately 4" further outward (or, if both hands are already placed out near the lane dividers, move the other hand inward). As the hand is walked over, it will be noticed that the shoulders also move in this same direction (perhaps 2") in order that they remain equidistant from each hand.

This action moves a considerable amount of upper body weight into closer alignment with the foot on the front pedal. When the gun is fired, this increased weight over the forward driving leg will allow that leg the opportunity to perform a really strong push forward. The author is not in favor of skewing the body out of alignment and this is offered as a possibility only if other measures fail to produce the desired result for the first stride.

Superimposed upon all the above, one will also want to experiment with different amounts of arm swing at the sound of the gun. A greater rearward swing of the arm associated with the rear foot will bring that leg forward faster but may decrease the amount of push received from the rear pedal. A more dramatic forward swing of the arm associated with the forward leg will increase the push received from the forward pedal but could delay too much, the forward motion of the leg from that pedal. The runner will have to determine what amount of arm swing works best in combination with the push being obtained by the legs.

One may also want to experiment with momentarily stopping the arms in their extended positions after their first swing. By slightly delaying the start of the second swing of the arms, more time will be allowed for the legs to perform their first motions. This will allow the leg on the forward pedal to perform a greater extension and thereby provide the body with more forward push.

If a runner continues to have difficulty obtaining sufficient drive off the pedals, a mental (or written) list of the things to be improved upon should be made. As an example, when the foot from the rear pedal makes its first touchdown, that touchdown is what signals the foot that is against the forward pedal to stop pushing and begin its forward motion. If a runner is replanting the rear foot too soon, this would rob the forward foot, which is still against its pedal, of the opportunity to deliver the maximum forward drive to the body. In this circumstance, a change is called for.

There may be a need to change the positions of the starting blocks. It may be necessary to swing the arms further. Perhaps a more pointed knee as the rear leg comes forward would allow it to swing further forward before touching down. This, in turn, would create more time to permit greater extension of the leg that is still in contact with the front pedal. Experiment until you get the drive off the front pedal that you seek.

If you feel you may want to give these same items more emphasis in *your* start, write down the motions you want to accentuate. Then, during your warm up go through these motions that you want to improve upon. While going through these motions, repeat the words to yourself: *arms, knee, extend,* or whatever the desired motion of each limb may be. This will more firmly implant the motions in your mind, and they will come easier to you when needed. Don't forget to revisit the placement of the feet in the starting blocks. One should occasionally check to see if a change in starting technique now requires a change in the setting of the pedals. Determine where you need to focus your attention in order to get your best start. Then devise a method that works for *you* in order to make the appropriate changes and achieve the desired result.

There is much to experiment with in order to obtain the best start for any particular runner. There is almost always some aspect of the start that can be improved. A better understanding of what goes into a good start will aid in implementing that improvement. Properly coordinating the pertinent factors will be, for many, the most difficult part of developing a good start.

It is important to note that no single factor operates independently of the others. Changing one will affect the others. Each is interrelated with the others by the common bonds of time and gravity. An adjustment to one will require a reevaluation of the combined total. This is what makes developing a good start so challenging. Many repetitions are required to attain the necessary precision. But stay with it. Remember, it all begins with the setting of the blocks and how your body utilizes that setting. The finish of your next race may be determined right here, in developing your start, before the next gun is even fired.

Don't forget the basics. Drive with the elbows and point the knees. One should not let the torso come fully erect until approaching top speed. Avoid too high a turnover rate that will prevent delivering full power to the track. Accelerate by pushing from behind and keep those elbows in a full amplitude swing.

We should note that a sprinter does not run every race exactly the same and we therefore cannot draw any conclusions from just a single race. But it was observed that the margin of victory held by Gail Devers over her rivals Merlene Ottey and Gwen Torrence in the 100m final of the 1996 Olympic Games was considerably less than the lead she held over them at the end of the start segment of the race. The importance of a good start cannot be overemphasized. Any advantage gained here may be needed further down the track.

The First Motion

If you have not already done so, stop and give serious thought to just what you want the first motion of your race to be. This first motion lays the foundation for all that follows. Spend some quality time and give it the serious consideration it deserves. When considering this first motion of your race, you are not necessarily confined to thinking of that motion in terms of only a single limb. If you will be looking for simultaneous motions from several body parts, you will want to consider each of those simultaneous motions as being part of your first motion.

Consideration of several simultaneous first motions could therefore lead to as many as five simultaneous first thoughts: left arm, right arm, rear leg, front leg, head/torso. With repetition, some of these will occur without any conscious thought process. When this happens, the runner will know that progress is being made in establishing the desired procedure for the start. This now allows the runner to think about only that motion that is needed to be most pronounced or exaggerated. The fewer motions one thinks of, the more definitive will be the physical responses with these motions. If, on the other hand, the runner will be looking for the first motion of one body part to begin after the first motion of another body part has begun, the first motion impressed in one's head will be the motion of only the first-moving body part(s).

The first motion of the foot that will press upon the forward pedal is *no motion*. But it is still a vital action and, as such, it will be considered here. You will want that foot to hold its position for some extended time—until after the first motions of all the other limbs have been completed. During this time, it will be exerting the maximum possible force against its pedal. This is why you carefully chose the foot position that you wanted to utilize for this action. Proper forethought is now paying its dividends.

As we have all observed, one is able to move a free limb (one that is not operating under an external load) considerably faster than one is able to move that same limb when it is operating under load (such as when lifting a weight). The second observation is that immediately after the starting gun, three of our limbs are operating freely while only the leg utilizing the forward pedal is operating under load.

The third observation introduced at this time is that the straightening of the leg by a longer-limbed runner will propel the body a greater distance forward than will the straightening of the leg by a shorter-limbed runner. The greater distance one's body is projected, the greater will be the elapsed time to complete this straightening of the leg. If both runners were allotted the same amount of time for straightening one's leg, the longer-limbed runner would not achieve the same degree of extension as did the shorter-limbed runner.

In connecting these three observations, the consideration is (depending upon where an individual is situated in the broad spectrum of leg lengths and leg strengths) the runner may be striving to complete the first motions of the three free limbs as quickly as possible. This endeavor may not produce the makings of the best start. When the free limbs complete their first actions, their natural inclinations will be to begin their second actions. For the leg that utilizes the rear pedal, the first action is its swing forward. Its second action is to touch down and begin its support of the runner. When this leg's second action begins, the opposite leg, which has been pushing on the forward pedal, will derive no further benefit from that pedal. With the other leg now in the commanding support position, the leg on the forward pedal will cease its valuable pushing action and begin its forward motion.

We do not want the leg from the rear pedal to complete its initial forward swing until the leg on the forward pedal has had the opportunity to complete its best extension while providing the push against its pedal. The completions of the first actions by the three free limbs must be controlled so they coincide with the most efficient completion time of the one limb acting under load. The degree of leg extension that will transmit the greatest power from the loaded leg to its pedal is what must dictate the first-action-completion-times of the free limbs. This will now also affect the turnover rate for the subsequent strides. Remain alert for the probability that extensive tweaking will be required in order to synchronize all four limbs to this point of coordination.

The first motions that are enacted at the start of one's race perform a transitional function for the runner. These motions transition the runner from a matched or same-mode type of action (no motion in any limb) that one holds while in the set position to an alternating type of action that one performs when in the running motion. While in the set position, the limbs are all doing the same thing at the same time. The *thing* in this case is no movement; all limbs are experiencing this non-movement at the same time and to the same degree. In contrast, when running, the arms are in an alternating action with each other, and similarly, the legs are in an alternating action with each other.

How well the athlete transitions from the simultaneity of limb motion identified with the set position to the alternating motion of limbs identified with the running motion is one of the elements of a runner's start. To this end, it appears appropriate that the initial swings of the arms (one swinging forward, the other swinging backward) should have similar carries to them and be performed in a manner that will most readily establish their equivalent alternating motions. The arms do not provide support for the body. Therefore, the only considerations to be given the intensity of their initial motions are their indirect effects upon the legs. These effects upon the legs will include the intensity of push from the leg on the forward pedal and the timing of the leg swing from the rear pedal.

The establishment of the alternating action of the legs requires a different line of thought because we are looking for different contributions from the legs than we were seeking from the arms. These contributions include the providing of proper support and balance for the body, the establishment of the turnover rate that will allow the most efficient degree of leg extension in the delivery of power to the track, and the greatest possible push from the leg associated with the forward pedal.

None of these responsibilities that we have placed upon the legs suggests that a high turnover rate should be employed in order to obtain the best result. Invoking too high a turnover at the start is one of the most common errors committed. Unfortunately, once this high turnover is initiated, it is virtually impossible to correct it part way down the track.

The most important consideration at the start is the pressure exerted by the runner's foot on the front pedal and the length of time this pressure can be maintained. It is this pressure that provides initial movement of the runner toward the finish line and begins the process of acceleration. Quite obviously then, the actions of the runner's other limbs should be controlled to best support the action of this one limb doing the driving at this moment.

The best thing the leg from the rear pedal can do to assist the leg on the forward pedal is to avoid moving forward and touching down too soon. As an additional benefit, this provides the rear foot the opportunity to give a quick flick to the rear pedal and add a very brief forward impulse to the body. If in this manner, the turnover of the legs is slightly lowered, there is no need to attempt any higher turnover by the arms. Their actions can be made more deliberate so that they match, and support, the actions of the legs.

The manner in which the athlete transitions to the alternating motions of the runner can enhance the manner in which one executes the start of the race. Give some serious consideration to that first motion you want to execute at the start of your race. Strongly maintain the image of that motion in your mind when you come to the set position. Inhale as you raise up to the set position and build up your internal pressure. Do NOT listen for the sound of the gun. Listening for the gun would encourage one to think about and analyze that sound. We don't care about any of the qualities of that sound; we only care that the sound has occurred. Instead, think of your first motion. The sound of the gun is the trigger that releases you to perform that motion. That sound allows you to release your fully-primed body parts to perform those first actions that you had thought through and trained yourself to perform. You're off to a good start.

We have often heard that to achieve a good start, one must think of the first motion that is to be initiated at the sound of the gun. We now have a better understanding of just what those words mean. As with everything involved with the sprint, not only are the *mechanics* of the actions significant, the *timing* of those actions is also important. If you have not already done so, stop and give serious thought to just what you want the first motion of your race to be.

The Standing Start

For Masters runners, a standing start without the use of starting blocks is permissible and some prefer to use this option. One drawback is that, in the standing position, the arms cannot be used for additional body support. Therefore, the legs must be placed under the center of weight in order to maintain balance while waiting for the starting signal. In this position, the legs cannot be extended behind the runner and it is more difficult to obtain a good push to begin the acceleration. But, for those who prefer the standing start, and if you are dissatisfied with your present method, the following alternative is offered.

To place oneself in this starting position, begin by placing the toes of both feet at the starting line with about 2" of clear space between them. Now move the foot of the stronger leg straight backward until it is about 15" behind the starting line. The toes of both feet are pointing forward. The feet are now set in their starting positions. Neither one should be moved backward from this location at the sound of the gun.

The arms are positioned with a slight crook in the elbows. The arm that is associated with the forward foot is extended forward and the other arm is extended to the rear. At the set command (if one is given), both knees are flexed and the runner goes into a semi-crouch. The hips and upper body should be shifted sideways so that ¾ of the body weight is on the rear foot and ¼ on the forward foot. Now the runner leans forward until both heels come off the track and balance is maintained on the ball of each foot and the pads of the toes. One should not look at the finish line, but instead, look down at the track approximately two meters in front of the starting line. Looking up tends to make one raise to the vertical too quickly. The runner is now ready for the gun.

The traditional standing start involves a sideways twist to the body, which in turn requires a sideways push on the track. In contrast, this alternative starting position places the runner facing straight ahead. The feet also point straight ahead for a strong push off without the need for a resetting of either foot when the gun sounds.

At the starting signal, the *forward* foot is raised off the track. This must be a decisive movement with the intent of keeping that foot off the track as long as possible. Placing that forward foot back onto the track prematurely would detract from the pushing action of the strong rear leg. The rear foot is already in the correct position to drive the body forward with a good push from behind. At the starting signal, that rear foot should remain right where it was placed earlier. As soon as the forward foot is raised, the rear foot will be supporting all the runner's weight. With the knee already flexed from being in the semi-crouch position, the rear leg will automatically begin its push forward.

At the same time that the forward foot is raised off the track, both arms are swung to their opposite positions. Replanting of the forward foot should be delayed as long as possible so that the rear foot can complete its first push with good weight on that leg. Again, we want the first three foot plants of each leg to be outside the point that would provide lateral balance.

From here on, the normal starting techniques will apply. The runner should strive for a strong push from the first few strides. This will push the body forward and build up good speed. This is preferable to a higher turnover rate that would result in one giving the track a good stomping but be less effective in accelerating the body to a higher speed. The runner should not look up until approaching top speed. One should concentrate on keeping those legs pushing from behind.

The raising of the forward foot when the gun sounds will be awkward at first, and there will be a tendency to put it back down too soon. Because of the semi-crouch starting position, that foot cannot be raised very far. That's okay. One should just make the lift a convincing movement with the intent of keeping the foot off the track as long as possible. This starting technique will take some getting used to, but give it a chance before discarding it as being "not for me."

This starting technique can also be used for longer races where no starting blocks are used. Here, all runners are lined up on the track with each trying to break free and avoid being crowded out upon reaching the first turn.

Psychological Preparation

So far, we have talked about the physical aspects of the start. Taking to the starting line psychologically prepared is also important. The runner should not be hesitant to put oneself *on the line* to be judged in a sporting competition. The runner should approach the line with the confidence of knowing the body is well prepared and is ready to perform at its best. The training program and race preparation must be conducted in a manner that will support this conviction. Be ready to run. Be ready to do your utmost. *Always believe in yourself.*

We will never achieve a perfectly honed body. Every time that anyone enters a race, it will be with a body that is less than ideal. That will never change, so there is no need to think further of this now as one enters the starting area. Likewise, it's too late to do anything further about an injury. To dwell on one's shortcomings is to set the stage for defeat before the race is started. It is essential that the runner think positive and have confidence in the training that has brought him to this race. Only by maintaining an optimistic frame of mind will one be capable of achieving a good performance.

As race time approaches, one's mind must be directed toward the start. One does not think about making the perfect lean at the finish, or of utilizing a particular high-speed technique. If one does not properly execute the start, properly performing those later portions of the race will be of far less consequence. It is at the start where one can make it or lose it. Make certain you are ready to do it right. At this moment, concentration is the runner's most important task. This concentration must not be allowed to stray. Unlike longer events, there is no opportunity to increase intensity later in the event. Later is too late. Full intensity must be attained when in the set position; the gun then releases it to action.

If the runner thinks only of the first movement to be made at the sound of the gun, a far better frame of mind will be engendered to grab the good start, which otherwise may only be dreamed about. While standing behind the starting blocks and staring in the direction of (but not seeing) the starting line, the movement that will be made for that first motion after the gun must be envisioned. The runner must know exactly how to respond to the sound of the gun. Staying focused on this immediate movement will help maintain the self-confidence needed to perform well. If the second and third motions are problem areas, have a plan in mind to deal with them, but they cannot be brought to mind until the first motion is completed.

The actions of others are of no concern to the runner. Remember, *you* are in total control of what happens in *your lane.* Think of the action of the shoulders, that first stride forward with a pointed knee, or the arm motion that is needed. Get that critical picture etched into the brain. Do not think any further ahead than just the first motion that will be performed at the sound of the gun. This is the most important one and sets the tone for all that follows.

After the runner has settled into the blocks, that single thought must continue to be kept in mind. If this key thought is strong enough, it will block out all extraneous activity that is always occurring. As one raises to the set position and takes a generous inhalation, that image must still be retained in mind. There is no point in having concentrated on that one image all this time if it is allowed to slip away now. One must hold that image in mind until it has been executed. The runner easily holds balance. There is no reason for a false start. One's level of aggression has now reached its peak. But this is a controlled aggression. This runner knows exactly what needs to be done at the sound of the gun.

The runner must react immediately to the sound of the gun. At the gun, the brain releases the body to perform that movement that has been ingrained in the mind. Once this first motion is executed, and *only* then, should the next order of business be considered: wide foot plants with both feet, strong evenly matched responses from both legs, knees driving forward, solid foot plants at a precise cadence, full swings of the elbows to the rear. Any faltering of a step here is a sign of improper balance.

Nowhere else in the race is precision so important. The runner must be totally focused upon the present moment. One must think of nothing except what must be happening at this instant. As the runner becomes nearly vertical and approaches running speed, the mental checklist of techniques needed to achieve top speed should now begin.

This is all predicated on having determined what must be concentrated on. You cannot approach the starting line having not yet decided what to do.

Make a decision. It may be the right decision, or it may be a wrong one. But you must have a plan and be ready to execute that plan. If it is the wrong plan, it can be changed for the next race. But it will never be the right plan if your thoughts are muddled. This can only lead to indecisive action. Only with decisive action can the right plan come to fruition. Understand what it is you need to accomplish; then use this knowledge to develop the start that works for you.

Afterthoughts

At the time of this writing, the rules pertaining to false starts are quite harsh. According to current rules, no one is disqualified upon the first false start in a field of runners. However, this false start is charged to the entire field. Any subsequent false start will result in that runner being disqualified, even if it is the runner's only false start.

I certainly believe false starts must be discouraged because they are sometimes an indicator that a runner is attempting to anticipate the gun and thereby gain an unfair advantage over the competition. But this may not always be the case. When being held in the set position, an unexpected twitch of a leg or shoulder muscle could result in the athlete being disqualified. This seems like an unduly harsh result for such an occurrence. The longer the starter official *holds* the runners, the greater are the chances of an unfortunate consequence.

In lieu of disqualification, perhaps some alternative is possible. One scenario could be that after the first false start has been charged to the field, any runner who commits a single false start, which causes a restart, would be allowed to remain in the race. The difference now being, that runner would carry a time penalty that would be added to one's actual finishing time on the subsequent successful start. Such a system would discourage false starts, yet still allow a full field of runners to compete except that two false starts by any runner would result in that runner being disqualified.

Instead of a time penalty, a distance penalty would be superior. In this instance, the faulted runner would start at some predetermined distance behind the other runners. Now, the order of finish as observed would be the order of finish as recorded. The starting line for faulted runners could be a distinctive color. A longer race would present more opportunity to make up such a penalty; therefore, a longer race would carry a heavier penalty for one who had false started.

If some such system were utilized in the early rounds of a meet, a runner charged with a false start would still have the possibility of advancing to the next round. If the handicapped runner were unable to make up the deficit, that runner would not qualify for advancement to the next round. However, a full field of eight runners would still have had the opportunity to compete in all rounds. This would be better for the athletes and the spectators alike. Consequently, it would be good for the sport.

Critics might argue that such a system would unfairly treat the slower runner (who has false started) since that runner would be less apt to overcome the imposed penalty than would the faster runner. A reasonable response to this criticism would be "Is not the purpose of the event to determine who is the fastest runner?" A system that discourages false starts and that also provides a means for runners to remain in the competition cannot be all bad.

On a different aspect of the start, in sprint events where no electrically activated speaker is placed on the starting blocks, the runner's start is governed by receipt of the sound directly from the starter's pistol. This introduces a slight delay that is not accounted for when assigning race times to individuals. For every 11 feet that a runner is positioned further from the starter's pistol, there is a 0.01 seconds delay in the time the runner receives the start signal. There does not seem to be a convenient way to account for this. It appears we will have to wait for the cost of individual electric starting devices to be lowered to the point they become more prevalent. We have the technology; unfortunately, cost is always an issue.

In the lane assignments for the 100m race, differences in condition of the track surface in each lane is always a consideration, but distance from the starter's pistol should not be ignored. Rather than an arbitrary system of lane assignment, it seems only fair that runners with the fastest times in qualifying heats of that event be given first choice of lane selection for subsequent races. It appears that technology is now sufficiently advanced that this choice could be offered the runners.

7

THE SPRINTER'S STRIDE

The start segment of the race has carried us to the point where the sprinter has completed the acceleration, has become fully erect and has achieved running speed. Now, the run segment of the race begins, often referred to as the fly phase. During the run segment, the runner must assume the form and employ the techniques that will provide the quickest means to the finish line. But, what is the correct form? What are the right techniques? Do not judge the right technique to be the one that feels most natural. The right technique is the one that gets you to the finish line the soonest. We will examine various techniques and each reader can judge then, not if the technique seems natural, but if it may make one faster.

The objective of any new technique is that it will offer an improvement to one's speed. After training for some period of time with a new technique, the body will come to accept it. The new technique will no longer seem new. The body will now view it to be quite normal. This process will have been exceedingly easy if the technique has shown itself to be an improvement to one's racing game. In this frame of mind, we will begin our analysis of the sprinter's stride.

When striving to cover more ground with each tick of the clock, a runner may want to reach further forward with the leg so that, with each stride, more distance is covered. This might work fine if this increased distance were the only factor involved. Unfortunately, with every touchdown there is a braking force transmitted from the track, up the leg and to the hip joint. This braking force dramatically reduces one's forward speed.

If a child were running through the house and came to the freshly mopped kitchen floor, we all know what would happen. The child's foot would slip *forward* of its body and the child would go down rear end first. Since the track is not nearly as slippery as the kitchen floor, a runner's foot does not slip forward at touchdown. Instead, the track applies a rearward braking force to the runner's foot that slows one's forward speed.

This braking action would be greater if the runner were to stretch the stride and move the point of touchdown further forward of the hip joint. The increase in braking would more than offset any gain in stride length obtained by reaching the leg forward. Increasing stride length by reaching further forward with the leg is not the way to increase forward speed; it slows the runner by increasing the braking action.

Since this braking action has such a profound effect upon the runner's speed, let us look at it more closely. The braking action can be viewed as having three components. Component No. 1 is due to the weight of the runner and it occurs when the leg that is supporting the runner is in contact with the track at a location in front of the runner. Because the weight of the runner presses down on the track, the track will exert a reactive force that will press upward on the runner's foot an equal amount. This is how the track supports the weight of the runner. Regardless that the leg is bent at the ankle and at the knee, this supporting force will act in a direction that is straight from the ball of the foot to the hip joint. Bone and muscle take care of routing the force along the bent path of the leg between these two end points.

Whenever the reactive force from the track, which is what supports the runner, is inclined in a direction that opposes the runner's forward motion, it has a slowing effect upon the runner. The angle by which this supporting force opposes the direction of travel is an indication of the braking effect this force is having. This inclination of the supporting force is most pronounced at the moment of touching down. The inclination becomes progressively less as the runner advances until the supporting force becomes vertical when the runner passes directly over the supporting foot. At this point, the braking component of the supporting force has diminished to zero. Component No. 1 of the braking force is shown in Figure 1.

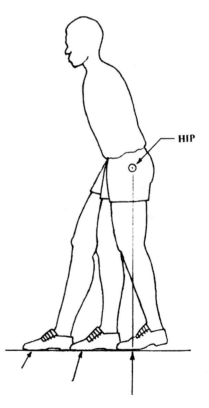

Figure 1. Braking Component No. 1.

Figure 1 shows the apparent motion of a runner's supporting foot moving rearward with respect to the advancing hip joint in three stages of stop action. At the moment of touching down, the foot is at a substantial distance in front of the runner's hip joint. Here, the reactive force from the track, because of its inclination to the runner's direction of motion, has a significant portion of its action opposing the runner's forward motion. A moment later, when the runner has advanced to a point where the foot is not extended as far forward, the braking portion of the supporting force is lessened. Finally, when the runner reaches a position directly over the foot, the supporting force is vertical and its braking portion is reduced to zero. There is not much we can do to lessen this component of the braking force that is due to the runner's weight except avoid reaching further forward with the foot, and perhaps, shed a few unwanted pounds.

We now move to component No. 2 of the braking action, which is an impact force occurring at the moment of touchdown. This is a consequence of the airborne portion of the runner's stride, during which no support is being provided by the track. At the conclusion of the airborne interval, the runner's body is descending because it has had no support. At the moment of touchdown, the descent is halted. In so doing, this puts an additional load on the supporting foot. This impact force is added to the static weight of the runner and, in effect, makes up for the time the runner was receiving no support from the track. The reactive force from the track due to impact, just like the static force due to the runner's weight, will travel in the same direction, from the foot to the hip joint. This is shown in Figure 2a.

Normally this impact force is very brief, but also very intense. Unfortunately, it occurs at the worst possible time, when the foot first touches down and is at the maximum distance in front of the runner. Here, the inclined impact force delivers a very undesirable braking effect. But, with a little ingenuity, its detrimental effect can be somewhat reduced. What we do is we *cushion* this impact force. This is accomplished by introducing a slightly bent knee to the touchdown. This is shown in Figure 2b.

If the impact force is cushioned, the total amount of the force is not changed, but its action is slightly altered. The initial intensity is reduced and the duration of the force is spread out over a longer period of time. In this way, the latter portion of the impact force will be acting at a time when the runner's body has advanced to a position that has reduced the horizontal distance between the foot and the hip joint. Consequently, the latter portion of this impact force is now acting on the runner in a more vertical direction and its braking effect is reduced accordingly.

In addition to spreading out the duration of impact and thereby lessen-

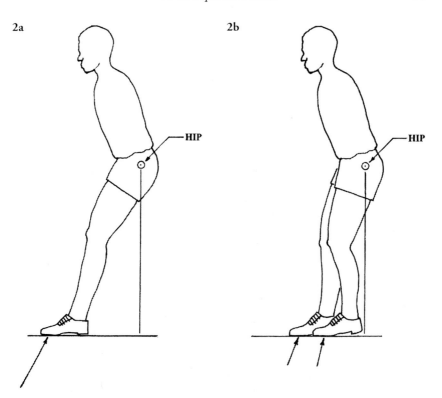

Figure 2. Braking Component No. 2.

ing the braking action, it can be seen that, by introducing a slightly bent knee, the point of *initial* contact will now be slightly closer to the runner. Therefore, the force will be somewhat more vertical, and again, the tendency is to reduce the braking effect. This gain, achieved by bringing the point of touchdown closer to the runner, will apply to both the impact force and also the force due to the runner's weight.

If the preceding got a bit heavy for some readers, it can be summed up in the following two sentences: Reaching one's stride further forward will accentuate the braking action and slow the runner's forward progress. The introduction of a slightly bent knee at touchdown will soften the foot plant, and immediately result in the runner realizing an increase in speed.

We should note at this time that braking action is *not* increased when a more powerful push from behind is utilized to increase the stride length. The reason for this is that the strong push off propels the entire body (including the hip joint) forward harder and faster. This faster speed of the runner carries the body further while it is airborne and the stride length is thereby increased. However, since the entire body has been propelled forward by the push off, the distance as measured (at the instant of touchdown) from the hip joint, forward to the point of touchdown, has not been altered. Since the relationship between the hip joint and point of touchdown remains the same, there is no change in detrimental braking action when the stride length is increased in this manner.

If the hips are slung forward, the braking action will be further reduced because the supporting force that points from foot to hip joint will point more upward rather than rearward. Note, however, that the harder one's foot strikes the ground, the slower one will run. One should not jam the foot down onto the track in an attempt to get a rebound effect. This would only accentuate the braking force. Similarly, a bobbing up-and-down running style also invites more braking action. The softer the touchdown that is attained, the faster one will run.

And now we come to the third of the three braking components. Component No. 3 of the braking action is attributed to the forward horizontal motion of the runner's foot as it contacts the stationary track. This braking effect occurs when the forward moving foot of the runner's forward moving body bite's the stationary track when touching down. The sudden stopping of the foot's forward motion when it first touches the track imparts a slowing effect to the entire runner. This is shown in Figure 3a. Fortunately, this braking component is completely under our control. It is an undesirable occurrence and can be completely eliminated by initiating proper technique as shown in Figure 3b.

To eliminate this braking effect, one must attempt to match the horizontal speed of the foot with the speed of the track so there is no jolt (in the horizontal) when the two meet. To accomplish this, one begins bending the knee just prior to touchdown. Bending the knee begins a retracting motion of the lower leg and foot. The foot is now moving inward toward the body, and its forward speed is therefore less than the forward speed of the runner's body. A more rapid bending of the knee will produce a more rapid retraction of the foot. With practice, one can retract the foot in such a manner that it has no forward speed at all at the moment it touches down on the track. This technique provides a smooth engagement and braking component No. 3 is totally eliminated. It also provides a beneficial knee bend for cushioning the impact of braking component No. 2.

A cautionary note is applicable here. Do not attempt to perform this retraction of the foot and lower leg by consciously employing a knee-bending motion. This would be too difficult to achieve, and its attempt would prove disastrous. A different approach to achieving this technique is most satisfactory and will be discussed shortly.

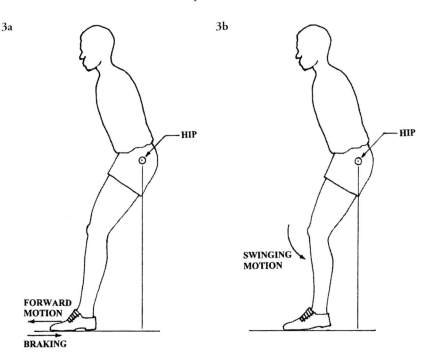

Figure 3. Braking Component No. 3.

If the foot were retracted even faster, it would be moving backward at the instant of touchdown. This would give the runner a slight impulse forward, but the lessening of stride length would outweigh this slight gain. To obtain the proper degree of foot retraction, one has only to pay close attention to the response from one's foot as it is laid down on the track. The proper amount of foot retraction will have been obtained when there is no tendency for the foot to slide either forward or backward inside the shoe. During practice, somewhat slackened shoelaces may facilitate the finding of this neutral point. When the touchdown feels the lightest, the proper match up of foot and track will have been achieved.

This technique of retracting the foot would, of itself, slightly reduce the stride length. But, the reduction of braking action is of greater importance and the runner's overall speed will increase. Because of this increase in speed, one will cover more ground during the airborne interval between each foot plant. A measurement on the track will indicate the stride length has actually increased. Take note, though, this is a technique that is applicable to high speed and is to be employed only during the run segment of the race after running speed has been attained. The runner will be able to feel a smoother running action by utilizing this technique. Once again, smoothness and speed progress hand-in-hand. The utilization of good form and the reduction of braking is not only necessary to attain top speed, but will help ward off the reduction in speed that occurs from fatigue in the second half of the race.

This feeling of improved smoothness is something that happens after the technique is employed, but does not tell the runner in advance that improved smoothness is needed. To fill this void we call upon another of our senses that we have so far used only sparingly, our eyesight. If we are reaching for too long a stride, or are landing too hard, the outward stretched leg in front of the body will land sharply. This sharp landing will cause the braking action just discussed, but it will also cause the body to bounce upward. The amount of this upward bounce at the instant of touchdown is an indicator of the amount of braking action the body is receiving.

During the run segment of the race, the runner should maintain the head in an erect posture. The eyes should be fixed in the head, looking straight ahead, focusing on nothing. In this attitude, the runner's peripheral vision will see the landscape bounce at every touchdown. By making a determined effort to minimize the bounce of the landscape, the runner will be automatically introducing the aforementioned foot-retracting technique. This is how the body naturally accomplishes this increased smoothness and a superior result is hereby produced than would be attained by attempting to directly control the retraction of the lower leg.

But first, the runner must consciously call upon the body to enact a smoother run. Experience will show just how much this landscape bounce can be minimized. The runner should keep this image in mind of ideally how much it is possible to minimize the landscape bounce. Then, on any future run, a comparison between the recalled image of what one is capable of achieving, and the amount of landscape bounce one actually sees, will indicate if the braking action has been satisfactorily reduced or if it can be reduced still further. A change in the landscape bounce brings an immediate change in the braking action, and as a consequence, an immediate change in smoothness and speed.

For proper implementation of this technique, it is necessary that the eyes focus on absolutely nothing. Experience will tell you which portion of your peripheral vision (upper, lower, side) will most keenly pick up the bouncing landscape. In most cases, the eyebrows will sharply limit the upper range of one's peripheral vision. This upper limit of vision will then be the location at which one can determine the amount of head bounce in one's running form. The goal is to lessen this bounce toward zero.

Braking action has a direct effect upon the runner's speed, and thereby an indirect effect upon the stride length. In explanation, when a softer touchdown is achieved, braking action is lessened. This reduces the amount by which the runner's speed is slowed at the beginning of the foot plant. Consequently, the push off from that foot plant will not have to regenerate the speed that braking would otherwise have taken away. With this burden removed, the push off is now able to use its power to propel the runner forward faster. This faster speed will cover more ground during the airborne portion of the stride, and the runner's stride length is increased accordingly. Only by employing this technique and experiencing the resulting gain in speed can one fully appreciate the detrimental effect of braking action and recognize the importance of taking action to minimize it.

If one has had occasion to run outdoors after darkness has fallen, it may have been noticed that with fewer visual distractions, it is easier to concentrate on one's running form. If there was the feeling that you were running better, it may not have been just your imagination. In general, we can better concentrate on a task if there are fewer distractions. When we run in daylight, we must try to duplicate that complete focus on our running. There is no need to look at objects that offer no reward for our having acknowledged their presence. This is another reason to not focus on other runners should you find yourself behind. Do not concentrate on what your eyes can see. Allow yourself only peripheral vision, which is also used to keep oneself in the center of the running lane and to assist in maintaining balance.

As a collateral advantage, not focusing on any single object frees up the mind to concentrate on the task at hand, running fast! When not concentrating on single visible objects, the brain is more receptive to messages being sent from other parts of the body. This better enables one to visualize the body and to feel one's running form. It is in this mode that the runner is best positioned to employ those techniques it is believed are most conducive to top speed.

* * *

There was a time when, at top speed, the author had the sensation of nearly falling forward over his feet. In talking with other runners, it was found that some of them also experienced a similar difficulty. This problem develops because the touchdown is, in fact, occurring too close in front of the runner. In addition to the stride being abbreviated, this foot plant will not produce a strong push off because the runner's weight is already on the toes instead of being able to roll from the ball of the foot onto the pads of the toes, pushing all the while. There can be several reasons for this shortened stride:

1. The strength of the quads and lower abdominal muscles is insufficient to swing the leg to a properly extended position in front of the runner within the time interval that the turnover rate provides for this action. Strength training should be helpful in improving this deficiency.
2. It is possible the runner is utilizing too fast a turnover instead of a more powerful stride. One may want to cut back on the turnover rate and strive to develop a stronger push off.
3. Leg mechanics may be at the root of the problem. If the knee splays outward instead of staying in alignment as the leg is swung forward, this misalignment compromises the ability of the quads to swing the leg forward. The stride length will be shortened accordingly. To correct this, make certain the feet are kept pointing straight ahead. This will assist in rotating the entire leg to a forward-facing orientation. Leg strengthening exercises should improve the alignment. In performing these exercises, do not let feet or knees point outward. Practice here the alignment you want to maintain on the track.
4. There may be an insufficiency of knee bend during the forward swing of the leg. More knee bend will allow the leg to be swung forward quicker and farther, thereby being better prepared for the touchdown.
5. There may be an insufficient momentum swing from the arms to allow the leg to properly carry forward. In this case the foot is forced to touch down early as the body attempts to limit the difference between the swinging leg momentum and the swinging arm momentum. This is discussed in more detail in a later chapter.

The foregoing was not an endorsement for longer-stride running. These are suggestions on how to get more out of a stride for which you have already expended a great deal of energy.

* * *

I'm sure that, at one time or another, most of us have determined that if we are to run faster, we must swing the free leg forward faster. In this way, it will be ready to make the touchdown sooner and we can then begin the next stride sooner. This does seem to make sense; this is the reason so many of us have attempted it.

When expending maximum effort to swing that free leg forward faster, we have, most probably, also driven the corresponding arm rearward more decisively. This also seems to make some sense. We were invoking Newton's Third Law of Motion, which is commonly stated as "for every action, there is an equal and opposite reaction." The action of driving the arm rearward more forcefully should invite the reaction of bringing the corresponding leg forward faster. And hence, we should run faster.

But experience has shown us that this effort to run faster by attempting to swing the free leg forward quicker has not resulted in the expected improvement. What has happened to our plan here? Are Mr. Newton's laws not what we thought they were?

Rest assured that Mr. Newton's laws hold true to their heralding. They will affect everything we do. But we should be aware that Newton's laws are not the only things with which the runner must contend. Another ingredient in the runner's mix of constraints is the fundamental matter of synchronism; more specifically, the underlying relationship between the movement of the left leg and the movement of the right leg; the lesson we taught ourselves when first learning to walk. No matter how hard we may try, we cannot break this bond of synchronism.

Therefore, we must be mindful that, because of this basic synchronism, the speed with which the free leg can be moved forward is directly related to how quickly the other leg (planted on the track) is moving rearward. The free leg cannot be swung forward at a faster tempo than the other leg, fixed to the track and moving backward (relative to the runner's forward motion), will allow.

When trying to swing the free leg forward faster, if nothing else is changed, the runner is fighting oneself. Here, the runner is attempting to swing the free leg at a tempo that is faster than the tempo of the planted leg. The harder we try, the more punishment we inflict upon ourselves. The pursuit of this folly leads only to frustration and despair when we discover there is no positive reward for having made such a strong effort. This absence of positive results (which I'm confident most runners can attest to) combined with the fatigue that ensues, can lead to only one inescapable conclusion: the effort to run faster by expending energy in this manner has been sorely misdirected.

Instead, use your efforts toward simultaneously moving all the body parts quicker. This will keep all the body parts synchronized. Yes, in order to swing the free leg forward faster, forward speed must first be increased so that the planted leg travels rearward faster. Do not get the physics backward. Attempting to swing the free leg forward quicker will not improve speed. Improved speed will enable the free leg to be swung forward quicker. This is a basic tenet that, all too frequently, is not correctly understood. Instead of expending strength, energy and a vast amount of practice time attempting to just swing the free leg quicker, that effort would be better spent concentrating on other techniques that will directly improve speed. Obviously, efforts are best directed toward those techniques that will offer the greatest reward right now.

A simplified version of running would tell us that it is the slowest moving of our four limbs that will determine our top speed. In general, that slowest moving limb will be the leg whose foot is anchored to the track at any given moment. Efforts spent attempting to move any one of the other three limbs faster will produce disappointing results. The three free limbs do not propel a runner down the track. Their effect on the runner is mostly in the realm of positional recovery and of momentum input to the torso and they should be viewed in that light. Momentum of our swinging limbs is discussed in greater detail in a later chapter.

In summary, those attempts to swing the leg and the associated arm harder and quicker have not yielded the desired result. We have only attempted to disrupt the natural synchronous cycle of the body. That will always be a futile struggle. If our present efforts to run faster are not showing the expected result, then we must accept what this experience is telling us. It is telling us we must try something different.

Therefore, let us not give up on Newton's law relating to action and its consequent reaction. What we must do is make certain that we apply it in a manner that will yield a positive result for us. We can do this by putting conscious emphasis on the *forward* arm swing (the action). The *rearward* push by the same-side foot that is in contact with the track at this time (the reaction) will then be similarly emphasized, even without any further direction from the runner.

If one accepts the premise that what pushes us forward is the leg action pushing rearward on the track, obviously then, a greater rearward push by that leg will increase the forward motion. When one forcefully drives the arm forward, the corresponding leg pushes more forcefully backward on the track. In response, the forward push from the track is now greater and the runner is propelled forward at a higher speed.

In order for this variation of arm movement to be successful, it will first be necessary to develop sufficient leg strength so that one will not feel the urge to emphasize the rearward arm motion in order to quickly swing the free leg forward. This leg strength and quickness must be readily available so that the forward leg swing does not have to be uppermost in one's mind when reaching for a higher speed. Let good leg strength, coupled with a beneficial knee bend, move that free leg forward so it will then automatically be in position for a proper touchdown. Now, you can concentrate on your forward arm movement.

There is nothing wrong per se with training to swing the free leg forward in a faster manner. This capability must be attained in order to permit the optimum stride length. It is necessary to have the leg swing forward in sufficient time to permit the proper lower leg retraction just prior to touchdown. But beyond that, spending valuable training time and effort to focus on bringing the free leg forward quicker as a method to run faster, is a misdirection of one's energies. That effort will not produce a faster runner. It will produce a tired runner. One's training would tend to stagnate at this point.

Once the free leg can be swung forward quickly enough to perform its proper touchdown, one's training efforts will be more fruitful if directed toward other factors that are directly curtailing one's running speed. Focus attention on determining which factor (or factors) is (are) currently preventing an increase in speed. Diligence in this direction will produce greater dividends than will the attempts to disrupt the body's natural synchronism.

*   *   *

One part of the striding motion that is sometimes given insufficient attention is the kickback. This is the rearward motion of the lower leg that occurs immediately after the foot breaks contact with the track. This is not lost or wasted motion. This is the action that folds the leg at the knee in preparation for the leg's forward swing. The amount of kickback determines the degree of knee bend produced. It is this knee bend that is critical to the ability to rapidly swing the leg forward.

Although the kickback occurs as a rearward motion, do not think of it in this light. It is preferable to think of the kickback as the commencement of the leg's forward cycle. It is this kickback that prepares the leg for its forward swing. When adjusting the amount of knee bend that is introduced to the forward leg swing, the adjustment is made here, in the kickback. More kickback provides greater knee bend. Exaggerated training movements such as butt kicks are an aid in developing good kickback and the resulting good knee bend. This portion of the training regimen is often not afforded sufficient recognition.

Good knee bend is imperative for a quick forward swing of the leg. The greater the amount of knee bend a runner is able to incorporate in his running style, the closer to the hip joint will be the lower leg, and the quicker one will be able to swing the leg forward. To achieve a good knee bend, one may also want to bring the mind into play. To get the mind to assist, instead of thinking about bringing the entire leg quickly forward, try thinking of just the knee. Think of bringing only the upper leg forward and getting the knee out directly in front. Think of that as being a pointed knee. Let the lower leg trail behind. Think of pointing the foot behind the lower leg. Not only will this foot position help in swinging the leg forward, it can also promote a quicker flick of the foot and thereby assist in obtaining a stronger push off. With these images in one's mind, the body can better duplicate that form when it goes into action.

*   *   *

We want to be capable of getting the free leg swung forward to its proper position for touchdown as quickly as possible. We have just discussed that bending of the knee will assist in accomplishing a quicker forward swing. But, another means to getting the leg forward quicker is also available to us. Adopting a running form that requires a shorter distance through which we have to swing the leg will also help achieve this desired result.

This is accomplished by restricting the backward swing of the *upper* leg after the spikes break free from the track. If the rearward swing of the upper leg is curtailed, it will then have a shorter distance to travel in its forward swing. It will be able to reach its destination sooner. Additionally, when the rearward swing of the upper leg is reduced, the rearward swinging momentum of the total leg will then be focused onto just the lower leg. This will aid in accentuating the knee bend. Thus, we get two benefits from curtailing the rearward swing of the upper leg: we now have a shorter distance through which to swing the leg to complete its forward cycle, and we also have encouraged a good knee bend for that swing. Please note, this curtailment of leg swing refers to the upper leg *after* the takeoff is completed.

*   *   *

If you are still having difficulty employing a good knee bend in your running form, you may want to try the following practice routine. While standing in place, begin a marching step but bring the knees all the way up to the chest. Raise the tempo to about two steps per second. After a few of these high knee lifts in place, lean slightly forward and gain a little forward motion while maintaining the high knee lifts. While maintaining the same stride tempo, keep increasing the forward speed. The knee motion will gradually transition from vertical to horizontal. Now, get the feel of this stride with the exaggerated knee lift. On your next run, try to approach the feel of knee bend that was used during the practice routine.

The search for ways to improve our body's running capabilities must be relentless. Just as muscle strength can be improved, the quickness of muscle contractions can also be improved. Quick high knee lifts while standing in place can help in this regard. While standing erect, raise one knee as quickly as possible to the chest. Then drive it just as quickly back down until the toes touch the ground. At the instant the toes touch the ground, quickly raise the other knee to the chest and repeat. Do not try for a high turnover rate here; one pair of steps per second is fine. Concentrate on quickness of movement, both up and down, with a short pause at top and bottom of each step.

Check with the mirror to make sure that good form is being maintained; foot plant directly under hip joint, foot pointing straight ahead, and knee in alignment with foot and hip joint. Small ankle weights can be added for more effect. A weight should not be added that perceptibly slows down the movement. Quick arm movements of a running style can accompany this exercise.

To improve quickness of the takeoff, bounding is one of the best training techniques available to us. At the same time, it is building strength in those muscles used in this movement. Long powerful strides with the takeoff made from well behind the runner, and exaggerated float time, is the form we are looking for here. Keep the knee folded and the foot pointing rearward for as long as possible. Strive for longer strides (not higher) by employing stronger quicker takeoffs and reduced ground contact time, but keep the motion smooth.

Bounding challenges the takeoff muscles from the toes all the way up through the muscles in the lower back. These muscles in the lower back are, unfortunately, often overlooked in the exercise regimen.

Quickness training vs. strength training is not an *all* or *nothing* proposition. Both are necessary, which consequently makes them both important. Which is more important? This will depend upon the individual and perhaps can best be viewed from the following perspective. "At this stage of my training and development, which of these is having the greatest impact on limiting my speed?" "Improvement in which area will advance my overall performance at this particular time?" Do not neglect one in favor of the other. Just put the emphasis where it will do the most good right now. The sprinter will utilize them concurrently; they must be developed concurrently.

We all understand that we run by contracting certain muscles that actuate the legs in a manner that will move us forward. But it must be remembered, this is only half the action. Between each muscle contraction there will be a muscle extension. The body does not have a mechanism for directly extending the muscles. The muscles are extended only by the action of the opposing muscles contracting and moving the limb in their direction. We cannot consciously extend our muscles; it only happens as a consequence of the limb moving away from them.

In repetitive movements, each contracted muscle must next undergo an extension before it can again perform its next contraction. The term *opposing muscles* is quite appropriate here. Each muscle contraction will happen easier if the opposing muscle is more relaxed. And, by extension, we can see that if a muscle contraction happens easier it will also happen faster. If a muscle is not adequately relaxed, the opposing muscle that is contracting will have to work harder. It now is working to not only move the limb it is also working to stretch the inadequately relaxed muscle. The more work a muscle is forced to do, the slower it will perform and the sooner it will fatigue. When training for the sprint, one must train to run relaxed. When training to run relaxed, we are training to run faster.

The action-reaction principle addressed earlier also applies between the two legs. If the effort to swing the forward-moving leg is considered to be the action, the reaction can be felt as an increased push against the track by the rearward-moving leg. Every part of the body is in communication with every other part and all must work both independently and jointly toward the common goal.

When running the 100m sprint, the athlete will be expending energy at an enormous rate. This all-out effort cannot continue for the full duration of the race. There is a necessity to pace oneself. Even so, in the second half of the race, there will usually be a slowing of even the most highly conditioned runners. Knowing ahead of time that this will happen, have a plan to deal with it. The plan should be "don't fight it." Keep the elbows low with a good swing to the rear. Don't let the hands go floppy. Make certain the arms are doing their utmost to support the efforts of the legs. Remain relaxed and let good form carry you toward the finish line.

8

WHERE THE FOOT
MEETS THE TRACK

In order to get the most benefit from each stride during the brief time the foot is in contact with the track, the location of that point of contact is extremely important. Location, as used in this context, means its location relative to the location of the hip joint. The term *foot plant* refers to this location of the point of contact and it also refers to the interval of time during which the foot is in contact with the track.

For this examination of the foot plant, we will consider that a full stride consists of three major components: a forward-reaching motion of the leg while in the air, the foot plant that, as just described, is the interval during which the foot is in contact with the track, and the kickback that folds the leg at the knee in preparation for its next forward motion. Here, we examine the foot plant portion of the stride, which has its own subcomponents. The foot plant begins with the touchdown, which is the instant the spikes bite the track. The location of the touchdown is forward of the hip joint if the runner has completed one's acceleration. During the latter portion of the foot plant we have the push off, which begins when the hip joint has moved forward to a location directly over the foot, and it ends with the takeoff, which is the final but powerful flick of the foot as it is about to break free from the track at a location behind the runner.

All the reactive forces from the track are incurred during the brief interval of the foot plant, and originate at the location where the spikes are engaging the track. From there, they travel through the foot and up the leg to the hip joint. These are the forces we use to propel ourselves down the track. However, we must remember that there are also negative forces acting on the runner during the plant time of each foot. Let us look at the forces acting on a runner's foot and how each affects one's speed.

We examine the reactive forces that are directed from the track to the runner by looking first at the foot when it is on the track at a location forward of the hip joint. When a foot is planted in front of the runner, its main function is to begin supporting one's weight. The runner gets no forward pull from the leg that is extended forward. It does just the opposite; it imparts a braking action to the body as discussed in the previous chapter.

If one were to draw a straight line from the ball of the foot at touchdown to the hip joint, it would be seen that the line points mainly upward, but it also points somewhat rearward. As you will recall, the degree to which this line points to the rear, is an indication of the amount of braking action imparted to the runner as the foot begins to support one's weight. The initial portion of the foot's plant time (when the foot is in front of the runner) slows the runner's forward progress.

During the time interval of the foot plant, the runner's body is moving forward. Relative to the runner, the point of contact passes under the body and then behind it where the pushing action then occurs. Only during the latter portion of the foot's plant time (when it is behind the runner) does it push the runner forward.

Let us now take a more in-depth look at this issue. A hypothetical run on a sandy beach will help illustrate the reaction of the track as it acts on the runner's foot. Let us start this demonstration on the beach with an imaginary person running easily at a moderate speed. We will watch what happens as our subject now attempts to accelerate.

One foot plants itself in the soft sand in front of the runner. The foot immediately makes its imprint in the sand. At this point, it begins to support the weight of the runner. The foot stays in this position while it waits for the body to pass over it. As the hip joint arrives at the point directly over the ball of the foot, there is now heavy weight on the foot and it begins to push backward on the sand.

As the hip joint passes forward of the foot, the runner pushes progressively more rearward on the sand until a point is reached where the foot slips in the sand. The runner cannot get the same forward push in the soft sand that could have been obtained on the track and a slight stumble ensues. The runner's speed is greatly slowed compared to what it would have been if there had been no slippage.

It is noted in passing that when the foot passed behind the runner, it would have eventually slipped anyway because of the combination of lessened vertical weight and strong horizontal push just before breaking contact with the sand. But the slippage to this runner occurred not because of lessened weight on the foot, but because of the strong forward push from the foot while there was still heavy weight on it. The fact that there was still heavy weight on the foot when it slipped is evidenced by the runner's stumble and tendency to fall. The imaginary person was forced to take a short quick step with the opposite leg in order to get that foot under the body and prevent the fall.

Before we leave the beach, let us note that it was when the foot was well behind the runner that the sand gave way and caused the runner's foot to slip. This is the portion of the stride where the leg pushes forward the hardest. This is the portion of the stride that contributes most toward our forward speed. As a matter of fact, when we want to slow down at the conclusion of a run, we emphasize the forward reach of the legs and de-emphasize the rearward stretch. Does this tell us something about what we should *not* do in order to run faster?

Obviously, the runner's feet have to be on the track some minimum amount of time in order for them to support the runner's weight and also to provide a forward push. From the experiment conducted during our virtual visit to the beach, we know that when considering the total time the feet are in contact with the track, the time spent with the feet behind the runner is more beneficial to one's speed than is the time spent with the feet in front of the runner.

One way to begin indoctrinating the body to the concept of striding with a stronger push from behind is what the author refers to as the Groucho Marx walk. That entertainer would sometimes use this unusual stride much to the delight of his audience. To perform this stride, stand fully erect, and then flex the knees enough to lower the body approximately eight or ten inches.

Now begin to walk. Do not lean forward; keep the torso erect. Extend one leg fully forward. Let the back of the heel plant on the ground. As the body passes over it, roll your weight onto the ball of the foot. Flex the knee so the torso does not bob up-and-down. As the body passes forward of the foot, keep the pads of the toes on the ground as long as possible.

The objective of this exercise is to push on the ground as far behind the runner as possible. Besides strengthening the knees, this routine will help the body get the feel of pushing off from behind. If one were to imagine a line from the pads of the toes to the hip joint, this would be the direction of the push off force. Obviously, the further behind the runner that the toes are positioned when they push off, the more horizontal is the force on the hip joint.

During this exercise, keep the feet, knees and hips in alignment. Keep the torso erect. Keep the motion smooth. This exercise readily lends itself to group participation. The routine may feel strange and will probably appear likewise. Fortunately, a low score in elegance on practice day does not carry over onto race day. The only score that really matters is your time at the finish line.

Let us now look at the aspect of the amount of forward lean used by a runner and how it relates to the foot plant. Figure 4 shows three runners, each with a different degree of forward lean. The foot is shown in the mean location of the supporting leg's foot plant. Note that it is always located behind the runner's center of gravity (C.G.).

In each case is shown the downward pull of gravity acting vertically through each runner's C.G. Also shown is the upward push of the track on the ball of the runner's foot. Note that the greater the degree of forward lean, the farther apart are these two forces. When there is a greater distance between these two forces, there is a greater tendency for the runner to topple forward (counterclockwise in these illustrations). To counter this tendency to topple forward, the runner pushes backward on the track. From the perspective of the runner's foot, the track is pushing it forward. This force pushes forward

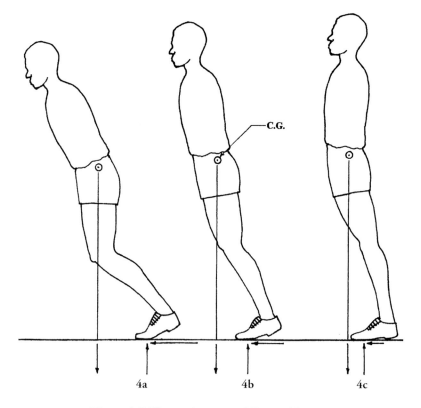

Figure 4. Different Amounts of Forward Lean.

on the lower portion of the runner and produces a turning tendency in the clockwise direction. This clockwise turning moment is used to balance against the counterclockwise moment and keep the runner upright. In this context, a moment of force is defined as the strength of a force multiplied by the length of its lever arm. The further a force is located from the point about which it acts, the greater will be the moment of that force.

The runner shown in Fig. 4a, with the most forward lean, is contending with the largest counterclockwise toppling moment. In this position, the runner must apply the greatest amount of force to the track in order to remain in balance. This large force to right the runner also affords the greatest forward thrust. This provides the runner with the greatest acceleration and is well suited to the start of a race.

The runner shown in Fig. 4b is utilizing a slight forward lean. This produces a moderate counterclockwise toppling effect and requires a substantial push on the track in order to maintain rotational balance. This substantial forward push will still afford the runner with a small acceleration and would be used for the greater part of the 100m race.

The runner shown in Fig. 4c is shown in the upright posture. This produces the shortest distance between the two vertical forces and therefore has the smallest counterclockwise toppling tendency. As a consequence, a smaller push on the track is required to maintain rotational balance. This configuration is best suited for maintaining speed rather than accelerating. (The runner always requires some force and a small forward lean to overcome the apparent headwind's tendency to slow and to topple the runner backward.)

The magnitudes of the horizontal pushing forces shown in Figure 4 are exaggerated in order to show more clearly the differences between the three runners as described in the text. If drawn to proper scale, the resultant of the horizontal and vertical forces on a runner's foot would point to the runner's C.G. Forces in the runner's leg were previously taken upward as far as the hip joint. But obviously, they don't stop there; the runner's torso distributes them about the body. In this section, we have introduced the force of gravity that, by definition, centers on the runner's C.G. Therefore, to be more meaningful, the forces in the runner's leg have been extended beyond the hip joint, and are now shown in relation to the runner's C.G.

Because of the human anatomy being what it is, the more forward lean that a runner utilizes, the greater the rearward reach that can be accomplished with the leg. Conversely, the more upright a runner holds the torso, the more difficult it is to reach backward in order to push off. We just don't bend backward at the waist very well. Four-legged animals have an advantage over us here. With their backbone in a horizontal position, they are able to extend their legs well behind them while still maintaining contact with the ground. This provides them with a longer, stronger push off from the legs.

Also, they are relieved of the requirement we humans have, that of balancing our weight over the two legs that also must do the driving. They are able to support their bodies alternately between front and rear legs. Besides being able to accentuate the push off portion of the foot plant, our four-legged friends have the additional advantage of being able to lay down a soft foot plant when the legs are extended forward. Upon touchdown, each leg does not have to support as much of their weight. This combination of a strong push off and a soft touchdown is a formula for speed. The big cats of Africa excel in this regard.

When we humans run in the upright posture, the rearward reach of the leg will usually be abbreviated. In order to maintain the vertical balance of forces about the runner's C.G., when the rearward reach of the leg is shortened, the forward reach of the leg must then be similarly shortened. The result is a shortened support platform. (The support platform is the distance traveled during the time interval of the foot plant.) When the support platform is shortened, the total push generated by the leg will be reduced. But, some good things are also happening. With the shortened forward reach of the leg, braking action will be lessened. Also, with the amplitude of the leg swing reduced, it can be swung to its forward position more easily. This, in turn, can allow for a higher turnover rate. Again it is noted, a good long-term stretching and flexibility program will allow the runner a broader spectrum from which to select the running style and stride length with which to run.

What is the best running posture for a particular runner? There is much for the coach and the runner to consider here. Obviously, one cannot take the one-size-fits-all approach. There is no single amount of forward lean that is best. Each amount of lean, under the correct circumstances, can be used to advantage. Which one to employ will depend upon the capabilities, limitations and potential of the particular runner, the event in which one is competing and the segment of that event under consideration (drive phase or fly phase).

When it comes to the case of forward lean, this may very well be an instance of what feels natural may also be what is best for a particular runner. The runner has, in all probability, assumed the amount of forward lean that one's body is most comfortable with, because this is how the body operates best. But now, with a little more knowledge in the basket, one may want to dabble with small changes to the lean to see if a modified attitude of the body will permit the attainment of slightly more speed.

In all instances though, just before the foot breaks free from the track, the leg and foot combine to exert a brief but powerful takeoff force to the track. This forward push is extremely strong and is evidenced by the runner's lower leg continuing to swing backward, in the kickback motion, as soon as the spikes are released from the track. Optimal use must be made of this takeoff push in order to reach one's full potential. The further behind the runner that the foot is positioned at takeoff, the more horizontal will be this takeoff push.

It would appear then, the further behind us the foot is located when it performs its takeoff from the track, the better. However, there is yet another factor at work that tends to negate this beneficial effect of pushing from further behind. We must be aware that the push off by the foot, while very quick, does occur over some short interval of time. In the interval of time during which the push off occurs, the body will travel forward some distance. (The reader is asked to note the distinction between the terms push off and takeoff.)

For simplicity, the push off is considered to begin when the toes are directly below the hip joint. It is completed, and the takeoff occurs, when the toes are at some distance behind the hip joint. Relative to the torso, the track will have moved backward this distance during the action of the push off. What is more significant, is that the point where the toes contact the track has moved away from the runner's hip joint some distance during the push off. This is the aspect of the push off that concerns us here.

Figures 5a and 5b illustrate two different runners as their foot is about to break free from the track. In each case, the hip joint is 3'0" above the track and each runner had begun the pushing action when the toes were directly below the hip joint. The runner in Figure 5a is shown completing the push off when the toes are 1'0" behind the hip joint. The distance from the hip joint to the point of contact, at the moment the push off is completed, is represented by the hypotenuse of a 90° triangle with a 1' base and a 3' height. Utilizing trigonometry, it is determined that this hypotenuse is 3'2" long.

This illustration tells us that when the runner started pushing off, the point of contact with the track was 3'0" from the hip joint. However, at the completion of the push off, the point of contact was 3'2" from the hip joint. The runner was dealing with the difficulty of getting a strong push off from a point that faded away from the hip joint a distance of 2" during the motion.

It is noted that here we are dealing with, not forces, but the geometry of leg mechanics. Since the leg swings about the hip joint, it is appropriate to relate this motion to the hip joint rather than the runner's C.G.

But, what if we push off from even further behind as shown in the morphed image of Figure 5b? Let us remember that this runner also began the push off when the toes were directly under the hip joint, but now it is completed when the toes are 2' behind the hip joint. Since the runner's foot, in this instance, is pushing from behind for a longer period of time, it appears that the foot should impart a greater total push forward. But the hypotenuse of this triangle shows us that adverse things are also happening. Utilizing trigonometry, it is determined the length of this hypotenuse is 3'7".

This tells us that the foot's contact point is 7" further away from the hip joint at the time of takeoff than it was when the push began. This also means that during the time interval that elapsed while this runner was performing the *final* 1' of the push off, the track receded 5" from the hip joint (7" during the time of the full 2' travel as shown in the triangle, minus 2" during the time of the first 1' travel same as runner "a," leaves us with 5" during the time of the final 1' of travel). Now compare this 5" recession for runner "b" with the 2" recession for runner "a" while they both traveled the 1' forward distance just before takeoff. Obviously, runner "b" is dealing with a more adverse situation. The position of the takeoff shown in these illustrations is not intended to reflect actual locations for real runners but is exaggerated in order to illustrate the point being made in the text. However, it is

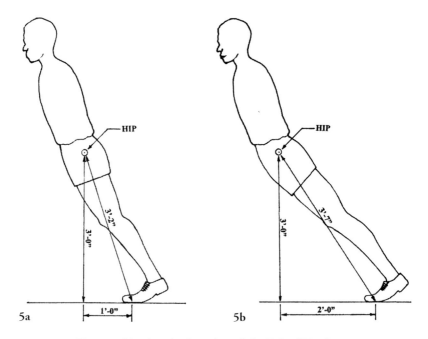

Figure 5. Varying the Location of the Takeoff Push.

indicative of a condition in the real world with which runners must contend (although probably subconsciously).

When the push off is viewed in this light, it is apparent that it will be difficult for the runner to obtain a strong push off from a point that is receding from the body in this manner. The further behind the runner that the point of takeoff is positioned, the more rapidly it will be receding. Of the total push that we receive from the foot during each stride, we rely heavily on a strong quick flick of the foot at takeoff to give the body a final push forward. As we attempt to move this point of takeoff further behind, we quickly reach a point of diminishing return.

If the contact point on the track were to be moving backward too quickly for the runner to obtain that final strong push by the foot, that portion of the push off would be lost and the total push given to the body would be diminished. In this scenario, the takeoff point would be too far behind the runner. This is not much different from walking up a downward-moving escalator. While one is trying to move upward, the step is receding downward, opposite to the direction of intended travel. If the downward speed of the escalator were sufficiently great, the passenger would be unable to make any forward progress.

The result of all this is that the further behind the runner is the point of that final push of the foot plant, the more efficient will be the *direction* of that push, but its *strength* will become progressively weaker. We are faced with the tradeoff of obtaining the best direction of that push vs. obtaining the best strength of that push. Here is an occasion where quick muscles will prevail. The action of the foot during takeoff must be quick enough to obtain a strong forward thrust even though the track is rapidly receding backward, away from one's forward moving body. We can now see that the optimum distance behind the runner for the takeoff to occur is, in large part, dependent upon the quickness of the takeoff push that can be obtained by the particular runner.

Sprinting is indeed a sport of speed. But strangely enough, the speed of movements of *most* of the individual motions performed during a sprint is slower than the maximum speed at which we can perform these movements individually under no-load conditions. In other words, the rapid movements of our limbs when under load are more dependent upon muscle power than upon quickness alone. What is suggested here is that, in general, quickness of muscle contraction, while important, is not the be-all and end-all of sprinting. If there is credence to this line of thought, then additional muscle strength can add quickness to limbs that operate under load. Lack of basic muscle quickness does not necessarily relate to lack of speed. The converse is also true; muscle quickness alone, without accompanying muscle strength, does not guarantee greater speed of action.

The preceding generality has one very important exception. This exception is the *final* push of the foot (discussed just above) that occurs just before losing contact with the track. During this motion, quickness of the takeoff mechanism is of utmost importance. While strength is good, it is no substitute for quickness of this particular motion.

If the foregoing is considered valid, then in addition to having the necessary strength in these takeoff muscles, we must work diligently on improving their quickness. Plyometrics! Bounding-type exercises can improve this capability. They cannot overcome a deficiency in fast-twitch muscle fibers, but they can help. Besides the practice of bounding, quickness of the takeoff muscles can also be improved by practicing jumps of all variety. Performance of vertical jumps can be tracked by marks placed on a wall when at the pinnacle of the jump.

Additionally, the author uses what he calls the hot deck jump. Most probably others use it, perhaps by a different name. This routine consists of a series of vertical jumps. The object being not to see how high one can jump, but rather to keep the feet in the air the *maximum* total time and on the ground the *minimum* total time. Think of the ground as being too hot to stand on as you jump upward as high and as soon after landing as possible. Concentrate on getting more spring from the feet. Immediately upon the feet leaving the ground bring the knees to a full flex. This encourages the leg/foot combination to react quickly and strongly. When running, this will become a quick strong forward motion with good knee bend to enhance the forward leg swing. We are primarily interested in improving the takeoff action. It is this very critical takeoff, at the end of the plant time, that makes the difference between good speed and better speed.

Quick takeoff action can make the difference between sprinters who are fast and sprinters who are faster. It can generally be said that quickness comes naturally to some, but unfortunately not to all. On the other hand, quickness can be worked with and improved. Whatever quickness you have, take it and make it better. Plyometrics—plyometrics—and plyometrics. Bounding, skipping, jumping and the like must be on the menu. These are very strenuous and demanding exercises. Do not attempt them when tired; that would be courting injury. Otherwise, their reward awaits you.

The running style that incorporates a strong push off by the foot will maximally stress the plantar fascia, the wide flat ligament on the underside of the foot. Be alert for any unusual pain in this area; particularly, a sharp pain in the center of the heel. Pain in the underside of the foot may be an indication of distress in this ligament. Do not attempt to run through this pain. Immediately stop running and see your medical doctor for a diagnosis. If caught early, a more serious injury may be averted.

There is also an advantage to flexing the toes upward before the foot touches down. This pre-tensioning action will stabilize the foot and it will be pre-conditioned to support the runner, which is its primary job upon touchdown. If there is no hesitancy in the foot, the entire leg assembly will be ready to work with a greater efficiency.

A somewhat more technical look at the foot plant would tell us that it takes work for a runner to move swiftly down the track. And this work must come from the runner. Because the work originates with the runner, we know that the direction of flow of this work must be from the runner to the track. We will designate this direction of flow as being positive because it produces a positive result. It accomplishes what we want; it moves the runner down the track.

But, what if there was a flow of work in the other direction, from the track to the runner? This would be a negative flow because the flow of work would be in the direction opposite to that described above as a positive flow. And when there is work flowing in the negative direction, it will have a negative consequence; it will slow the runner's forward progress.

If we do not use proper technique, this negative flow would be allowed to happen. The proper technique to be used in this scenario is for the runner to flex the toes upward before the foot plants on the track. If the runner does not do it before touchdown, the track will do it after touchdown as the foot begins to pass behind the runner. It will require work for the track to bend the runner's toes upward—negative work. This flow of work from the track to the runner will slow the runner's speed. If, on the other hand, the runner chooses to bend the toes upward before touchdown, this negative work by the track is eliminated. There is now one less impediment to the runner's forward progress.

This technique of bending the toes upward, which is called dorsiflexing, will be difficult to accomplish in a race that involves such a high turnover rate

But, if we are aware of the concept, we can more readily allow it to happen. It is understandable why athletes hate to give up their old shoes. The repetitive flexing endured by older shoes will have conditioned their soles so that the shape can be more easily changed. The toes can be bent upward with less effort, and the takeoff push by the forefoot will happen quicker when the action is not slowed by having to forcefully re-bend the shoes downward again. Toes bent upward before touchdown are faster; so are those old shoes.

As an aside, the chapter that addresses the start of a race describes the use of a wide foot plant for the first few strides of the race. Those wide push offs are pushing somewhat sideways on the track. This sideways push reduces, to some extent, the effect of the receding track just described. The amount the track recedes from the runner's forward motion is not altered, but the amount the track is receding from the runner's hip joint, *in the direction of its push,* is lessened by the amount of sideways push the runner utilizes. The more sideways push a runner uses, the less the track surface will be receding from that push. As the runner's stride length begins to increase in the first seconds after the start, the exaggerated sideways motion is reduced and the foot plant is brought under the hip joint to improve overall running efficiency.

Obtaining a strong push from the foot plant is one part of the speed formula. Turnover rate is the other part, and the foot plant can affect one's turnover rate. To explain: The location of the point of touchdown in front of the runner and the location of the point of takeoff behind the runner are interrelated to the extent that the body must receive vertical support both in front of, and behind, the location of the runner's C.G. to properly support the runner. The locations of the forward and the rearward supporting forces must comply with the requirement that the sum of all moments of force acting on the runner must total zero. If the moments of force did not total zero, the runner's body would be out of rotational balance and would be rotating forward or backward. Similar to balancing a seesaw, moving a vertical force that is behind the runner to a point closer under the runner's C.G., must be accompanied by moving a vertical force that is in front of the runner to a point closer under the C.G. in order to maintain balance. This, in effect, shortens the runner's support platform and will promote a higher turnover rate because the diminished amplitude of the leg swings can be completed quicker.

These moments of force are applied to the runner during the plant time of the foot. For each runner, there will be an optimum plant time. A longer plant time will provide greater time for forces to act, but a shorter plant time will allow a higher turnover rate. The runner's *feel* for the speed achieved may be helpful in deciding on the optimum tradeoff between greater plant-time forces and a higher turnover rate. However, this should be substantiated by reliable readings on the clock.

Often, the most effective combination embodies a shorter rearward leg extension. While this will reduce the total time for the forward push to act, it will facilitate a stronger impulse at takeoff. This impulse at takeoff will now be moved forward to a location that is closer to a point directly under the runner's C.G. To maintain rotational balance, this reduced rearward leg extension must be accompanied by a reduced forward leg extension at touchdown. This shortened forward foot placement will result in less braking action. Additionally, the shortened support platform means a shorter forward swing of the free leg is required and will allow for a higher turnover rate. The runner should consider the possibility that this change in stride may lead toward one's goal, the attainment of greater speed.

The amount that the total plant time can be shortened in this manner is limited to the time required to support the runner, and is also dependent upon other factors that limit one's achievable turnover rate. Shortening one end of the support platform must be accompanied by a shortening of the other end of the support platform in order to maintain rotational balance. Shortening the support platform to a point beyond where the body is capable of increasing its turnover rate is of no value; we would only shorten the stride length. We two-legged creatures have a very limited selection of available foot plants with which to run. However, understanding these limits puts one in a more commanding position when deciding the form with which we will perform that run. A small difference in foot plant can result in a big difference at the finish line.

In addition to the in-line location of the foot plant, the runner is also concerned with the lateral separation of the foot plants. One must be aware that it is not necessary that each foot plant pass directly under the body centerline in order to maintain balance. An eccentricity here is quite normal, even desirable. A foot plant that has a small eccentricity to one side of the body's centerline will be quickly followed by a foot plant that has an equal eccentricity to the other side of the body's centerline. The *average* location of these foot plants will properly support the body's center of weight without the body having any sensation of being out of balance. The body has the ability to accommodate these minor imbalances for short periods of time, particularly so if they are rhythmic in nature.

Not having to plant the feet directly under the centerline of the body affords us an advantage. As the foot plant moves outward from the body centerline, it comes closer to the vertical plane containing the hip joint. The running motion becomes more efficient when the motion of the foot is contained in the same vertical plane as the hip joint. This foot location allows the major portion of the pushing motion to be performed by the large strong toe on the inner side of the foot. This is preferable, as compared to the alternative of a push by the smaller toes. The smaller toes would be forced to do the work if the foot were placed closer to the body centerline as discussed in an earlier chapter.

Additionally, with the foot plant in line with the hip joint, the leg operates in a more vertical plane instead of such an inclined plane. A foot plant close to the body centerline would introduce leg crossover wherein the leg inclines from the point of ground contact, outward to the hip. When the leg is utilized in this inclined manner, sideways forces are introduced at the point of contact with the ground and thence travel through the foot and up the leg into the body.

The body must now accommodate these sideways forces, which introduces other muscles to the mix. The runner now has more muscle work to contend with, loses relaxation, tends to tie up from these additional forces and the speed is hampered. The introduction of any lateral forces to the body is detrimental to the overall running effort. Reducing leg crossover will reduce these lateral forces and permit a more rapid leg turnover since now the leg will operate in a straight fore-and-aft motion.

Widening the foot plant to the point that the leg operates in the same vertical plane as the hip joint will also have a beneficial effect on the kick-back motion. With the leg in this vertical attitude, the kickback action that begins when the track releases the foot will be a straight-line continuation of the preceding leg motion. The tendency for the foot to waggle sideways, out of the vertical plane of the hip, will have been eliminated. Corrective work for the muscles will be reduced and a smoother stride will result.

In a race, we must keep to a single lane and stay clear of the lane dividing lines. There is no requirement, however, that we must train this way. A good way to investigate different lateral distances between foot plants is to run with the foot plants straddling one of the lane dividing lines. The left foot should plant in one lane, the right foot in the adjacent lane. Both feet should clear the line. The amount by which each foot clears the line is what must be experimented with. Starting blocks can also be placed on a lane dividing line as the runner experiments with different lateral spacing of the foot plants for the start segment of the race.

If a runner's body rocks from side to side, too great a lateral spread is being used. However, one may want to start the experimentation from this position, and then begin moving the foot plant inward in the search for optimal lateral spread. The runner should be able to feel a greater forward push to the body when the proper lateral foot placement is achieved.

A coach or training partner can be of much help here. The runner can ask for the coach's observations as one searches for the optimal lateral spacing of foot plants for each segment of the race. This procedure can remove much of the vagueness associated with the foot plant. Such an investigation can provide a definitive quantity, expressed in inches, that the foot plant is clearing the lane line. A runner may believe a substantial spread to one's foot plants is being utilized. However, by making a comparison of the specific distance by which the lane dividing line is being cleared with the clearance that other runners in the group are utilizing, it may be decided that further experimentation of one's foot plant is warranted.

Lateral spacing of one's foot plants is an important factor in determining a runner's top speed. It is also a factor that can be readily adjusted if the runner knows exactly what one's current measurement of lateral foot plant is, and also has a target in mind of what lateral distance might provide an improvement to one's speed. Good cooperation among members of a group could provide this information to each member participating in the following interesting exercise.

Observations of each runner while straddling a lane dividing line when running at high speed would be fine, but the obtaining of accurate measurements by direct observation is difficult. However, an accurate measurement for each runner can be obtained if the group were to perform a similar exercise at a dirt field. Here, the running path can be given a light dusting of powdered lime. The runner would then run and leave footprints in the powder. A string line is then stretched through all of the left footprints and another string line is stretched through all of the right footprints. A measurement is then taken between the two string lines. This runner's lateral spacing of foot plants is now known. This is also a good opportunity to verify the stride lengths of both legs are equal and that the foot is pointing straight ahead. Irregularities can often be corrected with tailored stretching routines and mental concentration during strength exercises. The dusting would be renewed for each subsequent runner. This is something a runner could repeat on one's own time whenever desired. This can also be done to check one's starting technique. Look for converging string lines here.

In conjunction with this foot plant measurement, the distance between each runner's legs when they are vertical could also be obtained if so desired. This would provide a more meaningful picture of each runner's lateral foot plant, and offer information that would suggest a target figure that each runner may want to shoot for in order to improve one's top speed. The distance between a runner's legs could be easily obtained by having the runner stand erect and the coach take two measurements: one measurement from shinbone to shinbone just above the ankle, and the other measurement from thighbone to thighbone. The thighbone location can best be obtained by the runner probing the front of the leg with a finger of each hand. When the runner locates the thighbone, a measurement between the fingers can be made.

The runner now moves one of the feet sideways and the two measurements are repeated. When the upper and lower measurements are made to match, this dimension can be taken as the working distance between the legs when they are vertical.

This distance between the legs can be compared to the distance between foot plants. Each runner can now see how his two numbers compare to the numbers of other members in the group. With this information in hand, each runner will be in a better position to consider if a specific change in foot plant might yield an improvement to one's speed. Information assembled from an entire group can lead to advancement for each of its participating members. Progress can be tracked as individuals utilize revised foot plants.

Because of the offset that occurs in the thighbone at the hip joint, the legs will always angle inward toward the foot plant when the foot plant is placed under the hip joint. Any attempt to run with the legs in a truly vertical plane would therefore be doomed to failure. The distance that is measured between a runner's legs is to be used as a reference point, not a target point.

An observer running behind another runner on the track can look for consistency in the runner's stride. During this routine, it may be discovered that when running at a constant speed, a runner's foot plants do not clear a lane dividing line by a consistent amount. This may mean the runner is not maintaining a steady balance or direction, and must occasionally make a correction by adjusting the foot plant. The runner should concentrate on running in a straight line and on maintaining perfect balance. Any balance correction or alteration of position of the foot plant would require a change in running form and effort. The runner's maximum drive would be momentarily compromised while applying any correction. We should train with our best balance. We must then race with our best balance.

Do not expect that a wider foot plant can be practiced while in the jogging mode. The turnover rate of the jog is too slow to permit a wide foot plant. At a jogging pace the body would feel out of balance during each foot plant, because the time interval while waiting for the corrective foot plant on the opposite side of the body is just too long. When jogging, we must be content with a somewhat narrower foot plant. But, as the turnover rate is increased, we can widen the base of the foot plant to where it becomes a more efficient feature of our running form.

When the proper combination of turnover rate and lateral foot placement is incorporated in one's running, the body can feel quite comfortable when being supported by alternating off-center supports. While the body is being supported from one side, the torso's inertia (stability due to its weight) slows its immediate falling to the opposite side. If the foot plants are in sufficiently rapid succession, this inertia, combined with the body's resiliency, prevents the body from displaying any tendency to fall whatsoever. This inertial lateral stability of the runner's torso was utilized to the extreme during the first few very wide strides of the start, and now is continuing to be utilized for the runner's more normal strides during the fly phase of the race.

As the competition becomes keener, it becomes more important to explore each avenue that may lead to an improvement in performance. The foregoing analyses are presented with the intent of directing new light on some old issues in an effort to illuminate the way to better running. The more we know, the better prepared we will be to make the decisions and incorporate the techniques that will define our running ability.

9

THE ARM/LEG CONNECTION

The importance of the role of the arms in the sport of sprinting is, unfortunately, under-appreciated by most of the participants in the sport. It must not be overlooked that the two arms constitute 50 percent of the number of limbs in the runner's arsenal of moving parts. While the arms do not directly carry the runner down the track, it is believed that the top speed of many runners is limited, not by the ability of their legs, but by the inability of the arms to adequately support the efforts of those legs.

So, the single question is asked, "What is it that the arms can do to assist us in our search for top speed as we race down the track?" And in a single chapter, we will attempt to answer this question. The action of the arms can assist the running effort in two ways: First, the proper use of the arms will increase the stride length obtained by the legs. Second, the proper use of the arms will increase the maximum turnover rate achievable by the legs. Both of these functions are obvious contributors to the running effort. We will, therefore, look at each of them separately.

We begin our study of arm action by looking at those arm motions we can accentuate that will enhance the action of the legs and the consequent stride length. As a starting point, we will conduct some bounding exercises in order to determine what effect different arm actions will have on the stride length produced by the legs. First, perform a bounding sequence with the elbows fully crooked and with a minimum of elbow swing. Note the maximum stride length that can be obtained when there is minimum assistance from the arms. Now, try a second bounding sequence and add a dramatic powerful back swing of the arm. You will probably notice a considerable increase in your stride length. Finally, try a third bounding sequence and remove the exaggerated back swing of the arm. Add, in its place, a strong powerful forward arm swing. You may be surprised to find that your stride length in this sequence is even greater than it was before.

The increase in stride length of the second bounding sequence, when adding the strong back swing, was probably expected and is made possible because the greater rearward arm swing developed greater rearward momentum of the arm. This, in turn, permitted a greater forward carry to the same-side leg, which was in its free-swinging forward motion. On the other hand, when very little arm swing was employed in the first bounding exercise, the lack of arm momentum caused the leg to curtail its forward swing and drop to the ground sooner than it otherwise would. We will look closer at this momentum aspect of the swinging limbs later in this chapter.

Perhaps you found the increase in stride length in the third bounding sequence, when the strong forward arm swing was used, to be a surprise. Let us think about that. The forward arm swing occurs when the foot on the same side of the body is on the track passing beneath the runner, and continues through the time of the takeoff (that very important takeoff that cannot be stressed too strongly). We know from physics that for every action there is an equal and opposite reaction. In this case, the emphasized forward arm swing was the action. The reaction that developed was the additional backward push by the foot against the track. This added push by the foot was caused by the arm swing, but the foot and the track did not care about the reason. They only knew there was a stronger push. This stronger push forced the body forward at a greater speed and thereby resulted in a longer airborne portion of the stride. When running, this action will produce a very desirable increase in stride length.

The runner must remain aware of the obvious fact that the forward motion of the arm includes the action of closing the angle of the elbow. To obtain the greatest effect from the forward motion of the arm, this closing of the elbow must be performed as dynamically as possible. The more rapid this is made to happen, the greater will be the forward acceleration of the forearm. This, in turn, will place a still greater rearward force on the driving foot. This action will derive the greatest speed from the push off and thereby carry the body farther while it is airborne. The stride length has hereby been increased by a more effective use of the arm. If done properly, this will have been accomplished without detriment to the turnover rate.

In the 100m sprint, by the time the runners reach the 60-meter mark, all the starting and accelerating techniques have been left behind. Now, the race is to see who can achieve the greatest top speed. It is especially exciting if, at this point in the race, there remains a group of closely bunched athletes. While they are moving very rapidly down the track, any difference in their speeds is small.

One's eye is normally attracted to that single runner who is now moving at a slightly higher rate of speed than the others. A quick comparison between that runner and the others will often reveal that the fastest runner seems to be deriving greater benefit from the use of the arms. The arms are seen to pump forward with greater intensity and then retract just as quickly. The author believes this arm action to be one of the most significant, and one of the most under-appreciated, factors in the attainment of top speed.

Here, the laws of physics (action vs. reaction) are acting in *favor* of the runner. As sprinters, we should utilize the laws of physics to the best of our ability. While some knowledge of physics is helpful, it is not how well one understands the laws of physics that counts, it is how fully those laws are complied with and how well their ramifications are implemented that will yield the best results.

For the arms to best fulfill their role, it is imperative that we maintain stringent control over their motions. Random or detrimental motions should not be allowed to creep into one's form. The arms should not be swung across the chest. This would introduce a twisting motion to the torso. The forearms should be kept swinging forward and backward, similar to the leg motion. The complete arm motion should be in one vertical plane. The wrists should pass the same distance from the runner's sides as do the elbows. One must not lose control of the forearms and allow them to shimmy sideways. At the end of a race, when the legs are spent and the arms must take control to dictate the pace, a fore-and-aft alignment of the forearms will best permit the arms to perform this task.

Have you ever tried to run while wearing loose-fitting shoes or sandals? It is difficult to maintain a rhythm and you feel disconnected from the ground. It just doesn't work very well. The author feels the same way about allowing the hands to be loosely connected. Too much looseness at the wrists detracts from quick crisp arm movements that are necessary when realizing a high turnover rate.

The hands should not be so relaxed that they lose their rhythm and their motions become disconnected from the forearms. On the contrary, rather than loosely following the motions of the forearms, they should behave as extensions of the forearms. In this manner, they make a greater contribution to the swinging action of the arms. And just as the hands should be considered as extensions of the forearms, so should the fingers be considered as extensions of the hands. The complete assembly, from elbow to fingertips, should act as a single unit in order to derive the maximum benefit from each arm swing. Proper arm movement is best served with the thumbs pointing upward. This greater utilization of the complete arm unit will increase its effectiveness in both the forward swing, which will increase stride length as just discussed, and also in its rearward swing, the importance of which will be discussed later in this chapter.

And now, what arm actions can we incorporate into our running form that will allow us to increase our turnover rate? Presented next is what may be considered an unconventional perspective of what is occurring when we reach the top end of our running speed. It is requested that the reader maintain an open and receptive frame of mind in order to assimilate the information presented. You may or may not accept the concept that is proposed, but utilizing the techniques associated with it will make you a faster runner in either case.

Primarily the legs perform fore-and-aft swinging motions that pivot at the hip joints. Left unchecked this swinging of the legs would produce a consequent oscillating of the torso, clockwise then counterclockwise, when viewed from above. Such a motion of the torso would detract from the crisp and efficient action of the legs. To counter this motion, we call upon the arms to produce fore-and-aft swinging motions that pivot at the shoulder joints. This motion of the arms produces an oscillating tendency in the torso that opposes the oscillating tendency produced by the legs. In short, the arm motion counterbalances the leg motion and thereby stabilizes the torso. The arms must be encouraged to fulfill this role to the best of their ability. The better the arms do their job, the better the legs will be permitted to do their job.

At the conclusion of every sprint, one should ask, "What must I do differently (or do better) in the next sprint in order to improve my speed?" Often, the answer to this question is that improvement is needed in one or more of the techniques that have been employed. Techniques are those individual patterns that, when combined, make up our running form. Or, if it is believed a lack of muscle strength is limiting any of the techniques, additional time working the appropriate strength routine should be placed on the training menu. If it is believed a lack of quickness in the push off is the major culprit, more emphasis must be placed on bounding type exercises. The runner must be continually analyzing one's form, looking for weaknesses to be corrected, rather than looking at strengths (or worse, running but not looking for anything) in an open-minded and objective effort to see what the next step must be in order to improve one's top running speed.

But, when we believe we've done all the right things to enable ourselves to run faster, we may still find our top speed to be below that of which we believe we are capable. A *cap* has been placed upon how fast we run. We feel some mysterious unseen suppressant is working on us, preventing us from realizing the greater speed that we believe is contained somewhere within us.

We try to run faster by attempting to increase our turnover rate. We strive to move our limbs a little faster than they are now moving. All to no avail. The only thing that happens is, we expend more energy. But, there is no resulting reward of more speed. We know we have more body strength to expend. We know we can move our limbs faster than they are now moving. But, we are unable to make these things happen. What is occurring at this point? What is this invisible wall through which we cannot pass? What comprises this *cap* on our running speed? An attempt will be made to answer these questions here.

Many runners spend years building muscle strength, then toning and sharpening those muscles to provide quickness. Seemingly, endless time is spent improving one's techniques. What additional ingredient is needed in order to raise the running speed still further? Is it just more strength? More quickness? More tweaking of techniques? It is believed there is another fundamental factor that still controls our maximum attainable speed. We have talked about it before, but it generally receives such little attention it would be beneficial to explore it further. *MOMENTUM!* We now take a look at the momentum generated by each of our four limbs and how that momentum affects our turnover rate, and thereby our running speed.

What is momentum? The momentum of a body is a combination of its weight (mass) and its speed (velocity), and is expressed mathematically by the equation $M = mv$, or momentum equals mass times velocity. (When two quantities in a mathematical expression are shown side by side with no plus sign or minus sign between them, the operation of multiplication is automatically implied). From this formula, it can be seen that the mass (m) and the velocity (v) are of equal significance in the calculation of momentum. For example, if the mass of a body were increased by 10 percent, its momentum would be increased by 10 percent; and also, if the velocity of the body were increased by 10 percent, its momentum would likewise be increased by 10 percent. Both mass and velocity make an equal contribution when determining the momentum of a body.

We have all seen how figure skaters control the rate of their spin by retracting and extending their arms. The speed of their rotation is responding to the law of momentum as it applies to spinning bodies. A sprinter is also subject to the laws of momentum. In the case of the sprinter, it is the law of momentum as it applies to the forward and backward swinging of the arms and legs.

Let us now look at this momentum generated by the limbs as they swing forward and backward. This swinging of the four limbs are motions that are essentially fore-and-aft, and will be treated as such in this discussion. The alternating swings of the legs, which are offset to either side of the body's vertical centerline, create a tendency for the torso to twist in alternating directions in reaction to the leg swings.

If we were to look down on a runner at the time when the right leg is planted on the track, the left leg would, at this time, be swinging forward. From the overhead perspective, the legs would be swinging clockwise relative to the advancing torso. Newton's Third Law of Motion tells us that for every action there is a corresponding equal and opposite reaction. We will consider the clockwise motion of the legs to be the action in this case. The reaction is the tendency they produce in the torso to twist in the counterclockwise direction.

The main reason to swing the arms is to create a twisting tendency in the torso that is in the direction opposite to the twist created by the legs. When the swinging momentum of the legs and the swinging momentum of the arms are balanced against each other, the torso will be in equilibrium with no tendency to twist in either direction. When running, we must strive toward this goal.

But, look at those arms. They weigh *much* less than do the legs. How can they possibly create a momentum that equally balances that created by the legs? The answer is, they can't. But, the good news is they don't have to create a *complete* balance. Recall, if you will, the discussion of foot plant in the preceding chapter wherein it was stated that each foot plant does not have to pass directly under the centerline of the body. The body is able to accommodate being supported alternately from the left side and then from the right side, for short intervals of time, without feeling any imbalance. In the same way, the body can accommodate alternating imbalances between the swinging momentum of its legs and the swinging momentum of its arms, as long as these imbalances are not too great.

The formula from physics, $M = mv$, while accurate, does not tell the whole story. It does not indicate the ability of the runner's body to accommodate some alternating unbalanced momentum forces over short periods of time. The shorter the time interval of the imbalance, the greater is the amount of imbalance the body can accommodate.

Let us say the torso is receiving forces from the legs that would twist it clockwise. At the same time, it is receiving a smaller set of forces from the arms that would twist it counterclockwise. That's okay, for in just a moment, the torso will be receiving forces from these same limbs in the opposite directions. The torso is able to accommodate these alternating forces (if they are not too great) and carry itself with no perceptible twist at all.

We now want to take a closer look at these twisting forces imparted to the torso by the swinging legs and arms. Let us look at these forces in a 3-dimensional sense. For reference, we first place a horizontal axis through the central part of the body running from front to back; we will call this the X-axis. Any rotation of the torso about this axis would lean the shoulders to the left or to the right.

Secondly, place another horizontal axis through the body's center running from left to right; this will be the Y-axis. Any rotation of the torso about this axis would lean the shoulders forward or backward. Lastly, place a vertical axis passing through the head and crotch. No surprise, this is the Z-axis. Any torso rotation about this axis would twist the shoulders clockwise or counterclockwise (when viewed from above). For this discussion, the three axes will intersect at the average location of the body's center of gravity.

The general shape of the body is oblong, in the vertical direction. This shape places portions of the body's mass at relatively large distances from both the X-axis and the Y-axis. (Some parts are substantially higher and some parts are substantially lower than the center of gravity). This provides the body with a relatively high inertia (stability incurred due to weight and shape) about these two axes. The high inertia about these two axes can, in turn, accommodate a relatively large difference between the momentum of the legs and the momentum of the arms. The torso feels no inclination to lean alternately leftward and rightward as we run; nor does it feel any inclination to lean alternately forward and backward.

On the other hand, no part of the body is very far from the vertical Z-axis. The body, consequently, has a lower inertia about this Z-axis. Therefore, the body cannot accommodate as great a difference between the momentum of the legs and the momentum of the arms about this axis. Because of the difference in the momentum generated by the swinging legs and that generated by the swinging arms, our first awareness of a tendency for the body to twist will be about the Z-axis. The shoulders will want to twist alternately clockwise and counterclockwise when viewed from above.

This is evident in some runners who do not swing their arms very far; their shoulders twist clockwise and counterclockwise. Note however, that even here, there is still no evidence of the shoulders tending to roll about either the X-axis or the Y-axis. From this, we can see that the first visible sign of a momentum imbalance (between legs and arms) beginning to overpower the body's natural stability is movement of the shoulders about the Z-axis. It is this threshold of a twist about the vertical axis that concerns us here.

To review, we have discussed that the swinging arm momentum is used to counteract the swinging leg momentum. Both of these momentums act upon the torso. The swinging arm momentum is less than the swinging leg momentum; this is primarily due to the difference between the weights of these limbs. Further, the body can accommodate some imbalance between these two alternating momentums because of its inertia. But the momentum difference about the vertical Z-axis is the most critical. If you buy into this (even tentatively), let's continue further.

Now we must extrapolate from these *basics*. We place a subject runner in motion at medium speed. The limbs are swung and they each generate their own momentum. During any one swing, the combined momentum of the two legs will produce a tendency to twist the torso in one direction. At this same time, the combined momentum of the two arms will produce a smaller tendency to twist the torso in the opposite direction. It must be acknowledged that during each swing, the shape and the speed of each limb is changing. This, in turn, causes continuous changes in the momentum that they generate. The pursuit of that detailed analysis falls outside the scope of this book. For simplicity then, we will look at the *total* momentum generated by the two arms and the *total* momentum generated by the two legs over a full swing in one direction. This concept is no less accurate and is much more manageable. The study of the rotation of one's limbs rightfully introduces the theories of moment of inertia and also radius of gyration. For sanity though, we will continue to refer only to the concept of momentum.

And also, for simplicity, let us say that over a full swing of the limbs in one direction the arms generate ½ the momentum of that generated by the legs. Now recall the formula for momentum ($M = mv$) as our runner begins to increase speed by increasing the turnover rate. The momentum of the legs and the momentum of the arms will each increase as the runner swings these limbs progressively faster (the "v" is increasing here). However, the arms because they are lighter, will always develop ½ the momentum developed by the legs.

In the chart of Figure 6, the total momentum generated by the swinging legs is shown as the upper line; the total momentum generated by the swinging arms is shown as the lower line. It is seen that as the turnover rate is increased (toward the right) the momentums of these limbs increases (toward the top of the chart). And at all turnover rates, the arm momentum remains at ½ the leg momentum.

Now, if the runner's body was comfortable in accommodating this momentum difference while running at medium speed, then at higher speed, when the arms are still developing ½ the leg momentum, we might still expect that all would remain satisfactory.

However, while both momentums increase as the speed increases, and while the arm momentum remains ½ the leg momentum at all speeds, at

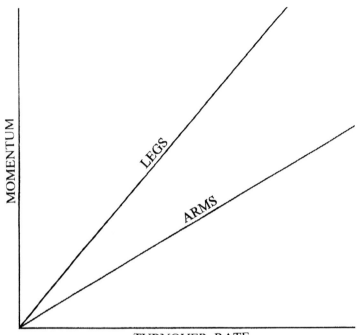

Figure 6. Momentum of Swinging Legs and Arms.

higher speed the *difference* between leg momentum and arm momentum *increases*. This is shown in Figure 7.

The concept being put forth is that when the *difference* between leg momentum and arm momentum becomes sufficiently large, the torso can no longer accommodate this imbalance without the tendency for it to begin oscillating about the Z-axis. This is the critical point where problems begin to develop. We utilize other muscles, both in the torso and in the limbs, in an attempt to control this twisting and we begin to *tie-up*. We know we have more strength in our muscles and more quickness in our limbs, but we are unable to release this power that we know is still within us. As we attempt to run faster, we only expend more power to control the resulting tendency for the torso to twist. There is no reward of increased speed. At this point, we have reached the *cap* that nature has placed upon our running speed.

Obviously, the greater the weights of a runner's arms and legs so greater will be their momentums, and consequently so greater will be the difference in their momentums. One might ask, "Would not these heavier arms and legs reach their critical momentum difference sooner that lighter limbs?" The

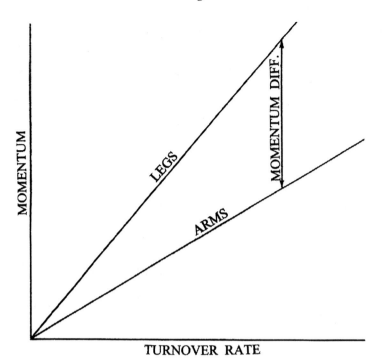

Figure 7. Difference in Momentum of Swinging Legs and Arms.

corollary to the above is that heavier arms and legs are usually attached to heavier torsos, and heavier torsos are capable of accommodating the greater imbalance of momentums caused by these heavier limbs. This tends to equalize the playing field between heavier runners and lighter runners.

The high turnover rate of the sprinter's limbs brings with it a rapid reversal of their momentums. For the torso to be effective in its role as stabilizer, its weight must be firm and of quite rigid makeup. This will allow its entire weight to be immediately available for the accommodation of each momentum shift generated by the limbs. For maximum effectiveness, the torso weight must act as a unit and not allow portions to contain random motion. Excess weight carried loosely on the body will be of virtually no benefit in enabling the torso to accommodate the rapidly alternating momentums of its limbs.

The torso's inertial stability prevents it from twisting in rapid response to normal alternating momentum imbalances. We encountered inertial stability of the torso when discussing its steadying influence on a runner's eccentric foot plants. At that time, we were concerned only with the weight of the runner's torso. We now again encounter inertial stability in discussing the runner's body twist. However, here we must acknowledge that it is dependent upon not only the torso's weight, but also its size and shape. The shape factor is what makes the Z-axis the critical reference line when experiencing this twisting force that results from a momentum imbalance between legs and arms. As the turnover rate is raised and the momentum imbalance is increased, the point is reached where the torso's stability begins to be overcome. The runner has now reached the maximum turnover that the body can tolerate.

Incidentally, have you ever had occasion to see a lizard that has lost its tail attempt to run? Without the stabilizing influence of its tail, the lizard's rear end waddles back and forth; the movements of its legs are slowed and it runs in an ungainly manner. By contrast, a lizard with its full tail, despite having to haul around that considerable amount of additional weight, runs very well. The tail does an excellent job of absorbing the alternating momentum caused by the alternating motion of the rear legs. The lizard's rear end, in this instance, is stabilized and the allowable turnover rate of its legs is much higher. The laws of physics are universal. They apply equally to all things, including lizards and people.

So where does this leave us? Is there nothing we can do to improve our speed above this point where the laws of physics appear to forbid any further increase in our running ability? After much reflection on the subject, it is believed that the means to gaining additional sprint speed is what we will refer to as *momentum management*. This factor is believed to be the shiniest key to unlock a runner's potential for achieving a still higher speed. The more successfully a sprinter controls and coordinates the momentum of the four limbs, the higher will be the attainable turnover rate, and the more speed one will be capable of developing.

Let's now take a closer look at the limbs whose momentum we must learn to manage. Here, we will look at the simultaneous action of the arm and the leg that are located on the same side of the body. We will look at the momentum that each limb develops and consider ways to minimize the difference between their momentums. First, we look at the leg. The maximum swinging momentum of the leg is developed during the period when it is performing its forward swing. The leg never really gets to perform a backward swing. The foot is planted on the track and the body passes over it. Don't misunderstand this; the leg in this mode does have momentum. It is just not as great, and therefore not as critical, as in its free swing forward.

Since the leg is the heavier of our limbs, the key to managing its momentum really means attempting to minimize its momentum during its forward swing. A reduction in momentum is best accomplished by increasing the amount of knee bend that is used while the leg is swinging forward. Utilizing a greater knee bend will bring the lower portion of the leg closer to the hip joint. Consequently, there will be a smaller generation of swinging momentum about that joint.

It is noted that this reduction in momentum is primarily about the Y-axis. However, because the lower leg is carried closer to the hip joint, it will be traveling slower than it would have been in the extended position. Because it is traveling slower, it will develop less momentum about all three axes.

Additionally, you may recall that we previously discussed the technique of curtailing the rearward swing of the upper leg immediately after the spikes have broken free from the track. This results in the leg having less distance to travel during its forward swing. Because it has less distance to travel, this upper portion of the leg can also move slower and still reach its target point in the proper amount of time. This slower motion will result in a lessened momentum about all three axes, with reduction about the Z-axis being the objective.

Since the motions of the leg will have a direct effect upon the momentum produced, these are skills that we must endeavor to master and incorporate into our running form. The reduction of leg momentum about the Z-axis is a primary means of reducing the critical momentum difference between legs and arms.

In the management of momentum, we must also look at the arms. How should we best use these lighter arms in order to develop the required countermomentum to adequately balance the leg momentum? We have greater freedom when working with the arms than with the legs. The arms do not have the constraint of having to periodically anchor themselves to the track in order to support the body and drive it forward.

Since it is during the forward swing of the leg when momentum balance about the body's Z-axis is most critical, we must determine what the arm is doing during this same time interval. At this time, the arm is performing its back swing. It is this motion that provides the opportunity for the arm to make its most important contribution toward closing the gap in the issue of momentum difference between legs and arms. Just as we wanted to *decrease* the forward swinging leg momentum, so do we now want to *increase* the rearward swinging arm momentum in order to bring the two closer into balance.

By reviewing the formula for momentum, we see that increasing the speed at which the arm is swung can increase the momentum of the arm. The rearward arm swing begins with the thumb at about the height of the shoulder. From here, the swing is downward and then rearward. This motion must be as brisk as possible. This briskness of the downward motion will continue of its own accord throughout the rearward-swinging portion of the motion. Quickness when applied at the beginning of a motion carries through, and is therefore the most effective way to increase the speed of the entire motion.

During the arm's back swing, the elbow angle between upper and lower arm opens up. This allows a broader swing of the hand. This broader swing will increase the momentum developed by the forearm. In striving for more speed, the runner will sometimes drive the arm harder in a rearward direction in an effort to force the corresponding leg to come forward just a bit quicker.

However, in this effort the forearm may be dropped too far, which will carry the hand too far rearward. The runner is now faced with the task of returning the forearm to its starting position so it can begin the next cycle of motion. This return of the arm to its starting position can conceivably take too long. This would adversely affect the turnover rate.

To avoid this, the elbow must be held with sufficient bend to bring the weight of the hand closer to the shoulder joint. One can swing the arm through a complete cycle much faster if the elbow is more closed and the hand is thereby more raised. Unfortunately, when the hand is carried closer to the shoulder the effectiveness of the arm swing is diminished. What is needed here is the arc of the forearm (and hand) that will create the greatest arm-swinging momentum without slowing its turnover rate to the point where it would slow the leg turnover rate. The arms should not be permitted to limit the turnover rate of the legs.

During the forward motion of the arm, the hand can be held higher than it is on its rearward motion. Since the forward arm swing is occurring at the same time that the same-side foot is anchored to the track and generating only a minimum amount of momentum, it is not necessary for the arm to generate as much momentum on its forward swing as compared to its rearward swing. If one closes the angle of the elbow sooner, the arm will swing forward more easily and be ready to begin the next back swing when needed. Depending on the runner's needs, this technique must be balanced against the desirability of an emphasized forward arm swing to accentuate the push off of the leg as previously discussed.

We never want the leg turnover rate curtailed because of the inability of the arm turnover rate to match the pace. If the arm turnover rate reaches its maximum, we cannot increase the leg turnover rate. We should strive toward not allowing the arms to dictate a running style or speed limitation to the legs. Strength training of the arms is paramount in this regard. Good arm and shoulder strength is necessary in order to achieve a high arm turnover rate and simultaneously maintain a high degree of arm momentum.

Running is generally thought of as a sport where the dominant action of the athlete is the movement of the legs. The swinging of the arms is generally considered a secondary response to the leg motion and only incidental to the running action. But a better understanding is now being formed of the function of the arms, and therefore a greater appreciation is had of their contribution to the finished product.

In the search for a more effective use of the arms, the author experimented with a more forward reach of the forearm instead of the traditional upward swing toward the chest. In that movement, the forearm motion was more akin to that of the drive rod on the wheels of a steam-driven locomotive. The forearm motion was more reciprocating rather than circular. This technique did not work well. It became apparent that this arm motion was less effective in creating the needed momentum. The reciprocating motion of that technique lacked the necessary speed that the more circular motion imparts to the forearm.

The traditional forearm motion that starts with the hand at about shoulder height begins with a brisk downward snap. The rearward swing of the upper arm combined with the simultaneous opening of the elbow joint transforms the downward motion of the forearm into a rapidly moving rearward motion. This speed of forearm motion is a major contributor to the momentum generated by the arm during its back swing. Note that a change in speed of any limb generally entails a change of momentum about one axis more than other axes. But, any desirable change in momentum about the Z-axis will be accepted.

The unsuccessful experiment described above was not completely wasted effort. It was informative. It pointed out the critical need for maximum arm momentum during its back swing in order to offset the momentum of the forward-swinging leg. The confirmation of this requirement led to the development of a more effective use of the hands. This includes extending rather than curling the fingers, and also utilizing the hand to initiate the swing of the forearm. The following paragraphs explain these more fully.

If the hands and fingers are left slack, there will be the tendency for them to be left behind when the forearm begins its downward and rearward swing. We want to use the forearm snap in order to gain the highest and the earliest momentum gain from this swing. The full momentum can only be achieved if the forearm motion brings the hands and the fingers immediately with it. This means hands and fingers must be held quite rigid and preferably fully extended so they become an extension of, and are snapped with, the forearm.

If the hand is bent slightly outward at the wrist, the fingers can be carried with a very gentle arc inward rather than being held bar straight. This still permits a relaxed running style while at the same time affords a means of extending the fingers in line with the forearm. This is an interim step to condition the runner away from the loose hand technique. Once this has been mastered, the runner can move to the next step.

Here, the fingers are held bar straight and in line with the forearm. This attitude of the hand ensures that the fingertips will be carried at the maximum distance from the elbow pivot point. It also ensures the fingers will swing in unison with the hand rather than be left behind when the hand quickly accelerates in the direction of the arm motion. With practice, the hands and fingers can be held rigid without tensing the rest of the body. This technique will squeeze slightly more momentum from each arm swing. It has been found that utilizing this *controlled* hand technique has advantage over the traditional loose-hand technique. This rigid-hand technique was the signature of Carl Lewis when he was at the top of his game.

Additionally, if the wrist is bent on each arm swing in the direction of that swing, the hand and fingers will travel in a longer arc during each arm swing than they otherwise would if the wrist were held straight. The wrist bends downward on the down swing and upward on the up swing. This exaggerated hand movement caused by the bending of the wrist, superimposed upon the normal movement caused by swinging the forearm, causes the hand to travel at greater speed over a longer distance, which in turn generates additional momentum during each arm swing. This technique is most readily incorporated into the running style by *initiating* each arm swing with the hand movement. Tell the hands to control the swing of the arms. It was seen that world-class runner Michael Marsh utilized this technique to his advantage.

The amount of momentum that the arm can generate is a critical factor in determining a runner's maximum turnover rate. Do not overlook any opportunity to maximize this very important ingredient when developing your recipe for speed. As compared to the unsuccessful experiment of utilizing a reciprocating motion of the forearm, the circular motion that begins with the hand at shoulder height affords the opportunity of increasing the forearm speed by opening the elbow joint during the motion and of increasing the hand speed by flexing the wrist. This more circular technique requires the use of more arm muscle, but the expenditure of this additional work is well worth the effort as it aids in generating much needed arm momentum. Expend arm power as though it were free; once developed it costs the sprinter nothing to utilize it.

Experiment with the height of the wrist (which is controlled by the angle to which the elbow is opened) during the back swing. If the wrist is carried lower, the runner will generate a greater momentum on each back swing, but the arm turnover rate may suffer. If the wrist is carried higher, a higher arm turnover rate can be attained but there may be an insufficient amount of arm momentum generated. Experiment with the height of the wrist to obtain the optimal compromise for your particular circumstance. Exercises designed to develop arm and shoulder strength now show their worth. It is most important you develop the arm swing that best complements your leg action.

Additional refinements can and should be employed to maximize the swinging momentum of the arms. Regardless of the height at which the wrist is carried, it is most important that the swing should carry the upper arm as far rearward as the shoulder joint will allow. This means bringing the upper arm to a nearly horizontal position behind the runner. This is a major assist in increasing the effectiveness of the arm swing. Do not twist the shoulders back and forth since that would introduce torso twist. Let the arms do the work. The arc of the elbow should be carried as low as possible. This will avoid shoulder hunch and permit the greatest freedom for the rearward travel of the arm swing. Another obvious way to increase arm momentum about the Z-axis is to move the entire assembly of the swinging forearm slightly further outward from one's side. The increased distance of this weight from the Z-axis will increase the momentum generated about that axis.

All these techniques are aimed at reducing the momentum difference between arms and legs. The runner will know when this momentum difference has been sufficiently reduced because a more free and easy running style can be maintained at the same turnover rate. This now opens the door to crank the turnover rate still higher.

If one were to look down on a runner from above, while he is attempting to increase the momentum of the arm swing about the vertical Z-axis, it would become apparent that a slight outward bending of the hands would increase their distance from that axis. This would be good. A slight momentum increase would be achieved without resorting to any further outward displacement of the vertical plane in which the forearm operates. Moving the forearm outward has a favorable impact on the momentum picture but becomes increasingly difficult to control. Moving just the hands can be an assist toward one's objective. The runner is encouraged to experiment with different hand motions and then adopt the total arm motion that works best for the particular individual.

Depending on one's current strength abilities, upper arm and shoulder conditioning exercises can be as important as upper leg conditioning exercises in enabling the runner to attain maximum speed. When speaking of upper arm and shoulder conditioning, this reference includes strengthening both the forward and the rearward arm movements.

The forearm constitutes a large portion of the total weight of the arm. The speed and the momentum contribution of this weight can be controlled by the extent that the angle of the elbow is opened. Additionally, the amplitude of the rearward swing of the upper arm determines not only how far the upper arm will swing, but also how far its connected forearm will swing. This combination provides the motion of the forearm with a huge influence when considering the momentum generated by the arm. To effectively incorporate this motion into one's running form, time must be spent in the weight room, properly conditioning the arm and shoulder muscles that will provide for a quick forward recovery motion from a rearward extended forearm. This can be a major contributor to one's top speed. Put it near the top of the list of exercises for necessary attention in the weight room. Maximum running speed can be achieved only when maximum arm swing is maintained. Maximum arm swing includes both maximum arm speed and maximum arm amplitude.

When developing a high momentum of the arms, one should be able to feel their weight swinging at one's sides. If their weight is not readily noticeable, they are probably not being used to their optimum. Swing the elbows more dramatically to the rear. Keep the arcs of the elbows low and try moving the paths of the forearms a little further out from the sides of the body. When these adjustments are properly made, one should be able to feel the reassuring weight of their swing as they develop the required countermomentum.

As a secondary effect, when sufficient momentum balance has been achieved, one will feel an immediate freedom in the movement of the legs, with a consequent increase in stride length and overall speed. Conversely, when running fast if the runner were to suddenly change to a less forceful arm swing, it would be immediately apparent that the body could not sustain the same stride length. The touchdown would occur closer than before and the stride would become shorter as the body attempts to reduce the momentum generated by the swinging legs to a point where the torso can accommodate it in conjunction with the reduced arm momentum.

Try letting arms and legs share in the responsibility to initiate their swinging motions rather than relying on one being solely a reaction to the other. Some runners may prefer to lead with the arms while still others may prefer to lead with the legs (this last option is the least desirable). Just be aware that these different options are available and after trying each, select what works for you.

In the early stages of a race, one's stride length is comparatively short. With this shorter stride, less momentum will be developed in each forward leg swing. On the other hand, the arms are free to utilize a full-length swing.

Therefore, at this stage of the race any momentum difference between legs and arms will be smaller. Do not concern yourself with this momentum issue during the acceleration portion of the race. Their momentum difference does not become critical until the leg swing nears its maximum.

During the process of developing optimum arm swing, the sprinter will come to better appreciate the importance of proper implementation of the arms. Without proper arm movement, the running speed will suffer. As has been indicated previously, it is believed there are many sprinters whose top speed is dictated by an insufficiency of arm movement, rather than by their legs. Don't be one of them. Remember, if we are to get more from our legs, we must demand more from our arms; they work in harmony with each other.

Unfortunately, we humans will never be able to bring the arms into complete balance with the legs. The arms are smaller, lighter and less muscular than are the legs. This prevents them from developing a momentum that is comparable to that developed by the legs. Because of this imbalance, the speed with which we can move our legs when running, will always be limited to the speed that the arm momentum can properly counterbalance. An obvious positive supplement to one's training regimen would be the addition of efforts to increase muscle mass of the upper limbs. An increased weight of the arms would contribute toward a narrowing of the gap between arm momentum and leg momentum. This, in turn, would allow for an increase in one's turnover rate.

It is believed that an increase in the mass of the arms can play a role in allowing a higher turnover rate. Therefore, just as the use of weights of any kind are forbidden in the long jump event, it is similarly believed they should be forbidden in the running events. It seems that proactively prohibiting weights in *all* track and field events would be a step forward in maintaining proper order and discipline in the sport.

We must remain cognizant that the arms do not directly connect to the legs. Their effect on the legs is transmitted through the conduit of the torso. Therefore, to obtain the proper interchange between arms and legs, the proper conditioning of the torso must occupy its appropriate place in one's training regimen. It is the entire body that must be trained to reach the finish line.

One of the aspects that limits the speed with which we run is the turnover rate that we can achieve. The relative weight of our upper and lower limbs is the primary feature of our body that establishes the maximum turnover rate we can achieve. By limiting the runner's turnover rate, and speed, Nature has ensured that we are positioned in the proper place in Her plan.

But, we inherently try to seek, and to stretch, the outer limits of those boundaries that help define who we are. We continuously search for ways to increase those limits that have been placed upon our speed. We have discussed that the imbalance of the momentums generated by our legs and arms imposes a limit on the maximum turnover rate we can achieve. Ways have been explored to reduce that imbalance and thereby push the boundary of our speed just a little higher. The better job we do of minimizing the momentum difference between arms and legs, the higher will be the turnover rate that we will be permitted to achieve in our running effort. Utilize every available technique toward this objective and you will be rewarded with the ability to attain a greater maximum speed.

In addition to the form factors that have been discussed, the runner should also look at one's equipment. A runner's equipment list is quite short, and right at the top of it should be shoes. Michael Johnson stated that the gold colored shoes he wore during the 1996 Olympic Games weighed only three ounces. That is incredibly light, only about one half the weight of most running shoes. It is also incredibly important because shoes are always placed at the location farthest from the runner's axes of rotation. This puts them in the position where it is most difficult to move them quickly. Particularly, when using a high turnover style of running (which he did) is it important to be able to move one's legs quickly.

Lighter shoes will permit quicker movement because they do not have as much inertia that the runner must overcome. And this brings up another, but less obvious advantage. The lighter shoes will produce less momentum in the swinging legs. Less momentum produced in the legs means less countermomentum is required from the arms. With less of a momentum demand on the arms, they don't have to swing as powerfully. This means they can cycle faster, thereby allowing a still higher turnover rate. Could there have been a little hidden magic in those golden shoes?

One might ask, "Would not a higher turnover rate, which requires the limbs to swing faster, increase the momentum difference between arms and legs, and thereby have a negative effect upon one's speed?" While it is true that a higher turnover rate will increase the momentum difference between arms and legs, it is the current school of thought that in order to run faster we must work harder and move our limbs faster. It therefore becomes necessary to improve one's physical abilities to the extent possible and to then train knowledgeably to best utilize one's body. Perform *your* training in the manner it will do *you* the most good.

There are some positive aspects to this momentum picture. As we manage the momentum of our limbs and are then able to improve our turnover rate, this faster oscillation of momentum reversals means that each momentum imbalance will be endured for a shorter interval of time. An integral part of this momentum concept is that the torso can accommodate somewhat higher momentum imbalances if their duration is shorter. This is one reason it is believed that the shorter stride/higher turnover style of running can be successful for the sprint and is helpful in allowing shorter athletes to be competitive.

As a correlating example of the body being able to accommodate greater momentum imbalances at higher turnover rates, one has only to look at the issue of lateral distance between foot plants that the body can accommodate at different turnover rates. The lateral distance between foot plants that is attained by placing the foot plant in the same vertical plane as the hip joint feels perfectly comfortable when running with a high-speed turnover rate. However, this same lateral distance between foot plants would be untenable at a jogging pace. The slower turnover rate of the jog will not allow the body to accommodate the same eccentricity of foot plants that it can accommodate at the higher turnover rate of a high-speed run. Alternating momentums follow this same pattern. The higher the turnover rate that is employed, the greater is the momentum imbalance that the body can accommodate.

In general, the strength and the mass of the arms and shoulders are less in women than they are in men. However, the women have a different trait that is to their advantage. As we mature, women appear to retain greater flexibility than do the men. This includes the amplitude of the upper arm swing, which carries with it a major means of producing the needed arm momentum. The amplitude of the arm swing is just as important as is the weight of the arm in developing the required momentum.

In the consideration of momentum balance, we discussed the importance of the rearward arm swing. The proper execution of this rearward arm swing has a major influence on the runner's momentum balance. The arm swing was thought of as commencing with a decisive rearward swing, which is then followed by the recovery motion of the forward arm swing to put the arm in position to repeat the cycle. The arm motion was generally considered to be rearward-forward—rearward-forward.

However, referring to the experiment relating stride length to different arm movements, we found that the forward arm movement was much more than just a recovery motion between rearward arm movements. The forward movement actually helped propel us forward because it placed additional rearward force on the foot in contact with the track.

It is believed this feature to be of such importance that the author prefers to think of the arm movement as *beginning* with the arm at its most *rearward* position. From this position it should make the strongest possible forward motion. When the arm reaches its forward position, it abruptly stops and begins its rearward motion as quickly as possible. The *rearward* motion is now considered to be the recovery motion. Think now of the arm motion as forward-rearward—forward-rearward.

The importance of developing maximum momentum of the rearward arm swing never diminishes. It is that we also have other things to consider. Arm motions in both directions require our focused attention. A rapidly moving forearm is to be accentuated. Only after the physical form of the complete arm swing has been decided upon, practiced and mastered, should the runner proceed to the next logical aspect of that swing, its timing.

We have seen that the intensity of the rearward arm swing and also the intensity of the forward arm swing both contribute to the speed of the runner, but for different reasons. Increasing the speed of the rearward arm swing assists in maintaining momentum balance during the forward swing of the same-side leg. This enables the runner to achieve a higher turnover rate. On the other hand, increasing the speed of the forward arm swing assists in obtaining a stronger push off. This improves the forward drive and consequently increases the stride length. To accomplish both of these objectives, we are now moving the arm most quickly in both directions.

If the arms are in good physical shape, this most rapid arm movement would result in their turnover rate exceeding the maximum turnover rate that the legs can achieve. This is a good capability, but it must be controlled. The arm turnover rate must be brought into sync with the leg turnover rate. A slowing of the arm motions is not an acceptable option, but the arm turnover rate can be adjusted in either of two other ways: by incorporating a slight pause at the end of the arm swing or by increasing the amplitude of the arm swing. Either method will increase the total time to complete the arm cycle so that it can be made to match the total time needed to complete the leg cycle. Let us look at each of these two choices.

First, we shall look at the choice of a short pause at the end of a swing. This involves the issue of timing. Since we are now considering the arm motion to be a forward-rearward flow, we will begin our look at the timing of the arm swing as it commences its forward movement.

One method to synchronize the arm turnover with a slower leg turnover is to introduce a momentary delay to the arm swing prior to the commencement of its forward swing. While this delay is occurring, the runner will have the opportunity to complete the airborne portion of the stride. A moment later, when the arm is undergoing a more effective portion of the forward swing, the same-side foot will now be in position to begin its rearward push. In this way, a greater benefit is derived from the forward-swinging arm because the delayed arm swing causes the foot to be in a more efficient pushing location when the arm-assisted push off is executed. The increased pushing action of the leg/foot will now project the runner forward faster than it otherwise would, and an increased stride length will result.

Additionally, because the initiation of the forward arm swing was delayed, that arm must now play catch-up and travel faster than it otherwise would. It will catch up to its synchronous position by the time it reaches its forward target point. This additional forward speed of the arm translates to a still greater rearward push by the foot that is in contact with the track. This greater push, in turn, develops a still greater speed of the runner.

A slight pause in the arm movement should not be allowed to occur upon the completion of its forward swing. At the completion of the forward arm swing, the motion is abruptly stopped and its rearward motion is begun immediately. This is done so the proper rearward arm momentum can be generated coincidental with the forward swing of the leg. Reversal of the direction of arm swing is accomplished as quickly as possible when the hand is in front of the runner. The quicker that the rearward arm momentum can be generated, the quicker will the same side leg be enticed to swing forward.

But the far more advantageous way to synchronize the arm turnover rate with the turnover rate of the legs is to increase the rearward amplitude of the arm swing. This will provide all the advantages previously described for introducing the slight delay at the end of the rearward swing, and it will also provide a greater swinging momentum of the arms. Unfortunately, we don't get all this advantage for free. It takes a very highly developed set of upper arms and shoulders to swing the arms further and still maintain the necessary high turnover rate. But every serious sprinter should spend serious time toward developing this ability. The arms should not be allowed to perform at anything less than their maximum. A greater arm swing will add noticeably to the output capability of the legs.

The following techniques have been found helpful in improving the effectiveness of the arm motion. The reader will see a relation between some of them and the momentum principles presented earlier.

- The forearms should not be allowed to swing across the chest. Their motion must be kept forward and rearward in much the same manner as the legs are moving forward and rearward.
- Swing the upper arm as far rearward as one's shoulder joint will permit. This action forces the forearm to swing farther and faster than it otherwise would. Shoulder hunch must be avoided if this is to be properly accomplished. Toward this end, swing the elbows as low as possible.

- Never allow the forearm to move outside the path of the elbow. If allowed to stray into that outer zone, a loss of control would result.
- The path of the elbow and forearm can be moved slightly outward from one's side. Allow a bit more air to pass between the elbow and the hip.
- The wrist should not be allowed to relax and lose control of the hand motion. The wrist has a job to do. The hand should not be allowed to flop about; it too has a job to do. Hand and fingers should be considered as an extension of the forearm and their actions must display this assignment. Additionally, the wrist should bend in the same direction as the arm is swinging. This will force the hand to move in a longer arc and at a higher speed than it otherwise would. This will increase the effectiveness of each swing of the arm.
- The angle of the elbow is opened for the back swing of the arm. This lowers the position of the forearm and increases its effectiveness. However, in this position it is more difficult to swing quickly and the risk is posed of unduly curtailing the turnover rate of the arms.
- The angle of the elbow can be more closed for the forward swing of the arm. This raises the position of the forearm making it easier for the arm to maintain a high turnover rate. Unfortunately, if the forearm is raised too far its effectiveness will be diminished.
- Emphasizing the forward swing of the arm will elicit a stronger rearward push of the foot. This will project the runner forward faster and farther.
- Aggressive upper arm and shoulder strength exercises must be undertaken if maximum benefit is to be derived from the arm swing.
- The turnover rate of the arms must match the turnover rate of the legs. At this turnover rate, the arms must be used in such ways as to generate the maximum momentum that their strength can develop.
- Let the arms share in the responsibility to initiate the action of the next stride rather than being merely a reaction to the leg action.

When training the legs to run faster, do not overlook the various techniques available for the arms to enhance those efforts of the legs. Do not be one of the many sprinters who allow an inadequate performance by the arms to hinder the performance of the legs.

Maximum strength in the arms and shoulders is essential for the sprinter to attain maximum turnover rate. Over the course of a week, estimate the number of hours spent training the legs. Compare this figure with the estimated hours spent training the arms. This comparison may lead you to rethink your training regimen so that adequate arm conditioning is incorporated in your training routines. The arms must be capable of properly supporting whatever you demand of the legs.

The total sum of the motions of the arms, hands and fingers may be considered to constitute the momentum of the arm swings. Emphasize those motions that will increase the momentum of the arm swings. This will allow them to more effectively complement the motions of the legs and thereby dislodge a huge barrier to increasing your present speed.

As sprinters age, we know that their race times begin to decline. It has also been observed that the cause of that decline in speed is primarily due to a reduced stride length. The turnover rate of the older sprinter seems to undergo less change. This is an intriguing observation. As we age, we know our muscle power declines. This decline directly affects the pushing power of the runner's leg and, as a consequence, the stride length decreases.

On the other hand, the turnover rate may be more dependent upon the swinging momentums of the runner's limbs rather than upon the athlete's strength used to perform those swings. These momentums remain relatively constant as we age, especially the ratio between upper and lower limbs. This suggests that since there is little change in the momentums of the limbs, we will see little change in the maximum turnover rate as one's strength declines. A further inference is that the younger sprinter is not able to utilize the accompanying greater strength of youth to increase turnover rate. That turnover rate is perhaps inhibited by another factor. Such a possibility has been explored in this chapter.

There is nothing new about the principle of momentum that has been presented in this chapter. What is new is its application to the actions of the sprinter. The author has endeavored to correlate an old scientific truth with an even older athletic sport. This, in an attempt to provide the sprinter with a better understanding of the challenge of running faster than ever before.

If you have not been able to release all the speed that you believe your body is capable of developing, if you feel a governor has been placed upon your speed machine, a review of the factors that govern the momentums of your limbs may reveal what needs to be addressed in order to make the next improvement in your top speed.

One cannot see momentum so the author cannot show you a sample of it to prove it exists, let alone prove it affects our top running speed. But nonetheless it is firmly believed momentum management (either instinctive or as a consciously acquired action) is an integral part of running, and like it or not is with us every step of the way.

10

ADDITIONAL ESSENTIALS

We have looked at the legs, the foot plant and the arms. These are the primary areas of interest to the sprinter when studying the upper end of one's speed range. However, they are certainly not the only areas. There are numerous other items of concern, and to the sprinter who is striving to extract the utmost from one's body, still essential. Let us look at these additional areas of concern.

Shoulders

Do not hunch the shoulders. This would inhibit the backward swing of the upper arms. To verify how readily a hunched shoulder would restrict the arm swing, stand sideways at a mirror. Utilizing the shoulder that is closest to the mirror, hunch it upward toward the ear. Now, with the forearm in a horizontal running attitude, swing the upper arm rearward until it will go no further. Note the position of the upper arm. Now return the arm to its starting position and drop the shoulder to its normal position. Repeat the arm swing. You will probably be surprised at how much the shoulder position can limit the amplitude of the upper arm swing. Shoulders must be kept low, and consequently the elbows will be low with a loose easy swing.

We are often told to not hunch the shoulders. It is not the shoulder position per se that hinders a runner. It is its consequential effect upon the arm swing that is the problem. Insufficient arm swing leads to a struggling by the legs, which carries with it the tendency for the runner to tie up.

Shoulder hunching is most apt to occur near the end of a race when the runner is tired and begins to work the arms hard to maintain the stride and the pace. This is exactly when a more effective arm swing would be most valuable in helping the runner avoid the dreaded tie-up. A strong, free-swinging arm motion is a major contributor toward maintaining a strong, free-swinging stride all the way to the finish line. Don't forget that image you saw in the mirror of an ineffective arm swing caused by shoulder hunch. Make a conscious effort to swing the elbows in as low an arc as possible. This will ensure no shoulder hunch creeps into one's form.

If desired, the runner can conduct a simple *road test* to see how well the shoulders are carried. Come up to approximately three fourths speed with a nice easy-flowing stride. Maintain an easy arm swing. All feels okay? Now make a conscious effort to lower the paths of the elbows as they swing past your sides. If there is a noticeable change in the feel of your gait, if it suddenly becomes more free and easy, perhaps you were not carrying your shoulders as low as you thought. This would be a good thought to recall when racing down the track searching for that next increment of speed. The lower one carries the elbows/shoulders, the greater will be the allowable output from the arms. The greater the output from the arms, the greater will be the allowable output from the legs.

Head

The head should be held erect, not tilted to one side. With the head held in alignment with the rest of the body it is in the best position to direct all the traffic below.

Also, this will afford the best setting for one's peripheral vision to inform the runner of one's location in the running lane, and to provide information regarding the body's vertical bounce. Provide your brain with the best vantage point to know what's going on.

Breathing

Once the runner is away from the vicinity of the starting line, the breathing should be steady and deep. Upon reaching the run segment of the race, a single violent exhalation can be useful in promoting relaxation and a freer knee lift. Then, one can put breathing on autopilot in the deep breathing mode. Do not synchronize it with one's stride; this would take it to a less-than-optimum rate.

Athletes who have reached a high degree of physical conditioning are afforded an additional option here; the entire sprinting event can be considered a high-exertion effort. These athletes can engage in the technique of exhaling through pursed lips for the length of the event. This elevates their internal pressure and allows them to achieve greater speed for a longer period of time than does the process of normal breathing.

Posture

Running posture has been discussed in detail in a previous chapter. At this point, the runner should know what posture is the most advantageous for the individual. Once the run segment of the race has been reached, the individual should assume that running posture. There will have been no point in assimilating all the reading material on that subject if, in the excitement of the moment, one disregards the techniques that were intended to be employed at this time.

Jaw

The jaw should not be clenched, nor the facial muscles tightened. Tense muscles here are an indication of tense muscles throughout the body. A relaxed jaw generally indicates a relaxed body. Oh yes, once the flight of runners has been called up to the starting line, no further *jawing* allowed.

Relaxed

Run with a relaxed style. When we run relaxed, the opposing muscles of our limbs are less apt to interfere with each other. When we call upon muscles to contract, we don't want them forced to fight against the opposing muscles if the latter are not sufficiently relaxed. After a muscle group has contracted and completed its job of moving the limb, it needs to be quickly relaxed so that it does not impede the action of the opposing muscle group that is contracting to move the limb in the opposite direction.

The simple exercise of running down a flight of steps, one step at a time, as fast as possible (with the railing handy for safety), is a good way to mimic the act of running relaxed. In this routine, the ball of each foot is made to just tap the nose of the step as gravity pulls the person downward. This can be good practice for encouraging quick relaxation of muscles.

Small but extremely rapid up-and-down foot movements will also help teach the legs both the quick contraction and the quick relaxation of muscles necessary for a high turnover rate. Another exercise designed to promote rapidity of movement is the backward shuffle. This is best done on grass or at home on the carpet in bare feet. In this exercise, both feet are kept in continuous contact with the ground. The feet are alternately shuffled backward as rapidly as possible. A 2" movement at each shuffle is fine. Rapidity and sameness of motion of each step is the goal here.

How relaxed is *relaxed*? How much is enough? How do we know if we are sufficiently relaxed? The answers to these questions are difficult to put into words. I believe the best way to get an understanding of relaxed is to get a taste of it. To get a sampling of relaxed, one may want to try this. Trot down the track at a slow jog. When it is time to swing each leg forward, try to do so with as quick, and as short, a contraction of the muscles as possible. Cause the muscles give the leg a quick kick forward. Then allow them to go relaxed again before the foot hits the track. Once you get the hang of it, try to slowly pick up the pace and still get that momentary relaxation just before touchdown.

Frankly, the author doesn't do this exercise very often because it rattles his tired old knees and they complain. Younger knees would probably perform better, but if they hurt, stop. This has been found to be a refresher course to remind the muscles how running *relaxed* feels. We cannot expect to run a race in this fashion, but by introducing the muscles to this relaxed feeling, hopefully they will be encouraged to get into this relaxed mode a moment sooner and thereby allow the opposing muscles to perform their contracting motion that much quicker.

The ability to quickly relax muscles should not be overlooked in our quest to optimize the quick contraction of muscles. When on the track, fight the *clock*, not *yourself*. If we can achieve muscle relaxation the slightest bit sooner, we can move our limbs just a little easier. We will have theoretically raised our running efficiency—one—more—notch.

Strength

The sprint is classified as a foot race. In some respects, this is an unfortunate label for the event to carry. It leads to the incorrect impression that it is the feet and legs that primarily represent the event. Let there be no doubt about it; the sprint is an *all-body* effort. Therefore, the entire body must be conditioned to withstand its rigors. A quick look at the bodies that have been called to the starting line of a world-class event will serve as evidence of this requirement.

Developing strength in one's legs and arms is an absolute necessity. But when doing so, do not overlook the need to also strengthen one's central body. Core strength is vital in order to obtain maximum performance from the limbs. The impulses relating the movements of the legs with the movements of the arms are transmitted through the conduit of the torso. The firmer one makes this conduit, the clearer will be these transmissions. The more stable we make the platform that supports the limbs, the crisper will be their movements. Central body strength should be developed that complements the limb strength. No body part should be granted a *free ride* to the finish line. Bring a completely conditioned body to the game.

In the sport of rowing, one ineffectual or out-of-sync rower can disrupt the efforts of the entire team. Each team member is expected to make the maximum contribution to the combined effort of propelling the shell to the finish line. And so it is in the sport of sprinting. Any single portion of the body that cannot support the efforts of the other components proves to be a detriment to the combined effort. Guard against weak spots. Once identified, they can be improved. When any one part of a dynamic system does not perform with an intensity that matches the others, the output from the entire system will suffer.

Limb Equality

When considering the relative importance of the body's limbs, one would not place more emphasis on limbs located on one side as compared to limbs located on the other side of the body. Likewise, one should not place emphasis on lower limbs to the detriment of attention to the upper limbs. For each pair of limbs that is scrutinized, it must be remembered there is another pair of limb swings happening simultaneously. And for each individual limb swing that is occurring, there are three other limb swings also occurring. No one limb is isolated from the actions of the other limbs. All limbs are performing motions and developing momentums that either reinforce or oppose one another. Each limb must play its assigned role to the maximum degree of perfection. All limbs must work in concert. When considering our four limbs, there are no *second chair* players in the ensemble.

It's a Breeze

If training is performed at a location where there is a breeze blowing, the question arises, "Should I run with the wind at my back or should I run with the wind in my face when making a speed run?" The author believes that a major reason to train on the track is to bring together all the separate techniques the runner will be utilizing and to use this occasion to perfect one's form for maximum speed. A base is thereby built from which to strive for still more speed.

To prepare the body to perform at a higher speed, the body must be introduced to that higher speed and develop the techniques, strength, quickness and coordination to support that higher speed. In short, one must run faster than the present top speed in order to prepare the body to routinely run at a higher speed in the future. The logical way to achieve this is to run with the wind aiding one's speed.

Running against the wind has its benefits too, but running with an assisting wind is generally more beneficial in the development of speed. Running with the wind aiding one's speed ninety percent of the time is not out of line. The other ten percent of the time, running against the wind is also useful but for a different purpose. Running against the wind will aid in developing power, which is also important. Think of running against the wind as a type of strength training. This will improve one's acceleration and assist in developing a more powerful push from behind. But, devote the greater part of your effort training for speed—this is what wins races.

Besides the wind, a training aid that can be even more effective is the bungee cord. Attached waist high to a harness, it can be arranged to either aid the runner's forward motion or to hinder the forward motion. It can be used independently by attaching the other end to a fixed object such as a goal post, or much more effectively, it can be used in conjunction with another runner where each take turns pulling the other.

Form

A runner should always maintain one's best form. No matter what running form one uses, there should be no shifting of gears as speed is increased from a slow jog all the way up to a full sprint. Gear shifting is of no positive value. It invokes an incorrect stride length for the speed that the runner has attained at the time. When running at any speed, the runner should have the ability to slide the speed up or slide the speed down with virtually no change in form. Running motions must be kept fluid.

All form techniques used in running can, and should, also be incorporated in the jog. Except for the heel strike and the magnitude and quickness of movement, the jogging form should be a close replica of the running form. Practice the desired techniques at all speeds, at all times. They will then become second nature on the day that it counts—race day.

When jogging, keep the head erect and the shoulders low. The forearms should be kept up (in the running position) and the elbows swung low with a good arc to the rear. The feet should not be allowed to come in too close to the body centerline. Lay down a soft foot plant. Each step should have a strong push off from the foot and a pronounced knee bend on the forward leg swing. Legs and arms must be kept in fore-and-aft motions. Good form should be maintained. IMPORTANT: Spend some practice time every week and concentrate on obtaining forward motion while expending the absolutely minimum amount of energy. When this groove is found, enjoy it and remember the feel of it. Then, speed can be increased—ever so slowly; no form changes allowed.

As speed is increased beyond a jog, the point is eventually reached where the weight of touchdown is no longer made on the heel. The weight of touchdown is now made on the ball of the foot. This should be the most significant change in the running form as one traverses the full range of speeds from slow jog to full sprint.

The runner must always be aware of exactly how the arms and the legs are operating. Subtle adjustments are made in order to maintain a free and relaxed running style. The concentration is on increasing speed while keeping energy expenditure to a minimum. Speed that is gradually increased in this manner will maintain smoothness of motion at the higher speeds. Once one breaks form, the energy consumption immediately escalates, and the fastest speed attained will be less than the fastest speed otherwise attainable. The runner should always be cognizant of what every part of the body is doing. Do not run in a vacuum. Practice your running form when you jog. Practice your jogging form when you run.

To improve our overall performance, we must improve both our speed and our endurance. Of the two, it is better to train for more speed first. In order to gain more speed, one may need to modify one or more of the techniques presently used. The speed techniques that are right for the particular runner should first be established and proven out by running faster. Once this is established, one can then train for endurance with these techniques. Otherwise, one may train for endurance while utilizing techniques that are later changed. Once the runner has achieved the form that he will be running with, training for endurance with that form can then be undertaken.

In this way, the runner will be better prepared to recognize a failure of good form should that occasion arise. Once recognized, a break in form can be dealt with, and steps taken to remedy the problem. Please note that the endurance referred to here is the peak endurance required for one's specific event. The more general endurance associated with overall body conditioning would have been accomplished as a prerequisite to any of the training referred to here.

Of course, we should be appreciative of those things that we do correctly. They are valuable and we don't want them to get lost. But we must continually be searching for some area where improvement can be made. Improvement in one's form will translate into an improvement in one's speed.

Sprinting is a game of finesse. Granted, strength is needed to sprint well, but strength alone will not do the job. Strength will not substitute for good form. Concentrate on form first, and then add strength. Speed will evolve naturally as strength is added to good form. Strength should be used as an additive to good form. Run with finesse, and then use strength to finesse—faster.

The Mind

The employment of proper body mechanics is certainly necessary for the runner to attain one's best speed. Utilizing mechanics alone, however, may not fully accomplish the desired result. Mechanics are good as far as they go, but unfortunately, they provide nothing in the realm of motivation. Mechanics alone provide no sense of urgency, which is necessary in order to reach one's extreme.

To supply this impetus, one's imagination can be put into play. The author does this by envisioning the devil itself is in pursuit. In the mind of the author, the devil is reaching out with its fiery hand to grab his butt from behind. Should the author be touched by the devil, surely a disastrous and most painful demise would result. With this incentive to avoid the devil's grasp, the very fastest run is realized. Here, self-control is critical. One must not break form in this final escalation of speed. Do the things you know are right for you. Just do them better; do them quicker.

Most of the author's training was performed as an individual, rather than under the watchful eye of a coach or training partner. As a result, upon the completion of each speed run that had been made in search of better form, the author would find himself in a mode of self-analysis. It was in this circumstance that a sense of self-awareness was observed that had previously gone unnoticed. During the first few minutes after a run, it is possible to re-create in one's mind the motions that the limbs had been performing during the run. The discovery that these sensations were available became a most valuable training tool.

When you have run off any tenseness in your system and begin to tire, you will be more attuned to hearing these tiny messages the body is continuously sending to the brain. If we listen to our body, it will often tell us what we had just been doing and to what intensity we were doing it. We will then be in a position to know what change we should next make to our running form as we mold it toward the form we believe we want.

Upon the completion of a run, every runner should allow oneself the opportunity to experience this awareness. The brain takes the information coming from the still-stimulated muscles and allows the runner to mentally relive the experience. Given the opportunity to learn in this manner, this knowledge can be utilized to make adjustments and thereby attain a better run on succeeding occasions. A coach should encourage the runner to fully utilize this perceptive ability (every person has this capability) and allow the runner the opportunity to go through this process. Then, the coach's observations can be combined with the runner's assessment of the run, and agreement reached on what seems to be working and what next needs improvement.

We all have a body *and* a mind, which we can apply as we see appropriate. During the development of one's running ability, they should *each* be utilized to the fullest. Then, on race day, bring them *both* to the game.

11

ASSEMBLING THE COMPONENTS

When sprinting, we use each of our four limbs in quite violent motions. Earlier, we looked at each of these individual motions, and methods were described to make each of those motions more effective. But now, the motions of the limbs must be brought together so they will act efficiently with each other and thereby produce one cohesive body; one very fast cohesive body.

If you believe you would like to try a different technique in the search for a faster *you*, thoroughly think through the new technique before attempting it. Decide at which stage of the race you intend to utilize the technique. Envision what characteristics the technique will present and anticipate what you might feel from it. What expectations do you have for its results? Later, this will better enable you to determine if you have properly implemented this change in your form, and if this change was right for you.

Be willing to accept the possibility that during the transition from one technique to another, there may be a period of adjustment before being able to realize the full advantage of implementing the change. Do not be tentative when making the trial change. Give it a decisive try. One should not decide to jump off the diving board and then attempt to get only the feet wet. Such an approach would be doomed to failure. Give any experimental attempt a full and honest opportunity to be successful. Only then will you know if the proposed change would be right for you, or if you must look elsewhere for the next improvement in your race time.

We have spent considerable time looking at individual techniques that are intended to improve one's running ability. In this chapter, we look at bringing it all together. This includes a review of most of the factors that comprise the running form, but is not intended to replace the more detailed descriptions of them that are found in earlier chapters.

The routine for getting the most out of each training session really begins at home. Here, a mental comparison is made between one's present running form and the desired running form. Also considered here are the mistakes that have been recently made. Just remembering all the factors that need to be concentrated upon can be a formidable chore. Therefore, a written list of those techniques that are still to be incorporated into one's form should be developed. Also included here are those techniques that need to be improved upon in order to make the next step forward in the never ending search for better form and more speed.

Through trial and error, it has been found that it is best to have certain techniques in place before others are initiated. During a slow and controlled acceleration, arm techniques should be established early, otherwise leg techniques won't *take hold* as one enters the higher speed zone. Therefore, when preparing a checklist, one must make provision for proper sequencing of individual techniques that are to be evaluated.

During your previous visits to the track and upon the completion of each short practice sprint, you have been encouraged to be self-critical and ask yourself questions. "Were all the techniques utilized as had been intended?" "What was limiting my speed on that run?" "What needs to be done better in order to make the next small improvement?" Your answers to these questions are what now form the basis for developing your list of *need tos.*

A mistake that the author found to be very disturbing when at the track was that while concentrating on some techniques, others were overlooked. The top speed that was achieved was therefore limited accordingly. The run then had to be repeated while remembering to check the feel of each of the techniques that were to be included in the run. As a result of these oversights, the routine of using an abbreviated checklist was resorted to. This shortlist of the most pressing items was prepared so that it could be easily memorized. It would permit each important item to be ticked off while the run was being performed. Depending upon what items were to be incorporated in the run, such a list might be:

wrists and forearms kept further from sides
elbows swinging low to avoid shoulder hunch
upper arms with a good swing to the rear
knees pointed forward
push off strongly from behind
eyebrows checked for minimal bounce

A prominent letter is then selected from the keyword in each line item and an acronym is formed for easy remembering. In this instance, the acronym *reanpy* is developed. Don't be concerned if the acronym makes little sense.

Its usefulness to *you* is what counts. By going through such a mental checklist as was prompted by an acronym, it was found that a desired technique was less apt to be overlooked. Thus, more efficient use of the training sessions was being achieved. Since the author is not a natural runner, the use of every available legal crutch has been resorted to in order to raise the speed one notch higher. Don't try to make the list all-inclusive. Just list the most critical items that are giving you difficulty at this time. Of course, the system that works best for an individual, is the one that should be used.

After some time interval of good effort, some of these things will begin to occur automatically without your conscious effort to implement them. This will signal you are making progress. Consideration can now be given to dropping them from the list. You will then be freed to direct your attention to other areas that need more effort to make them happen. Bring your checklist up to date. Change it as often as necessary in order to put the most meaningful items before you. This, so you can better concentrate upon and more quickly improve them.

You should walk onto the practice track with a plan of what will be worked on that day. Do not expect the plan to be perfect or without room for modification. But start with some written notes of what you intend to do that day. Making written notes forces one to begin thinking about each practice day before ever arriving at the track. Give the plan your best effort. After testing it, change it as needed. Try various techniques. Then, through trial and error, techniques will be retained or rejected from the plan.

Keep an open mind during the process of evaluating new techniques. If there is a particular technique that you thought would be good but does not seem to be working out for you, do not be too quick to discard it. Try to determine why it's not working. Perhaps some other factor is interfering with its execution and more time is needed to sort it out. This is why we have practice days. Eventually, the combination of techniques that works best for you will evolve. But without a plan you may find yourself just going through routines that you know, but with little chance of improving your race.

If you're not sure which way to go next, ask a coach or a friend. You can also go back and read the earlier chapters of this book to search for details that relate to your particular circumstance. Make notes as you read. Include page numbers of paragraphs you may want to return to. Maintain a positive and an optimistic attitude. Develop a plan for your trips to the practice track. Develop a plan to make yourself a faster runner.

As we attain higher speeds, our actions become quicker and the margin for error becomes progressively smaller. Our techniques must be executed more precisely if we are to consistently run at an even higher speed. To improve, we must scrutinize our actions ever more closely. Be objective in your self-analysis and the next step in self-improvement will become clearer.

There are some days that we have big plans for what we want to accomplish during our practice time on the track, but unfortunately not all days go as planned. Is this a day that your tune-up runs are not going well? Do the legs feel heavy and seem to have no zip in their stride? It just may be, for whatever reason, that you have reverted to a running form that incorporates too little push off and too little knee bend (they are closely related).

Try a practice run wherein you consciously employ a good strong push off with each foot. This will deliver a stronger forward push to the body. The foot and leg actions will continue from there and will carry through. A greater kickback will be provided, which will induce greater knee bend in the forward leg swing. This will promote a more lively swing of the legs. Go through this exercise a couple of times and you just might rescue a day that otherwise would have been a disappointing experience.

There are two basic ways to increase our top speed: (1) raise the turnover rate and (2) increase the stride length. The key to a higher turnover rate is with proper momentum management of the four moving limbs. The keys to increasing stride length lie in the foot plant: reducing braking action and increasing the push off, especially the takeoff, which occurs during those few milliseconds before the foot breaks contact with the track. Strangely enough, none of these are readily discernible to the eye of an observer. Only the basic motions of a runner can be directly seen. After that, we must rely on the runner's *feel* for those more subtle enhancements.

During the repetitions of everyday training, it is important that the sprinter not lose sight of those two most basic concepts. While training, you must stay focused on why a particular routine is being performed. The development of strength, technique, coordination and endurance must be carried out with the end goal always in sight so you can derive the most gain from each exercise and routine. Keep your eye on the mark. This will ensure you obtain the most benefit from the hours of hard work you devote to your sport.

That which follows summarizes the techniques that were discussed earlier. You may have other ones that you have found work well for you. Do not forsake what you know works well for you, but be open-minded to explore additional possibilities. This is how we improve.

- The feet must be kept pointing straight ahead. The feet are your foundation. If they are not properly set, all above them is compromised.
- Pay attention to the lateral distance between foot plants. A wider foot plant encourages greater use of the large toes rather than the small toes.

If the foot plants move outward, the forearms must likewise move outward.

- Proper lateral foot plant will minimize the amount of leg crossover. Crossover introduces unwanted twisting tendencies.
- Do not let the knees go astray and point outward. Keep the entire foot/leg assembly in alignment under the hip joint.
- Practice running higher on the toes to induce a livelier takeoff action. Think of flicking each foot to the rear in order to optimize the takeoff.
- When the plant foot has broken free from the track, encourage a generous kickback of the lower leg.
- Increase the amount of knee bend during the forward leg swing in order to attain better momentum balance between arms and legs at high turnover rates. Legs that are more folded will swing forward easier and quicker than will legs that are straighter.
- After takeoff, inhibit the amount of rearward swing of the upper leg. This will shorten the distance needed to swing the leg forward, and also enhance the kickback.
- Do not increase stride length by reaching forward with the legs. This increases the braking action of the touchdowns.
- Experiment with body posture as you train.
- Strive to develop the maximum amount of momentum from the arm swing. This will enhance the leg swing. There is no such thing as too much arm momentum unless it begins to slow the turnover rate. Strive to find that point of optimum arm momentum.
- Maintain the maximum amplitude of the upper arm motion by swinging the elbow low and in a long arc as far rearward as possible. It will require greater upper limb strength and a conscious effort to swing the elbow in this most productive arc.
- As the turnover rate increases, resist the tendency to curtail the back swing of the elbows. Instead, swing the arms more forcefully.
- Do not let the hands and fingers be left behind as the forearms begin their downward and rearward swings. Keep the fingers straight and cause the hands to lead the arm swings. Bend the wrists in the same direction as the arm swings.
- Move the paths of the elbows slightly outward from the sides in order to increase the momentum they generate about the Z-axis.
- Keep wrists directly in front of elbows. Do not let the forearms introduce any cross swing. *Never* allow the wrists to stray outside the planes of the swinging elbows, but bending the wrists outward will increase the momentum obtained from the hands.

- When practicing a gradual run-up to high speed, most techniques can begin to be put in place at 50 percent speed. Balance the arm and the leg momentums to the point where a free and easy leg swing is achieved. This results in a smooth running style that will require less energy from the legs.
- Incorporate stronger arm swings, both forward and rearward. We are looking for an extremely fine tune here between vigorous arm movement and overall smooth running motion. Open the angle of the elbow as much as one's upper limb strength will allow without it slowing the turnover rate.
- Match the arm turnover rate to the leg turnover rate by increasing the amplitude of the rearward arm swing. Upper arm and shoulder strength is needed here.
- The head and torso should remain motionless. Only the four limbs should be moving.
- Roll the pelvis forward and slightly lower the hips. Practice this when jogging, and then incorporate it in the running form. This will reduce braking action and aid in one's search for a softer touchdown.
- Use the vertical limit of peripheral vision to gauge the amount of vertical bobbing. Strive to minimize this vertical movement and its associated braking action by employing a softer touchdown. To properly control this motion, good strength in the knees and quads is required because of the more bent-leg configuration at the instant of touchdown.

The goal of every runner is to be able to run a faster race than one has run heretofore. Every sprinter wants to log a shorter time by running still faster than one's current performance. This raises the question "How best to go about accomplishing this better time?" One way is to continue doing those things that have gotten you to where you are, only train harder and more intensely. The second way of reaching your goal is to search for better ways of doing what you do. Both ways can improve your game. But you don't need this book to do the former. This book is intended to help you find your way along path No.2. This book is intended to help you via the route of innovation rather than the route of intensification.

Logic tells us that when we are running at our fastest speed, this is our fastest speed because something is preventing us from running still faster. The modus operandi that is advocated here is for the runner to analyze one's top speed and determine specifically what that something is that is preventing the runner from running faster. That item is then refined and improved to the point that it is no longer the limiting factor. This now allows the runner to improve the top speed by one tiny notch to where some other component of form is found to be the limiting factor. And the process is repeated. By improving each of the parts, we improve the whole. A coach can be very helpful here if you are fortunate enough to have one.

But very often, the person who must do the analyzing is the only one who is present, the runner. The key to making this process successful is two fold. First, the runner must be able to determine which of the many elements of the running form is presently limiting one's speed and therefore must be targeted for improvement. This determination requires that the runner be cognizant of what each body part is doing. One must not operate in a vacuum. The runner must be sufficiently aware of one's own body. Once the critical item is identified, it can be worked with.

Second, one must sufficiently understand the basic dynamics of running. The author has attempted to provide such an understanding herein, and is the primary objective of this book. This knowledge is utilized to recognize how each piece of the running system makes its contribution to the total effort. This, in turn, assists the runner in making the above-described determination of the weak link. Then, this knowledge is further used to determine specifically how to alter the critical item so it is no longer limiting one's speed.

The runner is in a very good position to make the determination of which of the many running elements should next be targeted. Only the runner can feel the run. Only the runner can feel the tired muscle. Only the runner can feel the force exerted in each limb. Only the runner can feel the location and the sharpness of the foot strike on the track. Only the runner can feel the timing of the arm swing. Only the runner can feel the push derived from the takeoff. Only the runner can feel the reward when it all comes into balance. Each of our many body parts is in constant communication with the brain. We must learn to listen to, and understand, these messages that are constantly being transmitted. Heeding these messages will lead the runner through the process of self-improvement. Only the runner can hear these internal messages. So, listen in. Understand what they are saying and use their input to your best advantage.

One should not merely plod through the daily workout. You can do better. Take the time to turn on those receptors in the mind. The author has found that those internal messages are clearest when one is fully relaxed or beginning to tire near the end of a workout. Upon the completion of each practice run, allow yourself to feel what your limbs and muscles were just doing. With this information, your mind will paint a mental image of your running form. Have also a mental image of what you would like your form to be. Then, compare these two images. Any disparity will tell you which techniques you must work with still further. The runner must get the picture in the mind before being able to achieve the action on the track. Also, listen to which muscles are complaining of fatigue. You will know that you must work to improve the strength and endurance of those specific muscles so they will not fail you near the end of a race.

The first minute after a run should be an introspective moment wherein the runner mentally re-creates one's running form, isolates critical techniques, determines what needs improvement and plans the training routine to improve those facets of the game so that future runs will be even better runs. This will prove more rewarding than idle chatter with your running mates. That can come later. Never assume there is nothing left to improve upon or that there is no faster time to be had.

The path to top speed requires the utilization of all the basic form factors previously discussed and then combining them with utmost smoothness. The key to smoothness is momentum harmony between arms and legs combined with a soft landing of the foot. Power is added by way of a vigorous arm motion, in both directions, and a quick powerful push off from behind. In putting all this together, remain relaxed. Relaxed muscles respond quicker than do tense muscles. Also, they don't tire as quickly.

It took only a moment to read this blueprint for greater speed. It will take considerably longer to implement it. But the runner will feel the rewards as incremental improvements to techniques are made. Demonstrating a steady improvement in one's race times can be more gratifying than winning a medal in a single race. Smoothness is key to improvement. If necessary, power should be sacrificed in order to maintain smoothness. *Never* sacrifice smoothness in order to expend more power. Because, without smoothness, that's all one does, expend more power. It doesn't necessarily make one faster.

While running does require physical strength, this is better technique we're studying here. Timing and smoothness of movement are critical; finesse is the operative word. Run with finesse and let the finesse draw upon your body strength as it is needed. This cannot be accomplished by utilizing a formula with inches, pounds and milliseconds. This can only be obtained through *feel*. This is where the art of the sport shines through.

High quality practice sessions are in order here. Getting that arm motion and stride to work for some individuals will require the practice of many run-ups to high speed. But they don't all have to go up to 100 percent. A greater number of run-ups to 90 percent will permit the runner to more finely tune one's form. Keep working at it. The reward of higher speed will eventually be achieved. No one said this sport is easy.

Be cognizant of the fact that one should not implement techniques that are applicable to higher speed running until that stage of the race is reached where one has actually attained that higher speed. As a comparative example, the ignition timing of a gasoline engine would not be the same for high-speed operation as it is for intermediate-speed operation. Only when the engine has been given the opportunity to respond to and speed up with the present ignition setting, should the timing be advanced for still higher-speed operation.

And so it also is with humans who want to run faster. All of the go-fast techniques should not be initially employed at lower speed just because the runner will want them in place as top speed is approached. For instance, concentrating on reducing vertical bounce, or thinking about momentum balance too early in the race, would have a detrimental effect upon one's acceleration.

The runner should employ those techniques that are appropriate for the speed that is currently being generated. Give them an opportunity to have a positive effect upon the speed, and thereafter utilize techniques that are applicable to the higher speed. As one's speed increases, subtle changes of which only the runner will be aware are employed that are applicable to that stage of the race through which the runner is passing.

The author believes the concept of running with looseness overstates the issue. Running with looseness carries the risk of running with poor form. Running in a *relaxed* manner creates all the looseness that is needed, and this concept engenders a better state of mind. Running relaxed rather than running loose must also be practiced during the warm up jog. This style of running allows the runner to practice the proper form to be utilized by all the limbs at all speeds.

Placing the touchdown at a shorter distance in front of the body will significantly reduce the braking effect. But there are consequences, both bad and good. When the support distance that is forward of the body is shortened, the support distance that is behind the body must also be shortened in order to keep the body in balance. This has the effect of shortening the stride length but also of allowing an increase in the turnover rate. When increasing turnover rate, we must be cognizant of momentum balance considerations. These considerations limit the amount the turnover rate can be increased. So, in reverse order, improving the body's momentum balance can be a method of reducing the braking effect. The entire body works in harmony with itself.

Running at full speed during a training session will aid in improving strength, endurance and coordination necessary for top speed. But, when running at full speed, the runner is committed to running with those techniques that are currently in place. Running at full speed is not conducive to improving or altering any individual technique. Therefore, if one will be looking to restructure any techniques, running at full speed does not provide the appropriate setting for this type of work.

Let us say this is a practice day during which the runner will be working on improving high-speed form. Here, in slow motion, we will follow through a practice run-up to high speed that will utilize what we have learned earlier. As we shall see, practicing our top-speed techniques does not necessarily require running at top speed. Running at a somewhat lower speed is a better forum in which to do this extremely precise work.

The runner starts off at a medium jog. Running high on the toes, a slightly exaggerated kickback and a higher knee lift are utilized somewhat akin to what a long jumper might use starting down the runway. This additional spring in each stride will evoke a greater bobbing up-and-down. We will decrease this excessive up-and-down movement shortly. For now, just let it happen. This gait will require more power than would running normally at this low speed, but the style will be of advantage as the higher speeds are reached. The push off occurs over a shorter period of time with this technique, and provides a quick strong takeoff from behind. The arm swing is made stronger than that which would be necessary to provide only a minimum momentum balance, but the proper basics of the swing are incorporated now. Acceleration is made under complete control until 50 percent speed is reached. Here the runner levels off.

At 50 percent speed, the runner goes through a checklist and takes stock of all relevant factors, starting at the feet and working up.

- Feet pointed straight ahead.
- A fairly wide foot plant.
- Running high on the inner toes; toes bent upward.
- Feet, knees and hips all operating in proper vertical planes.
- Head and torso erect.
- Elbows out comfortably to the side.
- No cross swing of the forearms; wrists kept in front of the elbows.
- The fingers extended straight but not bone tight at this time.
- Wrists bent slightly outward.
- Bending the wrist at each arm swing amplifies the hand motion, thereby enhancing the effect of the arm swing.

- It is the forward arm swing that is dominating the arm motion. This swing is not initiated until after the corresponding foot has touched down.
- The elbows are swung low.
- The arc of the elbow carries as far to the rear as the shoulder joint will permit. The maximum arm momentum that can be developed at this speed is incorporated (more than is necessary for this running speed), but the arm techniques are all in place and now other things can be concentrated on. It must be remembered that when accelerating from this point, none of the present arm techniques can be compromised.
- Breathing is deep and full.
- Eyes looking straight ahead but focused on nothing.
- The touchdown is softened to some extent.

If all is not comfortable and relaxed, one should not accelerate any further. If it isn't right at 50 percent, it won't feel right at 80 percent or 90 percent. This is an easy enough pace that the form can be analyzed and a decision reached as to why it doesn't feel comfortable. One should be expending only a small amount of energy at this point. When it is decided what specifically is not working correctly, one should stop running and practice just that troublesome movement. The body must become accustomed to the running action that will be used at higher speed. The mental checklist should be remade to emphasize the troublesome item.

The runner now restarts and comes up to 50 percent speed again. A check is made to see if the running feels any better. If so, the correct analysis was made. If not, one must try again to isolate the troublesome action. This process must be repeated until all the aforementioned form factors are comfortably in place at 50 percent speed. When this feels right, only then is a controlled acceleration above the 50 percent mark given consideration. One must not be impatient. A new running form will not take hold right away. It will take dedicated work and a lot of self-examination to bring it all together. Practicing on one's own time, at one's own pace, with no outside distractions, is best for this particular type of work. One must learn to look inward, not outward, for an answer to the question "what should I do next?" When you have attained the form you believe to be right for you, be proud to show it to your coach.

The runner is now ready to begin raising the speed above the 50 percent mark. This is done by increasing the turnover rate of the arms. Become accustomed to the arms acting as the lead dog of the pack. The legs are left to follow the pace naturally. This will make certain the arms are not just reacting to the leg motion. The arms are swung decisively to ensure the momentum of the arms stays ahead of the minimum momentum required to balance the legs. This helps to keep the legs relaxed.

The elbows are given long swings to the rear while their arcs are kept as low as possible. When increasing the turnover rate of the arms, it is initiated by the motion of the hands rather than the elbows. The runner thinks *hands*. The hands bend the wrist downward on the back swing and upward on the forward swing. The hands are now swinging in a longer arc than they otherwise would if the wrists were kept straight. This keeps the arm momentum as high as possible. All this is put in place now so that no major changes will be required when even higher arm momentum is needed later on.

As the speed is raised above the 50 percent level, the runner stays high on the toes in order to promote the quickest push off by the foot. On the forward leg swing, swinging the entire leg forward is not the thought. Instead, the runner thinks *knees*. This, to encourage an ample amount of knee bend so the legs can be swung forward more effortlessly. The rearward swing of the upper leg is held to a minimum. A good bounce is maintained in the step, but it is now developing into a more forward bounce rather than an upward bounce.

As speed is increased, the takeoff will be made from further behind. The takeoff push is now becoming more horizontal and the excessive up-and-down movement is decreased. A wide foot plant is maintained so that all power from the push off goes straight upward to the hip. The runner does not *reach* the stride in front of the body. For a smooth top speed, braking action must be minimized.

Methodically, the speed is raised to 80 percent. All the basic techniques continue to be monitored. Everything established at 50 percent is still working effectively. A double check is made that the path of the elbows is low and still swinging all the way rearward. Verify that a wide lateral foot plant is being maintained. The time the foot is in contact with the track has now become quite short. Using peripheral vision as a guide, the foot plant is softened still further to minimize as much as possible the amount of vertical head bobbing. All remains smooth and feels really right. When increasing the turnover rate, there should be no tendency to chop the stride short. Maintain the full carry of the stride that the push off provides. Check again that the leg motion is being freely maintained.

If the runner's form does not feel right during a run-up, one should not be bullheaded. It won't get better by doing more of the same. Finesse is better than force. One should back the speed down, mentally regroup, figure out what's not right, make an adjustment and try again. One of the fundamentals may have been allowed to go astray. A good place to begin looking is at the momentum picture. Obtain maximum momentum from the arm swing by optimizing the physical path of each of the arm's components. Minimize the momentum from the leg swing by increasing the knee bend and limiting the amount of back swing of the upper leg. Optimize these arm and leg motions. This is the cornerstone of momentum management.

The runner should consider 80 percent speed as the last opportunity for a *major* adjustment to form. Above this speed, the time to put the right techniques in place will have been passed. The runner is now committed to a running form. Above 80 percent speed, the runner is focusing on adding speed and power to those motions that are already in place. Be confident in your form before venturing above the 80 percent mark. Adding more power to an incorrect technique will not reward the runner with huge success. Doing the wrong thing quicker is not the way to go. Every technique to be utilized must be in place and working smoothly.

When approaching top speed, if it is felt that the quads are beginning to work much harder, this is an indication you are beginning to exceed your maximum allowable momentum imbalance. Continuing further in this direction, to exhort the quads to deliver still more, will achieve only limited results.

Instead, change your focus to limit the back swing of the upper leg, and at the same time think, "more powerful push off." If done correctly, you will be aware that you have increased the turnover rate and less demand is being made on the quads. Now, with maximum input from the arms, you are in position to increase speed still further.

The runner now gives oneself the green light to continue smoothly opening the throttle—90 percent—95 percent; level off. At these higher speeds, minimizing braking action is critical to maximizing speed. The peripheral vision is checked again; the hips are slid forward and the foot plant is softened as much as possible. The speed does not feel excessively difficult. This is why we love sprinting. We love the feel of the speed. We know we are running well.

If all feels well after a few strides at 95 percent, the really difficult work begins; concentrate to find the soft spots. Everything done at this time is critical. The runner increases speed to 96 percent, no more, and holds. A search is made to pinpoint which motion, limb or muscle has suddenly had to work much harder to achieve that 1 percent increase. There is a good chance this additional load will be felt in the quads as they work harder to pull the legs forward just a little bit quicker. If the speed were to be cranked up to 97 percent, it would probably be done in the same manner; struggle to pull the legs forward faster. Our runner resists this temptation. This is not the purpose of this training exercise.

A sharp increase in the effort expended by the quads in order to pull the legs forward quicker is an indication that the body has reached the upper limit of its ability to accommodate the inequality of leg momentum and arm momentum. The attempt to increase speed by exhorting the quads to pull the legs harder will have only limited success. The body will be fighting one of the laws of nature by ignoring the body's need to maintain a momentum balance.

Don't fight Mother Nature. Instead, heed her message. One should drop back to 95 percent speed and work on improving the momentum balance. The slightest improvement in this balance will reveal most surprising results when one next elevates speed to 96 percent. This speed can now be achieved with less expenditure of energy than before.

To improve one's momentum balance, look to improving momentum input from the arms. While maintaining the same turnover rate, see if the rearward swing of the upper arms can be increased. Lower the elbows as much as possible. Experiment with moving the forearm track more outward at the side. Check the fingers. When one considers the extremely high speed with which the hands are moving, the minor adjustment of changing the fingers from curled to straight can make a noticeable difference in freeing up one's running form as proper momentum balance is regained. The fingers are the most rapidly moving part of the upper body. The value of their effect on the total picture should not be underestimated. Flaring the hands and the fingers slightly outward from the forearm, by bending the wrist, will enhance their contribution to momentum generation. This is easier to control than moving the entire elbow/forearm outward.

If the proper adjustments are made, the runner will be able to effect an increase in top speed with only a nominal increase in energy expenditure. The body will carry further between foot plants, not because one is striding out, but because the higher speed will carry the runner further before the next touchdown. The combination of less effort to achieve the leg movement, along with a higher running speed, lets the runner know the body is operating within the limits of proper momentum balance. Let us consider that when running at 95 percent speed, one has reached the *momentum cap*. At this point, even minute changes of arm and leg momentum will make a difference in the attainable speed. The runner should use every method available to raise this speed cap to its highest.

Now, if our runner is going for 100 percent on this run, the muscling of the limbs is left until this point. For here is where one begins fighting the body's upper limit of stability. All other techniques must be maximized first. The runner will feel the exertion rate rise dramatically as power is added to the running form. When adding this power, one must make certain to not break form and relinquish any of the technique that has brought him to this level.

In addition to muscling the legs to go faster, one must also muscle the arms. Muscling the arms rearward assists in attaining the highest turnover rate. Muscling the arms forward enhances the push off by the feet and will project the runner further ahead with each stride. Peripheral vision must be repeatedly checked in order to monitor vertical bounce and the underlying braking action it indicates. The arm action must be consciously worked so that it encourages a greater productivity from the legs.

Be sensitive to the sound of, and the feel of, the touchdown on the balls of the feet. Be receptive to feeling how far in front of the body the touchdown is occurring. If the upper limbs are well conditioned, slightly opening the angle of the elbow to obtain a broader swing of the hand may decrease the momentum gap, and thereby allow an increase in speed. One must employ the broadest swing of the hand that one's arm and shoulder strength can generate. If a speed decrease is sensed, this attempt must be aborted and the hand swing must be brought back closer to the shoulder. The hand swing that yields optimum results must be found. Maximum energy must be directed to the arms. Without maximum output from the arms, one cannot expect maximum output from the legs.

Now that the runner is putting everything physical into the run, it is time to mentally add that sense of urgency. One must run as if winning depended upon it. But it must be done without any loss of control and smoothness that has brought the runner to this level of achievement. If done correctly, our runner is now running at his fastest speed—today. With this under one's belt, imagine what tomorrow might bring.

Each practice run must be undertaken for a purpose. Before initiating a run, fully understand what the objective of this run will be, and how you intend to achieve that objective. During the run, take notice of those items for which the run is being performed. At the conclusion of the run, assess *both* how well you incorporated the techniques you were evaluating, and also the effects they had on the run. Understand what you learned from the run. From the results of this run, what will you do on your next run? In order to derive the most benefit from each run, have a plan. Each run should be intended to yield both a better-trained body and also a better-informed mind. Make certain you are deriving the most benefit from your time and hard work on the practice track. Train with a plan!

The actions of our limbs can move us toward victory; the sound of that victory will be heard closer and stronger as we increase both the frequency and the amplitude of our stride. To be able to attain your best speed will take hard work. But don't lose sight of the basics or your hard work may be misdirected. Make certain that your efforts are directed toward that part of your running game that will give you the greatest reward at this particular time. A better understanding of what can produce *fast* is your best weapon against *slow*.

However, the athlete should not be deluded into thinking good technique can substitute for good training. That would be the fast road to failure. Introducing better technique should not be used as an excuse to reduce the hard work and intensity of training. Good technique is to be considered an additive to intensive training. When both are melded together, the athlete will have created the best opportunity for success.

If you are confident that you have already mastered the major aspects of the sprint, do not ignore those items that may appear to be of little consequence. Success is supported by many building blocks—some large, some small. But they all contribute to your endeavor to perform at the highest of your ability. If just a small contributor is absent, the peak of your accomplishment will be just a little lower.

When you bring it all into balance, you will sense an ease of running. You will experience the *sprinter's high* of greater speed. Come up to top speed using your head, not your guts. There will be ample opportunity to run on your guts before you reach the finish line.

12

SIZE OF ATHLETE

How does the size of the athlete affect one's performance? Although there are some exceptions (gymnasts and jockeys come to mind), there is often some advantage to the athlete who is larger than average. Of course, this is mainly true in contact sports, but even in noncontact sports one often sees a better performance from the larger competitor. From a practical standpoint, the fixed dimensions of our physical world may make it appear to be a more massive and formidable place from the viewpoint of a person who is 5'2" tall as compared to how it appears to a person who is 6'6" tall. To add some slight degree of credence to this thought, the author has noticed that when returning for a nostalgic visit to places of his childhood, they now do not seem to be as large as he remembers them appearing when viewed through the eyes of a child. Yes, it seems that one's size does make a difference.

Now, we know there is much more than size alone that determines the victor in the game of sport. But the question is posed, "Is the size of the athlete a factor in the equation of track and field?" The heavier, more muscular, people do well in the throwing events. Taller people do well in the high jump where one's C.G. begins the competition already closer to the bar. But, what about the straight running events? Lighter built runners generally dominate the distance events while additional muscle power is evident in topflight sprinters.

This book is about sprinters, so let us look closer at this group. No one can argue that extensive physical conditioning is not important to perform at one's best. But, what about something over which the runner has no control? I'm referring here to one's height. Does the longer-limbed athlete have an advantage here, in the sprint, similar to what is enjoyed in many other sporting events?

In the sprint, we are primarily concerned with speed. And from the basics of running, we know that speed is the product of two components: stride length and turnover rate. We will look at each of these components separately to see what can be learned. First under the microscope is stride length. Here we ask, "What are the elements that comprise a runner's stride length?" "What control does the runner have over these elements that comprise one's stride length?" For this discussion, stride length will be considered to consist of three separate, nonoverlapping components. We will look at each of these individually.

First, there is the portion of the stride that arises from the distance the runner advances when planting one foot in front of the other, as one would do in a nonbounding sense. The only forward movement being the result of the step distance from one foot position to the next when stepping forward, but while employing the form that would be utilized when performing the running action. This distance is the result only of the runner's leg motion relative to the torso and is largely dependent upon the length of the runner's legs. The longer are one's legs, the longer will be this step component of the stride.

The second component of stride length is the distance that is added to the first component by the bounding effect of a powerful push off produced by the driving foot. This bounding or jumping effort introduces the airborne portion of the stride, and increases the length of a runner's stride over that which is achieved by only a stepping action. The more powerful is one's push off, the longer will be this bounding component of the stride.

The third component of stride length is the additional airborne distance that is added to the sum of the first two components by virtue of the runner's speed. As an illustration, if a runner were to perform a stepping-bounding stride while traveling at 10 mph, this would provide the runner with a certain airborne distance. However, if the runner were to perform this same stepping-bounding stride while traveling at 20 mph, the *increase* in airborne distance is what comprises component No. 3. This third component of stride length is attributable only to an increase in speed of one's airborne time, and is completely independent of how that speed was produced.

Now that the elements that comprise a runner's stride length have been identified, let us assign some values to each of these stride components:

Step Component:	¾ meter
Bounding Component:	¾ meter
Speed Component:	½ meter
Total:	2 meters

What might we deduce from these admittedly arbitrary figures? We can hopefully agree that the runner has no voluntary input to element No. 1, the step component of the stride. One's leg length is determined before one ever takes to the starting line. The taller runner would enter the race with an advantage here, but this is not an element that can be improved with training.

What about element No. 3, the speed component? The speed component is not an input factor that one controls directly. It is strictly a *result* of one's speed; it is not a *contributor* to one's speed. It evolves only as a result of the first two factors. The runner exerts no *direct* control over the speed component.

This now leaves us with element No. 2, the bounding component. This factor is completely under the control of the runner, and according to the above noted values is an element that comprises a large portion of the total stride length. When this bounding component is improved, a longer airborne portion of the stride is obtained and a greater stride length is achieved. Additionally, because this action will increase the runner's speed, the speed component of stride length (No. 3 listed above) will also increase.

With the foregoing understanding, if the runner wants to investigate the possibility of increasing stride length, one can now be more analytical. The runner is encouraged to analyze one's own stride characteristics and thereby determine the appropriate value for each of the three stride components. The values so determined may be in variance with the values noted above. However, once the runner understands which variables can be controlled, and how to control them, the path to an improved stride length will become clearer.

If we are to increase speed by increasing stride length, we must focus on improving the component of stride we have labeled *bounding component*. This bounding component can be improved by increasing the effectiveness of the push off. A greater productivity can be derived from the push off in two ways. The first way is for the runner to reduce braking upon touchdown. This will then reduce the need for the push off to utilize its pushing power to regenerate the speed that was just lost. The second way is for the runner to utilize a quicker stronger push off to generate new speed.

In addition to a greater step length, the longer limbed runner will, in all probability, have developed a more powerful takeoff mechanism, commensurate with the larger-size limbs, than will have the shorter limbed runner. When grading stride length as a contributor to overall speed, we will have to give the edge to the longer-limbed runner.

Next up for scrutiny is turnover rate. For this analysis, we must resort to physics, and unfortunately, we will have to briefly endure a few formulas. Here the movements of the limbs are considered to be circular arcs as the limbs swing about their points of attachment.

We have previously discussed straight-line momentum where M = mv (mass times velocity). In circular motion, we have the analogous concept we call angular momentum. Angular momentum is defined as the mass of the body (m) times the tangential velocity (v_t) of the body's C.G. times the distance (r) of the C.G. from its axis of rotation, or $M_a = mv_t r$. But we also know that the value of tangential velocity (v_t) can be obtained by multiplying the angular velocity (ω) by the body's distance (r) from its axis of rotation, or v_t = ωr. Now, if in the first equation, we substitute ωr for v_t, we get the result that angular momentum M_a = m × ωr × r or M_a = mωr². We see that the angular momentum of a swinging body is extremely dependent upon how far the C.G. of that body is from the axis of its swing. The angular momentum of a body grows, not in direct proportion to the distance its C.G. is located from the pivot point, but grows much faster, i.e. as the *square* of the distance r that the C.G. is located from the point about which it rotates.

This momentum is also indicative of the difficulty one will have in starting the body into motion and of stopping the motion. A body that has a greater angular momentum will be more difficult to start and to stop.

We will now take the above information and apply it to two hypothetical runners; one large, the other small. For this discussion, it is assumed the large person has a limb that is twice as long, twice as heavy, and twice as strong as compared to the limb of the small person. Let us say the small runner has a limb that weighs 5 lb. and is 2' long. The angular momentum of that limb (with its C.G. at its center) is 5/g × ω × 1² = 5ω/g. Using the above stated criteria, the angular momentum of the large person's limb would be 10/g × ω × 2² = 40ω/g. The large runner has 8 times more angular momentum to overcome than does the small runner when swinging a limb. In this example, the large runner also has twice the strength of the small runner, but even with this added strength, the large runner will still have 4 times the difficulty in quickly swinging the limb.

Of course these figures do not resemble runners in the real world. These easily remembered figures were used to illustrate the principle of physics with which all runners must contend when rapidly swinging their limbs.

To summarize: As a runner's limb becomes heavier, it becomes increasingly difficult to swing rapidly. However, this heavier limb is generally controlled by stronger muscles that are quite capable of dealing with the increased weight. The problem for the taller runner is that a longer limb becomes exceedingly more difficult to swing rapidly due only to its increased length. Even excluding the change in weight, a limb that is twice as long has become four times more difficult to swing rapidly. This is a major reason for the decline in turnover rate of the taller runners.

The swinging of limbs correctly belongs in the purview of Moment of

Inertia and Radius of Gyration. The Radius of Gyration is normally slightly greater than is the distance to the C.G. that was used above. This fact serves to exacerbate still further, the difficulty encountered when swinging a longer limb. Since this is not intended to be a presentation of physics, that aspect of the picture is not expanded.

When grading turnover rate as a contributor to overall speed, we will have to give the edge to the shorter-limbed runner.

While this discussion has included some gross approximations, the purpose of this narrative has been to shed additional light on those two fundamentals that determine our speed: stride length and turnover rate. When applying the results of this narrative to what we see in real life situations, the conclusions that were drawn appear to be valid. This leads to the single inescapable conviction: for those who are short in stature, you can confidently serve notice that you're still in *this* game!

13

THE CURVE

Running the Curve

The 200-meter event adds another dimension to the sprint—the curve. Running the 200m requires much of the form, strength, finesse and quickness required to run the 100m plus greater endurance and cardiovascular capacity. But it also includes some additional idiosyncrasies. In this chapter, we will take a close look at the special challenges that are presented when we run the curve.

In order to run the curve, there are two separate and distinct motions that must be added to the straight-line run. In order to follow the curving lane, a runner must continually *move* the body to the left. If the runner did not keep moving the body to the left, the runner would continue running in a straight line. The second action a runner must accomplish is continually *turn* or rotate the body to the left. This is done in order to continue facing in the direction of travel. If one's body were not turned while running the curve, it would remain facing in the same direction as it was facing when the race started. By the time the runner came to the straightaway, one's body would be facing backward to the direction of travel.

Figure 8 shows the first portion of the 200m race. While all tracks are not alike, the one shown is representative of many of them. The layout of this 8-lane track places the starting line for lane No. 1 coincidental with the beginning of the curve. Unless indicated otherwise, the content of this chapter will be based on a track of this construction.

Although the leftward turning motion and the leftward moving motion are done simultaneously, there are differences in how they are accomplished. Therefore, each of these motions will be addressed separately.

The first action we will look at is the *turning* of one's body to the left. This is done incrementally during those brief intervals when a foot is in contact with the track. While the foot is anchored to the track, the leg muscles perform a quick twisting motion that turns the hips to the left.

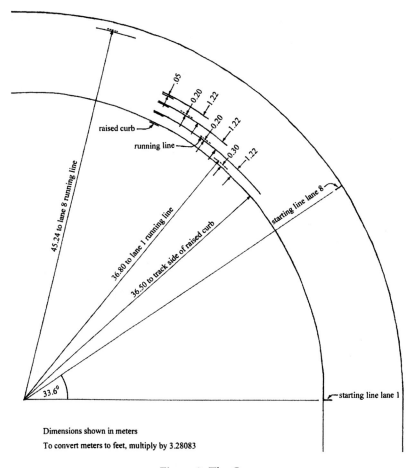

Figure 8. The Curve.

We must be more vigilant here. This twisting action, added to the running motion, makes the runner more prone to injury while on the curve as compared to running on the straightaway. The runner cannot avoid this twisting action when running the curve; the body must be turned during every foot plant.

Being aware that one will have to perform this twist while the foot is planted, the runner should consciously turn the foot to the left prior to touchdown. In this manner, after the twist is performed, the foot, leg and body will all be in alignment for performance of the takeoff.

If, in the alternative, the runner were to plant the foot pointing straight ahead, then the twisting action would take the leg from initially being in alignment to a twisted orientation for the takeoff portion of the stride. This would be less desirable than performing a well-aligned takeoff. The runner does not have a choice of whether or not to perform this twisting action. The choice that the runner has is whether to perform the takeoff with the leg in a twisted condition or to perform the takeoff with the leg in the aligned condition. This choice is made when the runner decides whether or not to twist the foot leftward prior to touchdown.

This twisting of the foot and leg takes care of the turning requirement for the lower extremities. But we still must accomplish the turning of the upper body. Because of the high turnover employed by the sprinter, there is very little time available in which to accomplish this turning of the complete body during each foot plant. We can assist the body in making this turn if we turn the upper body in advance of the touchdown. We accomplish this by employing a slightly diagonal motion to the right arm during its back swing. Again we are looking at the principle of action/reaction. The action of swinging the right arm rearward and rightward precipitates the reaction of pushing the right shoulder forward and leftward. This provides the necessary leftward turning of the upper body. This turning action occurs during the right leg's airborne motion. In this manner, the upper body will be fully turned leftward before touchdown occurs and the twisting of the leg can occur more easily. But now, there must also be a recovery motion for that right arm. It must swing forward and leftward to return to its starting position. During this motion, there will be the tendency to undo the leftward twisting that was just accomplished. During this recovery motion, the same-side foot will be anchored to the track. The body's muscle system is employed to prevent a rightward turning of the upper body. Unfortunately, the necessary twisting of the leg and turning of the body that is done on the curve prevent the runner from running in a relaxed fashion until the straightaway is reached.

It is much more difficult for the left arm to contribute toward any twisting of the upper body. It therefore seems to work out better if the upper body is over-twisted during the back swing of the right arm. This combination of foot twist and diagonal movement of the right arm provides the best means to accomplish the turning motion required for running the curve.

Because of the rapidity of the actions, the body does not respond with intermittent movements to each of these twisting impulses. But, just as in straight-line running, the body's inertia and resiliency average out these impulses so that it results in a smooth motion. What we have been describing is the series of quick impulses that will produce the smooth motion.

As has been stated, it is preferable to twist the leg leftward prior to touchdown so that the leg and body will be in alignment for the takeoff portion of the stride. But in performing this leg twist, one should not overly twist it and cause the leg to be out of alignment in the other direction. Knowing that we don't want an under-twisted or an over-twisted leg raises yet another question. How much does one have to turn the body during each foot plant? This can be ascertained by making a few short computations. For the runner in lane No. 1, we determine the length of the curved path by multiplying the radius of that path by π (36.80 meters × 3.1416) and find the length of the runner's curved portion of the race is 115.61 meters. (As an aside, this is 58 percent of the race on this track.) If our runner is using a stride length of 2 meters, we divide 115.61 by 2 and find the runner would take 57.8 strides to complete this portion of the race. This runner will have to turn the body through 180° in order to complete the curve. We divide 180° by 57.8 strides and find the runner must turn 3.1° during each stride.

Similar computations for the runner in lane No. 8 would show 57.8 strides are still required to run 115.61 meters but a total turning requirement of only 146.4° is required. This results in a turning requirement of 2.5° for each stride. The sharper the curve (inner lanes), the more turning will be required from the leg.

These rotations are not very large, and one should use care to not over-rotate the leg. To obtain a 3° rotation, a person with a 2-meter stride and a shoe that is 12" long would turn the toe ⅝" to the side. A person with a larger shoe would turn it somewhat further, but a person with a shorter stride would turn it less. With this information, each person can judge how much twist to put into one's own leg so that, at push off, it will match the orientation used in straight-line running. If this twisting issue should seem too small to be relevant, one has only to consider how difficult it is to run relaxed while hugging that inside lane line. It is the twisting of one's body that makes this so difficult.

A runner who utilizes a shorter stride will make a greater number of foot plants along the curve than will a longer-stride runner. This means that less turning will be required from each of those foot plants. This seems to offer an advantage to this runner. But on the other side of this coin, because of this runner's higher turnover rate, there is proportionately less time during each foot plant to perform that turning. Depending on the individual runner, the combination of these two inter-related factors could result in either an advantage or a disadvantage for the individual. Also, running the curve well in lane No. 8 is no guarantee this same runner could run the curve well in lane No. 1, or at the more intense pace of the 4 × 100m relay. The ability of the individual to quickly accomplish this turning will define how well a runner traverses the curve.

Now we will look at the second motion needed for a runner to run the curve, the *moving* of one's body to the left. When the runner adds a sideways motion to the normal straight run, one immediately feels the effect of centrifugal force. So, before proceeding further, we will examine that often-misunderstood effect called centrifugal force.

We know that centrifugal force comes into play when we run the curve, and can make it difficult to hug that inner stripe of our lane. This is especially true if we have drawn one of the inside lanes where the turn is sharper. But a unique force was not invented that would apply specifically to an object moving in a circle. While it is true that centrifugal force feels like something pulling on us toward the outer lanes, in reality what we are experiencing is the normal tendency for a body to continue moving in a straight line. The body is resisting our effort to keep forcing it to the left. This resistance of a body to any change in its direction (or its speed) is called inertia and is one of the universal properties of objects in the physical world.

When running the curve, the lane stripes continually curve to the left. In order to follow the lane to the left, we must continually apply a leftward force to our bodies so that we will stay within our curving lane. When we push our bodies to the left, we feel the resistance of inertia and it *feels* like some force is pulling us to the right. This resistance of the inertia that we must overcome we call centrifugal force. The force that we apply against that inertia with our feet we call centripetal force. No new system of forces, only some new names for these specific circumstances.

The runner pushes the feet against the track; the track, in return, pushes against the runner's feet. The component of this force from the track that is sideways to the direction of our travel is pointed toward the center of the circle around which we are running. This is the centripetal force we use to keep moving ourselves to the left and is equal in magnitude to the (so-called) centrifugal force. We actually apply the leftward centripetal force first as we continually drive ourselves to the left. The feeling of the rightward centrifugal force is, in reality, just a resistance to the forced leftward movement. This is not something that happens just once. Since the lane continually curves to the left, we must continually force ourselves further to the left. We continually push sideways against our own inertia so we continually seem to feel centrifugal force pulling us to the right. Confident that this has been cleared up, we will now move on.

Now that we know what centrifugal force is, let us investigate what effect it can have upon a runner. First, we will calculate the magnitude of this centrifugal force that a runner will be dealing with. At this point, we will create a runner to be placed on our standard curve. This runner will be quite fast, but will possess characteristics that can be easily remembered:

Weight	160 lb.
Speed	10 meters/sec.
Stride length	2 meters

The formula for calculating the centrifugal force acting on a runner who is following a curved path is: $F = (w \times v^2) \div (g \times R)$.

F is the centrifugal force in lbs.

w is the weight of the runner—established as 160 lb.

v is the speed of the runner—designated 10 meters per sec. = 32.81 ft. per sec.

g is the acceleration due to gravity—taken here as 32.16 ft. per sec.[2]

R is the radius of the runner's curved lane-

here the radius of the inner lane is assumed to be 36.80 meters = 120.73 ft.

and the radius of the outer lane is assumed to be 45.24 meters = 148.42 ft.

We will now enter these values into the above formula and calculate F for the inner lane:

$F = (160 \times 32.81^2) \div (32.16 \times 120.73) = 44.4$ lb.

For comparison, if this runner were in the outer lane, the centrifugal force would be 36.1 lb. The runner in the inner lane is experiencing a centrifugal force that is 23 percent greater than that experienced in the outer lane.

To counteract this centrifugal force, the runner will lean toward the center of the curve, thus putting one's C.G. inside the path being taken by the supporting feet. In this attitude, the downward-acting force of gravity creates a leftward toppling moment on the torso that will offset the rightward toppling centrifugal force. These two effects both act at the runner's C.G. and the rotational moment of each will exactly balance the other. The greater the amount of centrifugal force, the greater must be the runner's inward lean in order to generate the proper amount of leftward toppling moment of force. With the body in this attitude, in addition to driving the runner forward, the feet will also provide the leftward centripetal force. The leftward drive from the feet moves the runner to the left, but this force is at ground level. The leftward lean is required to allow the upper body to also move to the left and maintain its conformity with the leftward-moving feet. There are two ways a runner can assume this inward lean. One can lean leftward at the waist, or one can lean leftward at the ankles. The latter is the preferred method; this keeps the upper body aligned with the legs. A great deal of work is performed at the juncture of leg and torso; it should not be bent out of alignment.

The angle that the runner will lean inward can be ascertained by taking the centrifugal force, as computed above, and dividing it by the runner's weight. This value is the tangent of the runner's angle of lean. Utilizing a set of Natural Trigonometric Functions, it can be seen this represents an angle of 15½ degrees for a runner in the inner lane. This same runner, if in the outer lane, would lean inward 12½ degrees. Contrary to what one might assume, a taller runner who would have the centrifugal force acting at a location higher above the track, does not have to lean any differently than does a shorter runner who has the forces working at a location closer to the track. In the determination of the amount of lean, the height of a runner's C.G. does not enter into the calculation. One should also note that the runner's weight appears in both the numerator and denominator of the calculations and is therefore also canceled out as a factor. In considering the angle of a runner's lean, the only variables with which one should be concerned are the runner's speed and the sharpness of the curve.

Figure 9 shows our runner in the outer lane (lane 8) and also when in the inner lane (lane 1). The runner's weight and centrifugal force are shown, both of which act through the runner's C.G. The appropriate angle of lean for each runner is also shown. Shown acting on the runner's foot is the reactive force from the track opposing the runner's weight and also the reactive force from the track that is opposing the runner's sideways push against the track.

If desired, these two forces on the runner's foot could be combined and considered to be a single force applied at an angle to the runner. It would point from the supporting foot toward the C.G. and its strength would exactly offset both the runner's weight and the centrifugal force. This is shown as the "resultant" force in Figure 9.

Because this resultant force must offset both the runner's weight and the centrifugal force, its magnitude will always be greater than the runner's weight alone. What this means is, when running the curve, the force on the runner's feet will always be more than when running in a straight line. The magnitude of this resultant force can be calculated by dividing the runner's weight by the cosine of the angle representing the amount of lean. This would be the apparent weight that the runner's legs would be contending with when running the curve. A 160 lb. runner leaning at an angle of 15½ degrees would have an apparent weight of 166 lb. (160 divided by 0.964) or an increase of 6 lb. While the runner does not actually gain this amount of weight, the additional load exerted through the legs has exactly the same effect as if one had gained this amount of weight. The comparable number for this runner, if competing in lane 8, would be 164 or a gain of 4 lb.

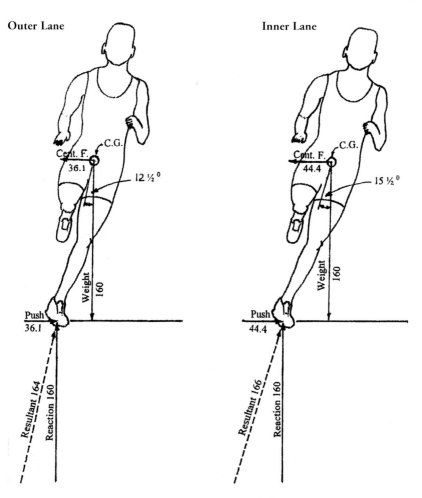

Figure 9. Forces Acting on Curve Runner.

The magnitudes of the forces are shown as their average intensity. Since the feet alternate their touchdown, coupled with the fact the runner experiences some airborne time, the instantaneous forces will vary considerably. The average forces shown here are accurate and considered to be appropriate for this discussion.

Note that the forces acting on the runner are either horizontal or vertical. They are not related to any slope of the track should the track be banked. Because the runner is leaning, the legs will be at an angle to a level track. The runner must rely on the flexibility of the ankle to permit the foot to lay flat against the track. We must also take note that a torso that leans sideways will lower one hip so that it is closer to the surface of a level track than is the other hip. This causes the actions in the two legs to be unequal. A runner who uses a lateral spread of 8" in the foot plant, who runs in lane No. 8, and has a sideways lean of 12½°, would experience an inequality of 1¾" in the distances from the hip joints to the surface of a level track. This same runner if in lane No. 1, would lean inward 15½° and experience an inequality of 2¼". The calculations for these figures are shown in conjunction with Figure 10, which follows. Because of this disparity in effective lengths between the left leg and the right leg, the runner will run with the left knee in a more flexed mode than the right knee in an effort to smooth out the running form. This has the unfortunate consequence of over-tiring the muscles in the left leg. This would suggest that the more-efficient wider foot plant recommended for the straight sprint should, perhaps, be suppressed for the curving portion of the 200m race.

Knowing in advance that it will be the left leg that will become the most tired, the runner may want to perform most of the turning with the right leg. Increasing the turning performed when the right foot is anchored to the track will allow the left leg to operate with less of a twisting burden. This will assist in equalizing the workload on the two legs.

Figure 10 shows the development of inequality between leg lengths as the runner assumes a sideways lean. The amount of this inequality is calculated by multiplying the runner's effective lateral foot plant by the tangent of the angle of lean.

A runner in lane 1 who uses an 8" lateral foot plant and leans 15½° would experience a difference of 8" × .277 = 2.2" = 2¼". This runner in lane 8, leaning at 12½°, would experience a difference of 8" × .226 = 1.8" = 1¾". A slower runner would utilize less angle of lean and would therefore experience less disparity between left leg and right leg.

For a given runner, one's speed and the sharpness of the curve determine the amount of centrifugal force that is developed. The amount of centrifugal force, in turn, determines the amount of lean a runner must utilize to counter this centrifugal force. The amount of lean is defined as the inclination of a line drawn from a point on the track midway between the left foot plant and the right foot plant upward to the runner's C.G. The most efficient running form for the runner is to maintain a straight line between these two points; this involves bending the body sideways at the ankles.

If, on the other hand, the runner were to introduce a bend at the waist, some things would change, but the angle of lean would still have the same inclination and would run from a point midway between the foot plants upward to the C.G. Physics will not allow this basic requirement to change.

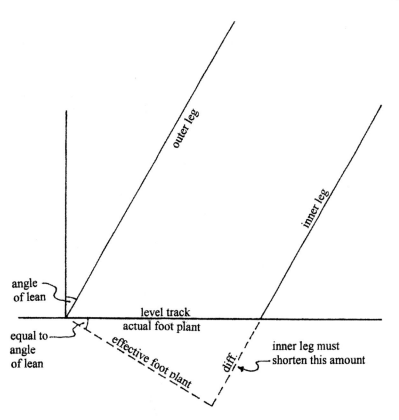

Figure 10. Leg Inequality.

One of the changes introduced in this manner would be favorable. Because the runner's body is no longer straight, the C.G. would move away from its position on the runner's centerline and be located closer to the left hip. This configuration will allow the runner's legs to operate more vertically and reduce the discrepancy in effective leg lengths.

But this non-alignment of the body would also introduce a lateral component of the supporting force at the foot plant location. This undesirable feature would outweigh any gain. The best posture for a runner on the curve is the one that maintains the body's alignment.

Banking the track would greatly alleviate both the sideways bend of the ankle and the apparent difference in the lengths of one's legs, but will not change the forces acting on the runner. The banking of the track is never a cure-all. To allow both legs to operate at identically equal lengths, the speed of the runner would have to be known when the track is designed. Runners at any other speed would still experience some effect of leg inequality. Also, to be completely fair, the banking of the inner lanes, where one's lean is greater, would have to be at a steeper angle than the banking of the outer lanes. This is just not practical.

The banking of the track at a motor speedway is most helpful because it provides a better gripping surface for the tires. This permits the attainment of higher speeds without spinning out. Sprinters do not approach speeds where lack of traction and spinning out is a problem. Since the banking of a running track would not change the forces acting on the runner, its value is of lesser importance. It should also be noted that outdoor track records can be established only on a track that is not banked.

Looking again at the runner in lane No. 1 of Figure 9, there is the centripetal force of 44.4 lb. that is developed at the runner's feet by virtue of the runner's lean. The question is posed, "Is this the only lateral force required from the runner's feet in order to hug the inside lane line, or must the runner exert some additional sideways force to make this happen?"

In order to answer this question, we must first determine what sideways distance the runner must gain at each stride. And we do this as follows.

The radius of the running line for the runner in lane No. 1 is 36.80 meters. As we determined earlier when looking at the turning motion required for the curve, this runner will turn 3.1° at each stride. The lateral distance a runner must push oneself during each stride is obtained by multiplying stride length by the sine of 3.1°. For a runner with a 2-meter stride length, this is 2 × .0543 = 0.1086 meters = 0.356 feet = 4.28 inches = 4¼". Similar computations for this runner in lane No. 8 who turns 2.5° per stride would show that a lateral displacement of 3½" is needed from the runner in order to match the curvature of the track. Runners with shorter strides would incorporate proportionately less lateral displacement.

Now we ask the question, "When considering the centripetal force previously calculated (44.4 lb. for runner in lane 1), how far sideways can we expect this force to project the runner during the time interval of one stride?" This distance will then be compared to the 4¼" required sideways distance per stride determined above.

As we begin the calculation, we take note that the runner's mass is determined by dividing one's weight (160) by the force of gravity (32.16). This runner has a speed of 10 meters/sec. and a stride length of 2 meters. This is a turnover rate of 5 strides per second or 0.2 seconds per stride. We will continue to use our runner in lane No. 1 as an example and call upon a few basic laws of motion to see what sideways distance we can expect this sideways force of 44.4 lb. to produce when it is applied to the runner for the duration of any one stride interval. In these calculations, we will utilize values that are averaged over the 0.2 seconds duration of the stride interval. The calculations will use the following terms:

F = average sideways force applied to runner

m = mass of the runner

a = average sideways acceleration of runner

v = average sideways velocity of runner

s = sideways distance gained by runner

t = time interval of each stride

$F = ma \rightarrow a = F \div m \rightarrow 44.4 \div \dfrac{160}{32.16} = 8.92$ ft. per sec.^{2}

$v = at \rightarrow 8.92 \times 0.2 = 1.784$ ft. per sec.

$s = vt \rightarrow 1.784 \times 0.2 = 0.357$ ft. $= 4.28$ inches $= 4\frac{1}{4}''$

These calculations tell us that the centripetal force of 44.4 lb. that is automatically produced by axially supporting the runner's weight when leaning 15½° produces a sideways motion of 4¼" during the time interval of one stride. This is exactly the amount of sideways motion that this runner needs in order to run a curved path that matches this track.

In more general terms, the sideways force that is automatically developed (when one acquires an angle of lean commensurate with speed and curvature) is the only force that is needed to produce the leftward movement necessary when one is running the curve. *NO* additional sideways force from the foot is required.

Maintain your form. Run as relaxed as possible and let the natural forces push you the necessary distance sideways. Only by maintaining the proper lean will the runner ensure that the proper lateral force will be developed that correctly matches the curvature of the track *without* the introduction of extraneous sideways forces to the leg. However, the runner will still have to institute the *turning* necessary to arrive at the top of the straightaway and be facing the finish line. Keep twisting the leg leftward before touching down and rely upon your peripheral vision to keep setting the left foot alongside the lane line. These are the basic actions for the feet. But, remain cognizant of the details so they are implemented correctly.

The runner's possibility of incurring an injury when running the curve is higher than it is on other occasions. The injuries incurred by Maurice Greene and Michael Johnson were noted earlier. Also, in the Olympic Trials of 2008, Tyson Gay, who previously in the week had accomplished a record-breaking wind-aided time of 9.68 seconds in the 100m finals, went down with a left hamstring injury in the quarterfinals of the 200m event. This injury not only eliminated him from competing in this event at the Olympic Games, it also interrupted his training for the 100m that he would run in

those Games. There are undoubtedly countless more injuries of a similar
nature that have occurred to runners under less-publicized circumstances.

Athletes competing in longer events also run the curve, but they do not
encounter it at as high a speed. When the curve is run at high speed, the
inward lean of the body is greater. This greater inward lean exaggerates the
inequality of the working distance under which the two legs must operate.
The left leg must operate in a more flexed configuration. This increases the
stress in the hamstring during push off. Also, the higher speed invokes a
higher turnover rate. This obviously increases the stress in the muscle system, but it also allows a shorter time interval in which to accomplish the
required turning motion. The leg must perform the twist more forcefully in
order to complete it in the shorter time that is allowed. This puts yet another
greater stress on the leg. And perhaps most importantly of all, the 200m and
the opening leg of the 4 × 100 are the only track events in which the athlete
is rapidly accelerating from a crouch start to near top speed while also contending with these special circumstances of the curve. When on the practice
track, one should avoid running the curve at full speed, especially in the inner
lanes.

Do not try to cut the curve short by bringing the right foot over close
to the inner line and letting the left foot float over the edge of the next inner
lane before it plants down again in your lane. A runner's stride is just too
short to permit this tactic to work. What it does accomplish is introduce
excessive leg crossover, which brings with it the *slows*. Instead, plant the left
foot alongside the line and let your normal lateral foot spread determine
where the right foot will plant. Note that the runner's foot is never allowed
to touch the line.

Placement of starting blocks on the curve is controversial, but the author
believes the runner should shift the blocks toward the outer side of one's lane.
Angle the blocks (and one's body) to the left so that a straight-line start can
be performed until the traveled path becomes tangent to the inside line of
the lane. This will allow the runner to complete a substantial portion of the
start segment before having to contend with the curve and its attendant special challenges to the legs. One may not, however, move the starting blocks
so far from the center of the lane that they touch one's outer lane line. The
fact that there may be no runner outside of you does not give you the right
to infringe upon the lane line.

With this arrangement, it will be necessary to keep the left hand back
from the starting line so it will be in alignment with the right hand, which
is at the line. The measurement to the first starting block will be from an
imaginary line between the two hands. It is not recommended that the start-

ing technique for the 200m be any different than the starting technique used in the 100m race. The start is difficult enough to bring off on a regular basis. Master one start and use it every time you come to the line.

There are additional considerations to also keep in mind. It is vitally important to maintain as much relaxation as possible on the curve so one will not reach the top of the straightaway with the fuel tank nearing empty. When not sufficiently relaxed, active muscles are, to a degree, fighting opposing muscles. This puts a severe drain on the running system. Because of the turning motion the runner must perform, the inability to totally relax is a normal occurrence. This underscores the need for the runner to be completely focused on maintaining as relaxed a form as possible.

To this end, one must think back to the strategies employed to improve the momentum balance between arms and legs. These must be employed here to the extent possible when running a curve. In this way, energy will be conserved. It is a wonderful feeling to arrive at the top of the straightaway in good position and with the feeling of still having something remaining in the tank for the straight-line run to the finish.

There is a natural tendency to watch that curving painted line as it comes toward you. From your present location to the point of tangency with the lane line is your directional target; it is instinctive to want to look at it. But remember, fixating one's vision on any specific object will reduce one's capability to sense the best running attitude.

Do not look at the curving lane line. Keep your eyes looking straight out from your head but focused on nothing. Let your peripheral vision tell you where the lane line is. Peripheral vision is perfectly capable of doing this while it is also giving you information regarding vertical bounce and the associated braking action. Sling the hips forward, soften the foot plant and reduce the vertical bounce to near zero.

Keep the body in alignment; lean leftward from the ankles. Concentrate on your form. Run the curve with all the expertise at your command and run as relaxed as hugging that inside line will allow. Upon reaching the straightaway, one's position and remaining strength can then be assessed and a strategy formed to reach the finish line.

Drifting toward the center of the lane would give one a momentary unencumbered feeling because the runner is momentarily running in a straighter line and consequently there is less of a turning requirement. But, do not surrender to that sweet invitation. It brings with it the heavy penalty of having to run farther to reach the top of the straightaway. Only as the end of the curve is approached should the runner allow sufficient relaxation so that drifting to the center of the lane will occur. This is referred to as *float*. Once on the straightaway, the runner can fully relax and bring it home.

Actually, upon reaching the *float zone*, the runner can permit relaxation that will allow drifting even further, to the *outside* of the curved lane, but only *as one reaches the straightaway*. This additional relaxation is more valuable than the slightly extra distance is detrimental. One can then relocate to the center of the lane on the straight sprint to the finish.

We have all seen the dramatic come-from-behind "kick" exhibited by a runner near the end of a race. But, do not delude yourself; this is not going to happen in the 200m race. The above-mentioned increase in speed is available only to runners in the longer races where race speed is well below sprint speed. In the 200m, racers are already traveling at a speed that is close to the upper limit attainable by the human body. There is just no further upper speed that the runner can access in a determined run to the finish.

It is folly to run the curve with the mindset you're going to pass the others when you reach the straightaway. This just doesn't work when the field is already running at a speed that is close to the human max. One cannot outrun the competition on the straightaway; one can only outlast the competition on the straightaway. Run the curve with your smarts; run the straightaway with your legs. To win the 200m, complete the curve at the front of the competition, then outlast them to the finish line.

To underscore the importance of running the curve well, one has only to note that the winner of this event is, more often than not, the runner who is in the lead upon reaching the top of the straightaway. It's that simple; win the curve, win the race. Do not hold back on the curve. Make every attempt to reach the top of the straightaway ahead of the other runners. If you lead them at this point, you have put them in a position where they would now have to run faster than you in order to beat you to the finish line. It is no longer a *fair* race. You hold them at a substantial disadvantage as long as you are slightly ahead of them. Do not relinquish this advantage easily. Make your rival work hard to pass you. If necessary to conserve energy for the next race, do so only after reaching the straightaway. The situation can be more accurately assessed here than on the curve. Run the curve well and strive to reach the top of the straightaway in good shape. The leader at the top of the straightaway is most often the leader at the finish line.

There are two basic strategies to keep in mind when running the 200m. Not surprisingly, they both relate to the first portion of the event, the curve:

1. Resist the temptation to run the curve conservatively in order to ensure reaching the finish line with a strong closure. Establish as the objec-

tive, your arrival at the top of the straightaway slightly ahead of your competition. At that point, most of the race is already behind you. It is much easier to maintain one's position within the field of runners than it is to run faster than the competition in order to catch up. Make the effort to reach the straightaway in the lead. If someone were to beat you, the burden would then be on him to now run faster than you. Not an easy task in those remaining strides of the 85 meters to the finish line. They are tired too.

2. Run the curve sufficiently relaxed so you don't empty the tank just to reach the straightaway. Running faster on the curve is not what will deplete one's reserves. Tightening up while performing the turning motion and poor body alignment for the lean is what will tire the runner. Use all the expertise at your command to run the curve as best you know how. Remain mindful of the details; concentrate on running relaxed and maintaining good form. Greater finesse is what will win the curve.

The 200m is really two separate races combined into a single event; the curved race and the straight race. Do not undervalue the first thinking you can make it up during the second. If you don't win the first one, you probably won't win the second one either; you will have started it under a huge disadvantage. Good technique is essential to winning the 200m. The place to gain the lead is on the curve where greater finesse can make the difference. The secret to winning this event is on the curve. At the gun, commit to winning race No. 1.

Thoughts on a Curve

The author feels that runners who qualify to run in a race by having placed sufficiently high in their previous heat should have a voice in deciding in which lane they will run. No logic is seen for the runner with the fastest qualifying time in the semifinal races, to be placed in a lane for the final race that this particular runner may not prefer.

Surely, our organizational, informational, and communicative skills have reached the point where the runner with the fastest semifinal time could be permitted to select the lane in which this individual prefers to run in the final race. The runner with the second fastest time in the semis would then have a choice of the remaining seven lanes and so on. It would be the runner's responsibility to be present and make a selection. If the runner did not select a lane, one would be assigned after other runners have made their selections.

A similar procedure could also be utilized in the semifinals and quarterfinals, all based on previous times turned in during that track meet. If the sprint events were ever to evolve to utilize some lane selection procedure such as this, it would be to the advantage of each runner to know the merits of the various lanes.

For the track geometry and the particular runner described earlier, the salient points of running in lane No. 1 and of running in lane No. 8 are summarized:

	Lane 1	*Lane 8*
Total turning required	180°	146.4°
Turning per foot plant	3.1°	2.5°
Centrifugal force	44.4 lb.	36.1 lb.
Angle of lean	15½°	12½°
Resultant weight on legs	166 lb.	164 lb.
Inequality of leg lengths	2¼"	1¾"
Leftward movement per stride	4¼"	3½"

The figures that apply to the runner in the inner lane compared to the figures that apply to the runner in the outer lane show advantages to the outer lane (or more accurately, disadvantages to the inner lane) that one cannot lightly dismiss.

In order to facilitate drainage of rainwater, the surface of an outdoor track is sometimes constructed with a slight slope. The direction of slope is normally from the outside lane downward toward the infield. This could be most pronounced on the curve. A 3¼" drop from lane 8 to lane 1 is within legal limits. A long careful look should allow a keen observer to determine if there is any slope to a particular track. It may be, that the runner in lane No. 8 will be starting at a slightly higher elevation than the runner in lane No.1 but both will finish at the same elevation. Even the slightest downgrade can be an assist in the sprint. This only adds to the disparity between the different lanes and enhances still further the desirability of running in the outer lanes.

When running in lane 8, there are no visual distractions of other runners. This enhances the ability to concentrate on one's running techniques. What about the advantage of being able to watch your rivals by running in an inner lane? Don't run your curve according to what someone else is doing. This is *your* race. Anywhere on the curve is too early in the 200m race to concern yourself with your position relative to runners in those lanes that are further to the outside. They are only a portion of your competition. When concerning yourself with your position relative to the runners you can see, you may lose track of those runners you can't see. Remember, they are competing also. Better to disregard the other runners until you have completed the curve. Run your own race on the curve as expertly as you know how. Only upon reaching the top of the straightaway should you concern yourself with your position in the race. This can be a concern if you find it desirable to not risk injury or to conserve energy for use in a later event. Unless you feel absolutely compelled to fixate on the fanny of the runner ahead, you should fare better by running in the outer lane.

It seems only fair that runners who have done well in their qualifying round be given the opportunity to select the lane in which they will next compete. To arbitrarily assign a runner who has won his qualifying round, to a lane in the succeeding round that this particular runner does not want, seems to be contrary to the basic tenet of fair play. Should some system come to fruition, which allows for the competitors to voice their lane preference, knowledge of the pros and cons of each of the lanes would be to the runner's advantage.

14

THE FINISH

The finish is often the only part of a race that we get to see in an abbreviated sportscast or picture in our newspaper. It is sometimes made to appear as an event unto itself. In actuality, the finish of the sprint is just the culmination of what has transpired before, during the start and the run segments of the race. The finish is the most publicized part of the race, but is really the part over which the sprinter, in general, has the least input. But not zero input. Let us look at what we *can* do during the final strides of a race.

No matter how you slice it, if you want additional speed from the body the legs will have to expend more power. The laws of physics will permit no different. How then, can we best induce those tired legs to expend still faster, their waning supply of power? There are two possibilities open to the runner. One possibility is to slightly increase the turnover rate of the arms. Because the turnover rate of the arms and the turnover rate of the legs are naturally synchronized, this will urge the legs to turn over faster and a speed increase will be realized. This will quickly sap whatever strength is remaining in the quads and would prove disastrous if invoked too soon. For this technique to be successful, the runner must still have some power left in the quads. Unfortunately, this is often not the case.

The lower quads will be especially tired; they have been doing an exceptional amount of work. They must repeatedly and rapidly resist the force of impact upon touchdown, which occurs with the knee partially bent. This takes a terrific toll on the limited number of fast-twitch muscle fibers. After touchdown, these muscles must begin to straighten the knee joint in contribution to the body's forward propulsion. They must also aid in the forward swinging motion and unfolding of the knee joint in preparation for the next touchdown. These muscles get no reprieve during a race. As the runner nears the finish line, these muscles will be very tired.

Let us look at the runner's other possibility. The quads have been driving the runner down the track and are now exhausted, but the muscle system on the back side of the leg may still have a little something left to give if that system is properly accessed. This is accomplished by consciously lowering the elbows, and forcing their swing further to the rear. Without changing the turnover rate, the forearms are then driven forward as powerfully as possible. As soon as the hand reaches its forward target point, the arm's rearward motion is immediately begun, making certain the elbows remain as low as possible. For this technique to be successful, the forearm must be kept in the same vertical plane as the elbow. Absolutely no sideways motion can be tolerated.

The intent of this maneuver in those last strides to the finish line is to cause a stronger push from the foot by the muscle system on the back side of the leg, create a longer stride, and thereby coax a bit more speed from that tiring body. To be of value, the runner must use maximum concentration to not allow the turnover rate to falter. If successful, a slightly longer stride will result and afford a short burst of additional speed.

If one attempts to achieve any increase in speed during those last few strides to the finish line, this should be considered a maximum-exertion effort. When one was performing a maximum-exertion effort in the weight room, the rule was to exhale through pursed lips in order to momentarily increase one's internal pressure. The rule for a maximum-exertion effort as one approaches the finish line is no different. Forcibly exhale through pursed lips and raise your internal pressure as you approach the finish line. This will squeeze just a little more power from those tired muscles. If one is in close company at the finish line, this technique of drawing still further on the body's strength reservoir can make a welcome difference when the race results are posted.

After working so hard to get the body to this point (all the months of training plus the earlier stages of this race), do not do yourself a disservice as you approach the finish line. In addition to doing things right, it is equally important to not discard good form and thereby begin to do things wrong. Continue to run your strongest right through the tape. Don't resort to panic motions. Run your best race and let the others lose their race for you.

Mistakes in this final second of the race do not just occur in an unprovoked manner. Through some conscious action, they are made to happen. Unfortunately, we see similar episodes repeat themselves time after time:

- The premature lean that disrupts a runner's form.
- Hunching of the shoulders in a final effort to exhaust the body.
- Stretching of the last few strides in order to get the feet to that white line painted across the track.

- An uncontrolled flailing of the arms.
- Turning the head sideways in order to observe another competitor cross the finish line.

In the final effort to do our best, we can inadvertently do our worst. To avoid the pitfalls, maintain full concentration until after you cross the line. Do not spoil an otherwise good performance with a crucial mistake at the end. Do not lean so early that your last strides are slowed because you have taken yourself out of the good form that had brought you this close to success. Also, instinctive use of the arms attempting to drive the legs faster will all too often cause the runner to hunch the shoulders. The results of this are an inability to properly swing the arms and a consequential shortening of the stride.

Resist the temptation to stretch the last two strides in order to get the feet to that white line painted across the track. The feet don't count. Reaching the legs forward for the point of touchdown is a natural tendency if one focuses attention on that finish line painted on the track. But reaching the touchdown further forward is not the fastest running form. Stretching the stride to reach the feet toward that line brings the *slows*. The antidote for this common ailment is *don't* focus on that painted line. The runner should continue looking straight ahead, but not allow the eyes to focus on any individual object. Let peripheral vision locate the finish line for determination of when to lean.

The runners who are about to finish just behind the leader will sometimes resort to full desperation. They abandon the good form that has brought them within two meters of a good finish, and exhibit a wild flail of the arms. Any chance of an effective drive to the finish is lost. Good form should be maintained all the way into the final lean.

Do not lose concentration in the last ½ second and think at this crucial moment that how someone else is finishing is more important than how you are finishing. Run your race to its conclusion. Keep looking straight ahead into nothingness and concentrate on running. The Finish Line Judges will determine the order of finish, not you.

The runner should maintain one's fastest running stride and push the torso across the line to stop the clock. Stretch the stride forward only after crossing the line in order to put the feet under the torso and regain balance.

A runner finishes the race when the torso reaches the finish line. This means the leading edge of the torso, which the eye and the camera can readily delineate. Obviously, any forward lean of the body will get the torso to the line sooner. There are two types of leans in general use.

One type of lean utilizes a straight body lean developing over the last several strides. The way to invoke this lean is to increase the turnover rate of the arms even more. The legs will follow suit and increase their turnover rate also. However, the legs will not be able to generate the stride length commensurate with this turnover rate. The point of touchdown will begin to fall short. The upper body will continue forward and a full body lean will thereby develop over the last few strides. In this attitude, the runner's normal stride, which directs its forward push from the feet upward into the body, will be directing that push more forward rather than upward; this favors a last-second increase in speed. One could also put forth an argument in favor of this type of lean using the tenet that as the body leans further forward, the body's C.G. is being slightly lowered. Since the C.G. is now becoming lower than where it had been previously, this is tantamount to running downhill for those last few strides.

Let this lean develop slowly, at its own pace. The runner must maintain sufficient concentration to not let the legs reach forward in an attempt to regain balance. If this lean is initiated too soon, the body will want to fall too far forward. The only way to now prevent this is for the runner to take a long stride to get the feet under the torso again. This long stride will very effectively put on the brakes and the runner will lose some very hard earned distance.

The other type of lean is accomplished by a sudden bend forward at the waist. This action projects just the upper body forward with minimum disruption of the body's vertical balance. This thrusts forward only that which will stop the clock, the chest. It is accomplished by a quick bend at the waist and accentuated with the flinging backward of both the arms in dramatic fashion. This lean requires only an instant to accomplish. Therefore, there is no need to break form and begin this lean prior to reaching the last stride.

The clock will not be interested in an upper body lean commenced prior to this time. A premature lean of the torso will only disrupt the runner's high-speed running form, slow him down and perhaps allow a nonleaner to pass. Since this is a quick forward lean, keen peripheral vision is necessary in order to know when it should be performed. On the downside, this lean does not project the chest as far in front of the feet as does a well-executed full body lean.

The lean for a particular runner to use is the one that the runner can execute the best.

The rule does not say the leading edge of the center of the torso must reach the finish line in order to stop the clock. The leading edge of any part of the torso will do. A slight twist of the upper body will immediately thrust one side of the torso even further ahead. It is when the first part of the torso reaches the finish line that you have finished the race. This technique was perhaps best illustrated by Olympic champion Gail Devers. This twist of the torso can afford a significant advantage to the runner who performs it competently. A well-executed twist can momentarily project a portion of the torso ahead of one's close rivals and provide an unexpected margin at the finish line. This is when it counts, when the camera is watching. The runner should envision the vertical plane that arises from the finish line. Then, push the chest through that plane.

Just as you have found it necessary to practice the start, so should you also practice the finish. Take every advantage for yourself that is available. Leave absolutely nothing undone that could conceivably help you win. Take care of every detail along the way while on your quest to be your best. Remember, $\frac{1}{10}$ of a second gained by a better start equals $\frac{1}{10}$ of a second gained by running faster equals $\frac{1}{10}$ of a second gained by performing a more efficient finish. They are all equal when measured on the clock, but you may find that the gains at each end of the race have greater potential for exploitation.

As a serious competitor, you must bring to the game everything you have, and then play it *all*. Do your best. There is no need to save anything for next time. And if you do well, it's okay to smile. There is never a guarantee that the good times will continue, so enjoy the moment for all it's worth. You've earned it.

15

POST-RACE

Post-race is commonly a period of celebration (or depression or bewilderment), and then a cool down routine to normalize the body and bring it back from the extremes to which it has just been pushed. A thorough cool down will help avoid next-day stiffness and thereby make the next training session more profitable.

As part of the cool down, a thorough stretching routine should be performed. Post-race stretching should be conducted in a manner that will encourage the muscles to remain lengthened rather than further abuse them and cause them to tighten. After a workout, the body will be more limber than it was during warm up. The limbs will be more easily held in the stretch position. This stretch should place a lighter pull on the muscles but hold the stretch over a longer period of time. For this stretch, a hold time in each position of approximately 50 percent longer than in warm up is recommended. This approach appears to be more conducive to the maintenance of long-term flexibility. This holding of a stretch for a longer period allows the muscle to favorably respond to the treatment and sets the stage for them to better serve you on your next practice day. The race has been run and there are other things to do. This stretching routine can be limited to only the primary running muscles rather than the more comprehensive routine engaged in before one's practice sessions.

Keep in mind that these are your muscles. Just because the race is over, don't think that it's okay now to wait until next Monday to resume taking care of them again. These are the muscles that you will rely upon to take you down the track and outperform the competition in your next race. Respect these muscles. Give them every opportunity to perform their best for you. Take care of them *now*.

But post-race can be much more than just cool down. This period can be one of the most valuable opportunities to begin planning the training for your next race. The first two minutes after a race present an opportunity for self-analysis that is impossible to replicate. One should make every effort to take full advantage of it.

You have just finished a race during which you have subjected your body to very violent motions. If you now permit an introspective moment, the race can still be felt in your limbs, their tiredness, yes, even their motions. This feeling is a form of proprioception whereby a person may be looking else-where, but retains the awareness of where the various parts of the body are and what they are doing. This awareness is accomplished by means of infor-mation being sent from the muscles to the brain, and is normal fare for one's body.

After crossing the finish line, the runner is breathing hard and the mus-cles that did most of the work are tired. The race is still very much alive within the runner. This is a moment that cannot be artificially re-created. There is nothing else that is its equal; it contains unique information. Do not let this valuable moment lapse into oblivion without extracting from it information that can be useful to you in preparation for your next race. Use this opportunity to note where emphasis in your training needs to be placed so that your next race will be a better race.

Utilizing the receptions coming from the still-excited limbs, re-create in your mind, in slow motion, an image of the movements you made during the race. Now move your body to match the form you are envisioning. The advantage is that now you can watch your actions, even stop the motion at will, and analyze your form.

While looking straight ahead, take a few steps and replicate the form you used during the race, using as your guide the lingering messages you are still receiving from your now-fatigued muscles. Re-create all the movements as accurately as you can without actually running fast. Concentrate on how closely you can match your running form. Now look at what you are doing and begin a process of self-analysis to see if what you are doing (and did dur-ing the race) is what you intended to do. Obviously, some of the motions cannot be exactly reproduced in slow motion, but with concentration you are able to feel these actions. Seeing your stride is less important than feel-ing it.

Many elements of your form can be accurately replicated and analyzed. You can ask yourself some questions. Were my feet pointing straight ahead? Was my lateral foot spacing what I wanted to utilize? Was my push off being done with the stronger inner toes? Was I obtaining maximum push from my takeoff? How much was my leg folded in the forward swing? Where was my touchdown taking place? What pattern was my forearm tracing? How quick was its downward snap? Were the hands leading the arm action? How much bend was in my elbow? Was I swinging my elbows low or were my shoulders hunched? Was my upper arm swinging sufficiently high to the rear? Was I putting sufficient power into my forward arm swing? Were my hands and fingers straight or curled? Did I minimize my vertical bounce as much as I should have? Which muscles fatigued the most?

At this time, you can still feel these actions. You can very quickly provide your own answers to these questions. Specifically question those aspects that gave you trouble during practice, or during your previous race, and that you believe are the most serious obstacles to attaining greater speed. A mental checklist (with a useful acronym) can be very helpful here. Decide right here and now what you specifically need to work on before your next race.

When I speak of listening to the messages within the body, I am not inferring that one must go into some trance-like state or that a special psychic ability is required. I'm speaking here of the messages coming from the limbs that we ordinary people feel. The only thing unnatural here has been the speed and intensity with which we have forced these body parts to move. It is because these motions were so extreme that we are now still able to feel their positions, their motions, their intensities.

Much can be gained from this routine. You should begin making mental notes of those things you want to work on during your next training sessions and, of course, what you want to do better in your next race. Afterward, make written notes of what you did, didn't do, want to change, and any other race-related things such as "I didn't take the time to check my spikes before the race and that distracting thought entered my head as I stepped into the starting blocks." Include notes on the weather, the starter, inadequate warm up, good feelings, bad feelings, your finish positions and times, and also those of other competitors, etc.

If you are fortunate enough to have the trained eye of a coach or training partner watching you, discuss freely with that person what and how you feel. Another person's input can be invaluable. As a team, incorporate any changes to the training plan. Do not leave the track on race day without deciding in your own mind, what single factor (or two) was limiting your speed and preventing you from running still faster. Be specific in your decision. Then begin thinking of how you can improve this in training. The next race will show how effective you have been in removing this speed barrier. Oh yes, check the results board to make certain it is correct and that no error was made in recording your finish.

Later that evening, it can be helpful to create a quiet and reminiscent atmosphere. Equip yourself with pencil and paper or a computer keyboard. Think back through the events of the day. Jot down thoughts as they come to you, in whatever sequence you happen to think of them. Make specific notes of how you prepared for and how you ran your race. Make note of any pre-race preparation that could be improved upon. Note how long it took to become race ready, and how well that coincided with when your race actually started. Include your field notes and thoughts that occurred to you during the post-race reenactment of your running form. When you have committed the relevant thoughts to written text, take a few extra minutes. Study these notes, and put them in an orderly fashion so they can be quickly and understandably reviewed at a later date.

At this time, fix your thoughts on those refinements and changes you want to include in your next training sessions. Decide where you need to next place the emphasis in your training. Make note of what you want to keep uppermost in your mind when the next race day arrives. Expect to modify this plan as you proceed through the process of injecting these revised techniques into your running form. Training plans should be thoroughly thought through, but they will not be perfect nor will they be complete. Plans should remain sufficiently flexible to meet the runner's needs.

The race result may be what you wanted or it may be less. But the result will always be zero if you learn nothing from the experience. Each race is an event that provides us the opportunity to learn.

There are numerous factors that that add up to the sum of the race. While the race is still fresh in your mind, evaluate how you performed each of those factors. Beginning with the warm up and stretching that was performed, go through each factor, including: setting of the blocks, body posture when in the set position, readiness for the gun and your consequent reaction, the push derived from the pedals, the rate at which your body came erect, the stride rate utilized, the actions of arms and hands, the push derived from the feet, amount of knee bend, the breathing technique utilized and how you approached and crossed the finish line.

In your next race, you will be called upon to again perform each of these actions. How will you perform them next time? If we do not learn from our experiences, we will be destined to have future results that are no better. Do not condemn yourself to always perform at your present level. Learn from your experiences and plan how to perform better in the future. This is the manner in which we advance. The performance of each race provides an occasion to learn. Do not waste this opportunity. It costs nothing to absorb the information available. Make the most of each opportunity and make yourself a better runner.

Before trying any new technique, be sure to think it through first. Fully understand what you want it to do for you so you will be better able to evaluate its effectiveness. Envision how you run now. Then envision how you might run while utilizing this different technique. Consider the following questions:

- What do I hope to gain with this technique?
- What other facets of my running style will it affect?
- Is this change really right for me?
- What criteria will I use in deciding whether or not the change has been successful?

Set realistic mileposts for yourself while en route to your goal. This aids in avoiding unnecessary disappointments. Working toward your next milestone keeps you informed of your current needs and in touch with your progress. This generally has better results than does merely dreaming of a distant goal. A milestone does not necessarily need to be one of a timed performance or the winning of a race. It is more likely to be the proper incorporation of a particular technique into one's running form.

If you really want to give another technique an honest try, then go do it! But remember, any change will not fit into an established pattern easily. The mind and body will have to adjust in order to accept a change. You may also have to revise your strength/training regimen in order to gain the most from this change. Don't give up on it too easily. That's why you thought it through before you started on this path—to convince yourself you really wanted to give this a good try. Be patient. Be persistent. If this technique is not right for you, then you will have learned that you need to look elsewhere for the next improvement. But never end the search.

Know your strengths, your weaknesses, your goals. Every runner's immediate goal is to run faster than one is running now. Some runners may have goals that are more far-reaching. Ask yourself, "Do I have the commitment?" Only with total commitment, will you reach a more difficult goal.

It is a wonderful feeling to have just run your personal best. But, do not confuse this with having just run the best that you ever will. Never accept the thought that you cannot run any faster. Keep searching for better form. Keep working at better training. Maintain as your premise that somewhere within you is a still better race. It's just up to you to find it, to be specific in your training, to bring it out, to make it happen.

It is simple logic that no matter at what speed you ran your last race, there was some thing, some aspect of your running that prevented you from running still faster. Keep searching for that limiting factor. Once you understand it, you can improve upon it. Search for a small incremental improvement. There is always something limiting your speed. Find it. Work on it. Always know that you can run still faster once that limiting factor is improved.

Ask, "To carry myself to the next higher level of performance, what must I do differently?" "What must I change?" "What must I do better?" "What must I concentrate on right *now* to improve my performance the next time out?" A good self-analysis will tell you what to do next. Never believe that you cannot do still better.

Visualization is an excellent tool to cement the correct movements of the body to the nervous system that will control those movements. The body motion is envisioned, then via this visualization the associated neural connections are joined to it. This can be done when resting at home, when at the starting line of the race and at all times in between. This technique can be used in reverse mode when evaluating your form immediately after a race, whereby sensations coming through the nerves are interpreted and then utilized to perform the associated motion, and also in rapidly alternating modes when establishing your best form during the race.

"I gave it everything I had; I ran as fast as I could." If this is your appraisal of your race effort, the statement is, in all probability, correct. You *did* give it everything you had; you *did* run as fast as you could. However, the thrust of this book is *improvement*. The key to improvement is to not let the thought process stop when the race clock stops. If one truly wants to create improvement, thoughts of the race will continue to permeate the mind long after the race is over. Always believe that you can do still better than your present times. Master the elements of speed and then put them together as only your mind and body are capable. Be meticulous. Stay focused. Leave no stone unturned in your quest for more speed. Believe in yourself. Be pleased with what you are doing. Be happy with yourself and your accomplishments. Enjoy the search for still more speed.

16

THE CLASS LEADERS

Frequently, serious thought concerning a specific topic leaves the person with more questions than answers. Have you at times found yourself in that situation? In the presentation of this book, the author has attempted to remove the nondirectional contour of the question mark and offer, in its place, some straightforward detailed information and advice! Some of the concepts that have been described may seem radical to you, others may not. The author believes in them, practices them and uses them to the best of his ability. It is asked that you think about them. Try them. Work with them. See if they are for you.

Small Increments Can Produce Large Differences

Some of the offerings contained in this book will, for many, appear to be of too little consequence to warrant much attention. One might be inclined to ask, "How much significance should I place on such a really small item?" To this, the author can only respond, "How difficult would it be for you to implement that small item?" "How fast do you really want to run?" The devil is in the details. If you do not master them, they will prevent you from attaining your best.

Yes, some of the techniques put forth may appear too minuscule to be of any real concern. But these running events are timed to $\frac{1}{100}$ of a second, and the placement results are sometimes dependent upon even closer intervals. The women's 100-meter races at the 1996 Olympic Games in Atlanta exemplify this point.

In one quarterfinal race, two runners posted a time of 11.38 seconds. One moved on to the semifinals; the other did not.

In one semifinal race, two runners posted a time of 11.14 seconds. One moved on to the final; the other did not.

In the other semifinal race, three runners posted a time of 11.07 seconds. Two moved on to the final; one did not.

In the final race, two runners posted a time of 10.94 seconds. One received the gold medal and was acclaimed the world's fastest woman; the other was awarded the silver medal.

One hundreth of a second is not something to take seriously? The competitors in that Olympic event might take issue with such a statement. This was a tightly contested, topnotch performance by the best female runners of the day. All should be extremely proud of their superb accomplishment.

Performances of the Elite

What are they doing at the head of the class? Let us look at some statistics for a moment. Not necessarily world record holders, but what the top echelon has been doing. For this, the author looked at major track and field events beginning with the 2000 U.S. Trials in Sacramento and continuing through the 2008 Olympic Games in Beijing, China. The results of the first four finishers in the women's 100m and the first four finishers in the men's 100m event at each of the observed venues are listed in the following tables. Some additional data relating to the performance of each competitor in those events is also noted.

Table I: 2000 U.S. Trials—Sacramento

Women	Time (sec's)	No. of Strides	Average Stride	Turnover Rate	Wind -1.0 m/s
Marion Jones	10.88	48½	2.06	4.46	
Inger Miller	11.05	50	2.00	4.52	
Chryste Gaines	11.13	50½	1.98	4.54	
Torri Edwards	11.15	50½	1.98	4.53	
Avg.	11.05	49.9	2.01	4.51	

Men	Time (sec's)	No. of Strides	Average Stride	Turnover Rate	Wind -1.7 m/s
Maurice Greene	10.01	46	2.17	4.60	
Curtis Johnson	10.07	47	2.13	4.67	
Jon Drummond	10.07	46	2.17	4.57	
Brian Lewis	10.09	48½	2.06	4.81	
Avg.	10.06	46.9	2.13	4.66	
Difference	9%	6%	6%	3%	

The last line labeled "Difference" shows that compared to women, men in this event:

1. Ran 9 percent faster.
2. Took 6 percent fewer strides.

3. Took 6 percent longer strides. (Stride length is expressed in meters.)
4. Had a 3 percent faster turnover rate. (Turnover rate is expressed as strides per second.)

Table II: 2000 Olympic Games—Sydney

Women	Time (sec's)	No. of Strides	Average Stride	Turnover Rate	Wind -0.4 m/s
Marion Jones	10.75	48½	2.06	4.51	
Ekaterini Thanou	11.12	53½	1.87	4.81	
Tanya Lawrence	11.18	51½	1.94	4.61	
Merlene Ottey	11.19	48½	2.06	4.33	
Avg.	11.06	50.5	1.98	4.57	

Men	Time (sec's)	No. of Strides	Average Stride	Turnover Rate	Wind -0.3 m/s
Maurice Greene	9.87	45½	2.20	4.61	
Ato Boldon	9.99	45	2.22	4.50	
Obadele Thompson	10.04	44	2.27	4.38	
Dwain Chambers	10.08	45	2.22	4.46	
Avg.	10.00	44.9	2.23	4.49	
Difference	10%	11%	13%	2%	

The last line labeled "Difference" shows that compared to women, men in this event:

1. Ran 10 percent faster.
2. Took 11 percent fewer strides.
3. Took 13 percent longer strides. (Stride length is expressed in meters.)
4. Had a 2 percent slower turnover rate. (Turnover rate is expressed as strides per second.)

Table III: 2003 U.S. Nationals—Stanford University

Women	Time (sec's)	No. of Strides	Average Stride	Turnover Rate	Wind -1.1 m/s
Torri Edwards	11.13	51	1.96	4.58	
Gail Devers	11.16	49	2.04	4.39	
Inger Miller	11.17	50	2.00	4.48	
Angela Williams	11.23	51½	1.94	4.59	
Avg.	11.17	50.4	1.99	4.51	

Men	Time (sec's)	No. of Strides	Average Stride	Turnover Rate	Wind 1.6 m/s
Bernard Williams	10.11	48	2.08	4.75	
Jon Drummond	10.18	46½	2.15	4.57	

Men	Time (sec's)	No. of Strides	Average Stride	Turnover Rate	Wind 1.6 m/s
Coby Miller	10.23	47½	2.11	4.64	
Joshua Johnson	10.24	47	2.13	4.59	
Avg.	10.19	47.3	2.12	4.64	
Difference	9%	6%	7%	3%	

The last line labeled "Difference" shows that compared to women, men in this event:

1. Ran 9 percent faster.
2. Took 6 percent fewer strides.
3. Took 7 percent longer strides. (Stride length is expressed in meters.)
4. Had a 3 percent faster turnover rate. (Turnover rate is expressed as strides per second.)

Table IV: 2003 World Championships—Paris

Women	Time (sec's)	No. of Strides	Average Stride	Turnover Rate	Wind 0.9 m/s
Torri Edwards	10.93	50½	1.98	4.63	
Zhanna Block	10.99	49½	2.02	4.50	
Chandra Sturrup	11.02	51	1.96	4.63	
Ekaterini Thanou	11.03	52½	1.90	4.76	
Avg.	10.99	50.9	1.97	4.63	

Men	Time (sec's)	No. of Strides	Average Stride	Turnover Rate	Wind 0.0 m/s
Kim Collins	10.07	47½	2.11	4.72	
Darrel Brown	10.08	45	2.22	4.46	
Darren Campbell	10.08	44½	2.25	4.41	
Bernard Williams	10.13	47	2.13	4.64	
Avg.	10.09	46.0	2.18	4.56	
Difference	8%	10%	10%	2%	

The last line labeled "Difference" shows that compared to women, men in this event:

1. Ran 8 percent faster.
2. Took 10 percent fewer strides.
3. Took 10 percent longer strides. (Stride length is expressed in meters.)
4. Had a 2 percent slower turnover rate. (Turnover rate is expressed as strides per second.)

Table V: 2004 U.S. Trials—Sacramento

Women	Time (sec's)	No. of Strides	Average Stride	Turnover Rate	Wind 0.1 m/s
Latasha Colander	10.97	51	1.96	4.65	
Lauryn Williams	11.10	53	1.89	4.77	
Gail Devers	11.11	48	2.08	4.32	
Marion Jones	11.14	48	2.08	4.31	
Avg.	11.08	50.0	2.00	4.51	

Men	Time (sec's)	No. of Strides	Average Stride	Turnover Rate	Wind 0.0 m/s
Maurice Greene	9.91	47	2.13	4.74	
Justin Gatlin	9.92	42	2.38	4.23	
Shawn Crawford	9.93	47	2.13	4.73	
Coby Miller	9.99	46½	2.15	4.65	
Avg.	9.94	45.6	2.20	4.59	
Difference	10%	9%	10%	2%	

The last line labeled "Difference" shows that compared to women, men in this event:

1. Ran 10 percent faster.
2. Took 9 percent fewer strides.
3. Took 10 percent longer strides. (Stride length is expressed in meters.)
4. Had a 2 percent faster turnover rate. (Turnover rate is expressed as strides per second.)

Table VI: 2004 Olympic Games—Athens

Women	Time (sec's)	No. of Strides	Average Stride	Turnover Rate	Wind -0.1 m/s
Yulia Nestsiarenka	10.93	48½	2.06	4.44	
Lauryn Williams	10.96	52	1.92	4.74	
Veronica Campbell	10.97	49	2.04	4.47	
Ivet Lalova	11.00	49½	2.02	4.50	
Avg.	10.96	49.8	2.01	4.54	

Men	Time (sec's)	No. of Strides	Average Stride	Turnover Rate	Wind 0.6 m/s
Justin Gatlin	9.85	42	2.38	4.26	
Francis Obikwelu	9.86	43½	2.30	4.41	
Maurice Greene	9.87	46½	2.15	4.71	
Shawn Crawford	9.89	47½	2.11	4.80	
Avg.	9.87	44.9	2.23	4.55	
Difference	10%	10%	11%	0%	

The last line labeled "Difference" shows that compared to women, men in this event:

1. Ran 10 percent faster.
2. Took 10 percent fewer strides.
3. Took 11 percent longer strides. (Stride length is expressed in meters.)
4. Had a 0 percent faster turnover rate. (Turnover rate is expressed as strides per second.)

Table VII: 2006 U.S. Nationals—Indianapolis

Women	Time (sec's)	No. of Strides	Average Stride	Turnover Rate	Wind -0.9 m/s
Marion Jones	11.10	48½	2.06	4.37	
Lauryn Williams	11.17	53	1.89	4.74	
Torri Edwards	11.17	51	1.96	4.57	
Rachelle Boone-Smith	11.21	48	2.08	4.28	
Avg.	11.16	50.1	2.00	4.49	

Men	Time (sec's)	No. of Strides	Average Stride	Turnover Rate	Wind -1.2 m/s
Tyson Gay	10.07	46½	2.15	4.62	
Shawn Crawford	10.26	47	2.13	4.58	
Jordan Vaden	10.27	45	2.22	4.38	
Jason Smoots	10.29	45½	2.20	4.42	
Avg.	10.22	46.0	2.17	4.50	
Difference	8%	8%	9%	0%	

The last line labeled "Difference" shows that compared to women, men in this event:

1. Ran 8 percent faster.
2. Took 8 percent fewer strides.
3. Took 9 percent longer strides. (Stride length is expressed in meters.)
4. Had a 0 percent faster turnover rate. (Turnover rate is expressed as strides per second.)

Table VIII: 2007 U.S. Nationals—Indianapolis

Women	Time (sec's)	No. of Strides	Average Stride	Turnover Rate	Wind -0.9 m/s
Torri Edwards	11.02	50½	1.98	4.58	
Lauryn Williams	11.16	53	1.89	4.75	
Carmelita Jeter	11.17	50½	1.98	4.52	
Allyson Felix	11.25	46	2.17	4.09	
Avg.	11.15	50.0	2.01	4.49	

Men	Time (sec's)	No. of Strides	Average Stride	Turnover Rate	Wind -0.5 m/s
Tyson Gay	9.84	45½	2.20	4.62	
Trindon Holliday	10.07	50½	1.98	5.01	
Walter Dix	10.09	50	2.00	4.96	
Mark Jelks	10.13	47	2.13	4.64	
Avg.	10.03	48.3	2.08	4.81	
Difference	10%	4%	4%	7%	

The last line labeled "Difference" shows that compared to women, men in this event:

1. Ran 10 percent faster.
2. Took 4 percent fewer strides.
3. Took 4 percent longer strides. (Stride length is expressed in meters.)
4. Had a 7 percent faster turnover rate. (Turnover rate is expressed as strides per second.)

Table IX: 2007 World Championships—Osaka, Japan

Women	Time (sec's)	No. of Strides	Average Stride	Turnover Rate	Wind -0.2 m/s
Veronica Campbell	11.01	49½	2.02	4.50	
Lauryn Williams	11.01	52½	1.90	4.77	
Carmelita Jeter	11.02	49½	2.02	4.49	
Torri Edwards	11.05	51	1.96	4.62	
Avg.	11.02	50.6	1.98	4.59	

Men	Time (sec's)	No. of Strides	Average Stride	Turnover Rate	Wind -0.5 m/s
Tyson Gay	9.85	45½	2.20	4.62	
Derrick Atkins	9.91	44½	2.25	4.49	
Asafa Powell	9.96	46	2.17	4.62	
Olusoji A. Fasuba	10.07	47	2.13	4.67	
Avg.	9.95	45.8	2.19	4.60	
Difference	10%	10%	11%	0%	

The last line labeled "Difference" shows that compared to women, men in this event:

1. Ran 10 percent faster.
2. Took 10 percent fewer strides.
3. Took 11 percent longer strides. (Stride length is expressed in meters.)
4. Had a 0 percent faster turnover rate. (Turnover rate is expressed as strides per second.)

Table X: 2008 U.S. Trials—Eugene

Women	Time (sec's)	No. of Strides	Average Stride	Turnover Rate	Wind 1.0 m/s
Muna Lee	10.85	47	2.13	4.33	
Torri Edwards	10.90	50	2.00	4.59	
Lauryn Williams	10.90	52	1.92	4.77	
Marshevet Hooker	10.93	47½	2.11	4.35	
Avg.	10.90	49.1	2.04	4.51	

Men	Time (sec's)	No. of Strides	Average Stride	Turnover Rate	Wind 4.1 m/s
Tyson Gay	9.68	44½	2.25	4.60	
Walter Dix	9.80	48½	2.06	4.95	
Darvis Patton	9.84	44½	2.25	4.52	
Travis Padgett	9.85	49½	2.02	5.03	
Avg.	9.79	46.8	2.14	4.77	
Difference	10%	5%	5%	6%	

The last line labeled "Difference" shows that compared to women, men in this event:

1. Ran 10 percent faster.
2. Took 5 percent fewer strides.
3. Took 5 percent longer strides. (Stride length is expressed in meters.)
4. Had a 6 percent faster turnover rate. (Turnover rate is expressed as strides per second.)

Table XI: 2008 Olympic Games—Beijing

Women	Time (sec's)	No. of Strides	Average Stride	Turnover Rate	Wind 0.0 m/s
Shelly-Ann Fraser	10.78	50	2.00	4.64	
Sherone Simpson	10.98	49½	2.02	4.51	
Kerron Stewart	10.98	48	2.08	4.37	
Lauryn Williams	11.03	53	1.89	4.81	
Avg.	10.94	50.1	2.00	4.58	

Men	Time (sec's)	No. of Strides	Average Stride	Turnover Rate	Wind 0.0 m/s
Usain Bolt	9.69	41	2.44	4.23	
Richard Thompson	9.89	44	2.27	4.45	
Walter Dix	9.91	48½	2.06	4.89	
Churandy Martina	9.93	46½	2.15	4.68	
Avg.	9.86	45.0	2.23	4.56	
Difference	10%	10%	12%	0%	

The last line labeled "Difference" shows that compared to women, men in this event:

1. Ran 10 percent faster.
2. Took 10 percent fewer strides.
3. Took 12 percent longer strides. (Stride length is expressed in meters.)
4. Had a 0 percent slower turnover rate. (Turnover rate is expressed as strides per second.)

Analysis of the Data

Before beginning an analysis of the foregoing data, a few notations are made regarding the tabulated figures. The stride lengths shown are not measured distances. Instead, they are secondary figures calculated by dividing 100 meters by the total number of strides taken to travel that distance. No special consideration has been given to the shorter strides utilized at the beginning of a race because these shorter strides are common to all the runners. Since we are looking at comparisons *between* the runners, rather than at absolutes, this would not significantly change the comparisons, nor the conclusions drawn from those comparisons.

A runner of average ability should not attempt to achieve a stride length that is equal to the stride length achieved by these runners. Such an effort would be counterproductive. It must be remembered that the stride length is achieved while being completely airborne. A faster runner will travel a greater distance while airborne than will the average athlete. A greater stride length evolves naturally through higher speed. Any attempt by a slower runner to match the stride length of a faster runner would require a stretched-out stride. This would increase braking action and have an overall detrimental effect upon one's speed. A particular stride length should not be one's goal. Greater speed must remain as one's goal. Stride length will increase of its own accord as one becomes a faster runner.

As can be deduced from a look at the column showing the number of strides taken by each runner, these figures are listed to the nearest ½ stride (1 percent accuracy). No attempt should be made to infer a greater accuracy into these figures or the calculated figures of stride length and turnover rate that are derived from these figures. This has been deemed sufficiently accurate for the purposes stated herein.

Now, to the tabulated data. A comparison of individual runners in the races that have been documented shows that there are notable differences in the data listed in all four columns. There are too few sets of data to make a sound mathematical comparison. In general though, as expected, the taller runners used fewer, longer strides and these strides were slower than those of the shorter runners.

A comparison of the sexes shows that there are notable differences in the data listed in *most* of the columns. The figures below each table show that between the sexes: the difference in the average time varies between 8 percent and 10 percent, the difference in the average number of strides varies between 4 percent and 12 percent, the difference in the average length of stride varies between 4 percent and 13 percent.

Regarding the anomaly that generally shows the difference in stride length to be a larger percentage than the difference in stride number, it is to be noted that in all four columns of the tabulated data, the women's mark is taken as the basis for comparison. In comparing number of strides, the women's base number is the larger of the two numbers compared (men used fewer strides). Since this larger number is used as the basis of comparison, the difference between the sexes shows up as a smaller percentage of it. And similarly for the comparison of stride length, the women's base number is the smaller of the two numbers compared (men took longer strides). Since this smaller number is used as the basis of comparison, the difference between the sexes shows up as a larger percentage of it.

A summary of these eleven track meets shows that regarding the times, on the average, men ran 9 percent faster than women; regarding the number of strides, on the average, men took 8 percent fewer strides than women; and regarding the stride length, on the average, men took 9 percent longer strides than women.

What stands out, however, is the *close* comparison of the average turnover rates; men utilized, on the average, a mere 2 percent higher turnover rate than women. Compared to the other listed characteristics, this appears most intriguing. In fact, of the eleven track meets studied, approximately one half of this difference in turnover rates is attributable to just the one meet examined in Table VIII. Compared to the others, this meet appears to be an anomaly. If it were not included, the difference in average turnover rates between men and women would be only 1 percent.

This departure from the apparent norm of the average turnover rates shown in Table VIII is primarily due to two factors. In the women's race, an extremely long stride is utilized by Allyson Felix who's strongest event is the 200m—being crowned world champion at that distance several weeks later. This longer stride results in a lower than average turnover rate. In the men's race, there were some short stature runners such as Trindon Holliday who has a reported height of 5'5" and who utilizes a shorter stride. This shorter stride results in a higher than average turnover rate. The combination of these two unusual factors tends to skew the resulting turnover comparison at this meet.

The variation in individual turnover rates exhibited in Table VIII is important. It shows that deviations from the closely-grouped turnover rates otherwise seen, can work very well for some runners. It underscores the possibility for others that a tweaking of turnover rates remains a strong possibility when searching for ways to achieve a higher top speed.

Considering all the differences that exist between runners such as their body size, weight, stride length and muscle mass, the overall close grouping of average turnover rates is found to be interesting. Is this just coincidence or is there some underlying cause for the clustering of these figures? The author does not believe in coincidences. Are the laws of physics at work here? Since the author is a believer in the concept that the turnover rate is subject to a cap, it is believed that such a cap is a major contributing factor to the close grouping of the average turnover rates. It is believed that the cap imposed by momentum imbalance may have clustered these turnover rates so closely together. Methods for individuals to raise this cap were discussed in earlier chapters.

17

BY THE NUMBERS

Avenues to a Faster You

As noted earlier, two avenues are available if we are to run faster: increased turnover rate and increased stride length. Let us look at what each of these avenues might offer. The 44 entries of time and stride count in the tables were averaged to begin the investigation. Averages are shown to a higher accuracy than are individual entries.

Female:

        50.13 avg. number of strides
        4.538 strides per sec. avg. turnover rate
        1.995 meters avg. stride length
        11.045 seconds avg. time

Male:

        46.11 avg. number of strides
        4.612 strides per sec. avg. turnover rate
        2.169 meters avg. stride length
        9.999 seconds avg. time

Difference:

        4.02 avg. number of strides
        0.074 strides per sec. avg. turnover rate
        0.174 meters avg. stride length
        1.046 seconds avg. time

From the point of view of the female, the combination of an increase of 0.074 strides per sec. in the turnover rate and an increase of 0.174 meters in the stride length would produce a time equal to that of the male. We will now take a closer look at each of these two constituents of the faster time.

Using these averaged figures, if the female were to increase only the turnover rate by 0.074 strides per sec., the time would be lowered by 0.18 seconds. And, if only the stride length were increased by 0.174 meters, the time would be lowered by 0.89 seconds. These total 1.07 seconds, which is 2 percent accurate compared to the 1.046 seconds listed above. The computations to arrive at these figures are shown at the end of this section.

Since the runner has no control over the length of one's leg, and consequently the stepping distance of one's stride, we will remove that aspect from our investigation. This is intended to remove from the calculations, the fact that the average male runner is larger in size than the average female. Of the total difference in stride length (0.174 meters), let us assign a value of 10 percent of this difference as being attributable to the longer step distance of the larger male. The remaining 90 percent of the difference (0.157 meters) would then be attributable to a more powerful push off. If the female were to increase stride length by 0.157 meters, this would reduce her time by 0.80 seconds. The sum of 0.18 seconds attributable to turnover rate and 0.80 seconds attributable to stride length brings us to a total of 0.98 seconds as a comparable time difference.

To summarize; setting aside the aspect of a person's size and its accompanying difference in stepping distance, the female is looking at increasing the turnover rate by 0.074 strides per sec. and increasing the stride length by 0.157 meters (6") to lower the time by 0.98 seconds in order to match the performance of the male of the same size.

This, of course, has been a hypothetical exercise that involves several approximations. But, it provides some insight into the framework within which we operate, and what one might expect to encounter when any runner, male or female, is searching for ways to improve the present race time.

A training partner with a keen eye can count the number of strides in your 100m run. It will be easier to count just the number of strides taken with the foot that comes off the rear pedal; then double this figure. If the other foot touches down just before the finish line is reached, there will have been an even number of complete strides and the doubled figure will be valid. However, if the other foot touches down after the finish line, there will have been an odd number of complete strides and the doubled figure must be corrected by 1. This stride count can then be used in the calculation of improvements potentially available to you.

Which of these alternatives (turnover rate or stride length) appears to be the most attractive is a question to be answered by each individual runner. If you believe you have already pushed your body about as far as it will go physically, increasing the turnover rate may be your best option. In this case, greater attention to momentum balance should take priority. By choosing to train for a higher turnover rate, the runner will not have entered a short dead-end street where one's path would be immediately blocked by higher momentum considerations. While a higher turnover rate does incur a greater momentum difference between arms and legs, it also incurs a shorter time interval of the momentum difference. This shorter time interval will allow for a greater momentum difference to be comfortably carried by the runner's body. When one considers the appreciable differences that exist between individual runner's turnover rates, it is suggested that a long and introspective look at one's own running form may indicate if there could be some room for improvement in this area.

On the other hand, one might do well to look at the means to improve the stride length. One's present physical abilities should be evaluated to determine if substantial improvement in this area might be available. Stride length is affected by the power of the push off. This does not necessarily suggest an inordinate amount of time be spent in the exercise room. Remember, these are fast-twitch muscle fibers we're talking here. Plyometrics are key! Minimizing braking effect is also a requirement. The more braking that one acquires at touchdown, the greater will be the portion of the push off power that must be consumed in regenerating that lost speed. Efficiency of the complete stride, including arm motions, is needed. The ability to increase one's stride length while continuing to maintain the requisite techniques requires unusual strength. The ability to reach a stride length as noted above, without slowing the turnover rate, requires a muscular power that most of us will never know.

These examples are laid out here so that each reader will be in a better position to judge his present circumstance and thereby make a more informed decision as to which avenue offers the brightest prospects for an improved running speed.

What follows, for those interested, are the computations for the described comparison:

Computation for an improved women's turnover rate:

Present: 4.538 strides/sec. → 1 ÷ 4.538 = 0.2204 secs./stride

Improved: 4.612 strides/sec. → 1 ÷ 4.612 = 0.2168 secs./stride

Difference is 0.0036 secs./stride 0.0036 secs./stride × 50.13 strides = 0.18 seconds

This is the improvement available in women's time by increasing only the turnover rate.

Computation for an improved women's stride length:

Present: 1.995 meters × 4.538 strides/sec. = 9.053 meters/sec. speed
100 meters ÷ 9.053 meters/sec. = 11.046 secs. time

Improved: 2.169 meters × 4.538 strides/sec. = 9.843 meters/sec. speed
100 meters ÷ 9.843 meters/sec. = 10.160 secs. time

Difference: 11.046—10.160 = 0.89 seconds

Correction for Size: 0.89 seconds × 90% = 0.80 seconds
  This is the improvement available in women's time by increasing only the stride length.

Total: 0.18 secs. available from turnover + 0.80 secs. available from stride length = 0.98 secs.

This is the time savings available if turnover were increased from 4.538 to 4.612 strides/sec. and if stride length were increased from 1.995 to 2.152 meters. (2.152 is 2.169 adjusted downward to agree with the smaller time savings of 0.98 seconds for the smaller athlete who has been used as the basis throughout these calculations).

The 4 × 100 Relay

Perhaps the rule No. 1, "Get the stick around," should be dropped from the lexicon of the 4 × 100 relay. It is a good objective, but it does not focus on *how* to get the stick around. Without focusing on how to achieve the desired result, the desired result might not be achieved. Just as in the start of the sprint, one should not focus on the intended result; one should focus on the immediate action to be performed.

And there are a series of immediate actions that are required for a good relay. The first action to be performed is the incoming runner must drift to the proper side of the lane so the baton can be passed straight forward. It's almost certain death if it becomes necessary to pass the baton diagonally across the lane. Both runners must remain in their proper side of the lane until the exchange is completed.

It is the incoming runner's responsibility to *find* the hand of the receiving runner. The outgoing runner must not panic if the end of the exchange zone is approaching and the exchange has not yet been made. The worst thing to do, and we see it time and again, is for the outgoing runner to begin waving the hand, *looking* for the baton. Once this occurs, failure is assured. The incoming runner cannot align the baton with a moving hand.

The receiving runner should discuss, ahead of time, where the incoming runner prefers the receiving hand to be. Normally, the receiving runner holds the arm rearward at 30° to 45° below the horizontal. Palm up usually offers the best target. Keep the fingers horizontal and the thumb out of the way so that it is not an obstruction to the placement of the baton. The receiving runner must get the *feel* of what it's like when the hand is held in the orientation that the incoming runner prefers. When the receiving runner feels the baton in the hand, grip it first; swing the arm second. Relays are aborted when this sequence is reversed. When the exchange is completed, the incoming runner must not then get careless and stray from the team's assigned lane until all runners have cleared the area.

The generally accepted method of running the 4 × 100 relay is for runners No. 1 and No. 3 to carry the baton in the right hand. These are the runners who run most of their race on the curve. Holding the baton in the right hand allows them to stay on the inside of their lane when making the exchange to runners No. 2 and No. 4. This is a good arrangement, but there are some additional thoughts that should also be given consideration.

The 24 baton exchanges that occur in the eight lanes of a 4 × 100 relay have the following characteristics. Runners No. 1 and No. 3 will be handing off the baton with the same hand; 13 times on a curve, 3 on a straight. Runner No. 2 will be handing off with the other hand; all 8 on a curve.

Because of the turning requirement a runner must contend with when negotiating the curve at high speed relaxation is reduced, which makes the handoff more difficult than when running straight. There is the school of thought that the float technique used by sprinters in the 200m can also be used in the handoff of the 4 × 100 relay. If the baton exchange occurs on a curve, the incoming runner can float from the inside of the lane to the outside of the lane just before handing off, thus allowing increased relaxation and improved ability to hand off the baton.

Floating to the outside of the lane as the handoff is approached has no downside because the runner does not have to make a recovery and come back to the inside of the lane. This runner's race is concluded after the benefits of the float have been collected. Additionally, the outgoing runner is already positioned on the inside of the lane which provides this runner with the shortest race. The best use of this technique requires runners No. 1 and No. 3 to carry the baton in the left hand and runners No. 2 and No. 4 to carry the baton in the right hand.

The teams in lane Nos. 1 through 5 would be able to use this technique in two of the three baton exchanges. The teams in lane Nos. 6 through 8 have their first exchange on the back straight, but their leadoff runners would still be allowed to utilize the float as they neared the end of the curve. They would then be on the outside of their lane and aligned for the handoff. All teams would use this technique for the third exchange.

All lanes of runners will have to hug the inside of the land for exchange No. 2. Hugging the inside of a curving land during an exchange is more difficult, but with this arrangement it occurs only this once during the race.

If the incoming runner is allowed to float to the outside of the lane in the majority of cases, there is less likelihood this will happen accidentally. An unwanted drift to the outside of the lane would necessitate a diagonal passing of the baton. With a diagonal passing of the baton, the team is more apt to experience a failed pass.

The 4 × 100 relay uses a blind pass. If the float technique is to be used, the outgoing runner must remember that the incoming runner will be changing position since last seen. Each runner must stay on the designated side of the lane. Yes, unforeseen things happen. One responsibility of the outgoing runner is to *always* check in which hand the incoming runner is holding the baton. That one glance will dictate which side of the lane the outgoing runner will take and which hand to extend. Getting the baton around remains as the top consideration for the team. Getting it around quicker is what wins the races.

Temperature vs. Performance

Prior to a race, it is a reassuring sensation to feel the warming rays of the sun on one's warm-up pants. As the sun creates warmth, you just know that good things are going on inside your skin as the blood flows freely to one's muscles. Your body is getting ready for a good race.

But that warming sun can also make good things happen outside your skin. Again, physics tells us what and why. As the air temperature becomes warmer, the air expands and becomes lighter (to wit, a hot air balloon will rise). A simplified explanation of why the warmer air is lighter is that the warmer, more excited molecules of air keep knocking elbows with each other and tend to spread apart so each has more room. This warmer air now has fewer molecules remaining in each cubic foot, and therefore, fewer air molecules all around us. Because there are fewer air molecules for us to push aside as we run forward, we can run forward more easily, and for a sprinter more rapidly. Warm sunny days do more than raise the temperature; they raise your speed.

Just how much does an increase in temperature help a runner? If the temperature were to begin at 70° F. in the morning, the density of air at sea level would be .07488 lb. per cu. ft. But when afternoon arrives, the temperature might climb to 90° F. Now the density of the air, which varies inversely as the absolute temperature, would be only .07216 lb. per cu. ft. The density of the air through which the runner must pass is 3¾ percent lower in the afternoon than it was in the morning.

This density change relates to a corresponding lowering of the apparent wind resistance encountered by a runner. We must remember that air resistance is only one small factor in the determination of a runner's speed, so a reduction of 3¾ percent in air density will not result in a 3¾ percent increase in speed. But, when an event is timed to ¹⁄₁₀₀ of a second, one should accept any advantage that may present itself. Warmer days set the stage for faster times.

Elevation of Venue

The elevation at which we compete also has an effect upon the amount of air resistance we encounter as we force our way forward. If the venue is at an elevation close to sea level, the athlete will be competing at the bottom of a sea of air. Here, the air is most dense because it is being compressed by the weight of all the air above it.

If we were to ascend higher up a mountainside there would be less air above us, and therefore, the air around us would not be compressed as much. This air would be less dense than the air below us. When the air is less dense, we can move through it more easily. This favors the sprinters and the jumpers. However, this higher altitude does a disfavor to the discus and the javelin people because the thinner air provides less aerodynamic lift on the implements. It also presents a problem for the distance runners because there is less air (and less oxygen) in each lungful the runner breathes in. An oxygen deficit is more easily acquired.

But now, let us look at the event of sprinting and how a change in elevation might have an effect upon the times registered. When making comment about an athlete's performance at a venue such as Mexico City, the nearly automatic response one hears is, "Yeah, but that was at altitude." Recorded times achieved by sprinters at higher elevations are not treated with the same respect as are recorded times achieved at venues closer to sea level. This is unfortunate, because their performance has not been enhanced to the degree that popular belief would attribute.

By reason of a runner's forward motion, he will encounter what is tantamount to running against a headwind that is equal in speed to the forward speed of the runner. The faster one runs, the stronger will be this apparent headwind. If a runner's forward speed were 10 meters per second (mps), that runner would experience an apparent 10 mps headwind. If, however, there is blowing a 1 mps tailwind, that runner would now experience only a 9 mps apparent headwind. Similarly, if a 2 mps tailwind were blowing, the runner would experience an 8 mps apparent headwind. A 2.00 mps tailwind (approx. 4.5 mph) is allowable under the international rules of competition and no apologies are required if one establishes a record time under this condition.

Now, it is no secret that a sprinter will reap some benefit when running at an elevated venue. But just how high must an athlete travel in order to find the same aerodynamic advantage as is realized by running with a tail wind at sea level? Well, at the same temperature, an elevation of 7000 ft. will suffice if one wants to replicate a 1 mps tail wind at sea level. But one would have to climb much higher, up to nearly 15,000 ft., in order to replicate a 2 mps tailwind at sea level. To add some perspective to these figures, Mexico City is 7400 ft. and Denver boasts an elevation of 5280 ft.

Since sprinting with a 2 mps tailwind is perfectly acceptable, it appears from the foregoing that no explanatory remarks should be necessary and records could be fully validated when recording a sprinter's time that was established at a high-altitude site. It seems that it would be fair to all athletes to assign to each competition site a *modified* allowable tail wind, the calculation of which would be unique to that site and be dependent upon its altitude. Venues at higher elevations would have smaller allowable tail winds. In this way, performances at all venues would be on an even footing when recording the times of sprinters.

The decisions to build a track and stadium at a particular location, and to thereafter conduct a competitive meet at that site are human decisions. Therefore, we humans can also decide to assign an allowable envelope to that site, within which performances could be acknowledged as being worthy of record status. Conversely, rain, sunshine, temperature and daily variations of barometric pressure can also affect us humans. But these remain within the purview of Mother Nature and we, as guests in Her domain, should accept whatever she deems to be an appropriate serving on any given day.

Wind Speed Variation

A 100m race that is held at a sanctioned track meet will have a wind gauge constructed to read the velocity of wind component that is aligned with the track. It is read for a 10-second period beginning at the start of the race. These readings are then averaged. This averaged figure is then cited as the wind speed applicable to that race. If this averaged figure is greater than 2.00 meters per second in the direction of running, the performance is deemed to be wind aided. Some variation in the wind speed during a race is normal fare. Hence the need for determining the *average* wind speed.

If one is very lucky, the average wind speed will have been a 2.00 mps tail wind for your race. And if one is outlandishly lucky, the momentary wind speeds that were above the 2.00 average will have occurred during the second half of the race where the runner's speed is the maximum. To offset these highest momentary wind speeds, the lowest momentary wind speeds should preferably occur at the beginning of the race when the runner's speed is the lowest. The maximum favorable tail wind will be of most benefit if it occurs at the same time the athlete is running at his maximum speed.

When a runner has achieved maximum speed in a race, his acceleration is zero, which means that the total of forces in the direction of motion must exactly equal the total of forces opposite to the direction of motion. The *net* force now acting on a runner is zero. Under this condition, even the slightest assist by a following breeze will boost a runner's forward speed. Conversely, at the beginning of a race when the runner is rapidly accelerating, there is a large imbalance of forces in the direction of motion. The *net* force acting on a runner is comparatively large. Under this condition, the slight assist by a following breeze will have very little effect upon the runner's speed. A breeze (either headwind or tailwind) will have the greatest effect upon the runner's speed when the runner has reached the upper end of the speed range. At this point, the runner's input will have produced the maximum speed of which one is capable. Now, any force from a breeze will produce the most noticeable change to that speed.

But, do these winds affect all runners equally? It seems reasonable that a heavier, more muscular runner, would be less affected by the external force imparted by a breeze, either headwind or tailwind, than would a slightly built (presumably weaker) runner. In the latter instance, the small force of a breeze would be a more significant portion of the total force being experienced by the runner and would therefore have greater consequence. A breeze can be a fickle guest when it visits the sprint.

What's the Difference?

What's the difference between the champion runners and the many, many runners whose performance falls just short of that status? One might flippantly respond, "A few tenths of a second." But, the question was not about the difference in their times. The question was about the difference in the runners. Yes, this answer may be somewhat more elusive, but by now, we should be able to come pretty close to it. Let us look at some possibilities.

What about training? The training regimen of the also-rans is, in all probability, no less demanding than that of their more famous counterparts. Unquestionably, each has devoted years of training to the honing of one's body for this event. It is difficult to discern much in the way of difference here.

Perhaps motivation? At every level of the sport, there are competitors who desperately want a winning performance. Throughout the sport, one will find a strong desire to excel. I don't believe we can find much difference here either.

There cannot be so few with the innate ability to run a sub-eleven-second 100-meter race in the women's ranks and a sub-ten-second 100-meter race for the men. A cursory look at the playgrounds, basketball courts and school athletic fields that abound will provide ample testimony that natural physical ability is not reserved for the very few currently at the top.

Where does this leave us? What do those very few possess that sets them apart from all those who want to become one of the so-very-few? What has produced the difference in performance of several good runners in a race? Only one was the winner. Through the process of elimination, there is only one factor still remaining. TECHNIQUE! Better technique leads to faster times.

The techniques incorporated by those who have achieved champion status are better suited to them than have been the techniques incorporated by the supporting cast of near-champions. The difference has been in the techniques used, or perhaps more accurately, in the techniques not used.

But as more sprinters become better acquainted with good technique, more sprinters will find their way to the front. Before a race, if one were to handicap each participant's chances of winning, instead of just a very few with any real chance of doing so, those *in the running* could number many times what it does now.

When good technique is added to the prerequisites of natural ability, thorough training and the competitive desire to win, the sport will have many faces from which to choose its next champion. There should be much company at the head of the class. Perhaps you can be one of them.

What's the Time?

As the top runners become ever faster, the timed differences between their performances tend to become smaller. Race times are recorded to ¹⁄₁₀₀ of a second, with placements sometimes decided by thousandths of a second. The recorded time is established when the electronic cursor of the timing system is placed on the image of the runner's torso. But, as can sometimes happen, this recorded time is identical to the recorded time of the winner of a different race. Were the two times really the same? Were the two runners equally fast?

Perhaps it is time for our technical committee to consider those questions. The present system is quite capable of discerning to within ¹⁄₁₀₀₀ of a second, the *difference* in times of the runners in a single race. But, if it is desired to determine the faster of two runners who have competed in different races, the challenge is much more demanding. The question becomes, "Is the time of 9.999 seconds as determined by one timing device at one venue on one day, exactly the same as 9.999 seconds as determined by a different timing device at a different venue on a different day?" This is a much more difficult question to answer with a great amount of conviction. But, perhaps the time has arrived for our technical people to determine if our technology will permit this degree of delineation.

Yes, if there is some degree of uncertainty when evaluating identical times of runners in different meets, it obviously adds to the excitement of the moment when these two athletes have the opportunity to compete head-to-head at a later meet. This can be good for the sport.

But, what if one runner's performance was actually faster than the other runner's performance. That runner will never be able to claim that record time as his alone. That athlete's accomplishment will always be somewhat dimmed by having to share the record with someone else whose performance was actually slower. Perhaps it is time to consider bringing additional technological advancements into the sport so that every runner's assigned time can be looked upon with greater confidence.

And let's see now, if a runner takes 10 seconds to travel 100 meters, then in 1 second 10 meters would be traveled, and in .001 seconds .01 meters would be traveled. This is approximately ⅜ of an inch. Surely, we are capable of marking the track to at least this degree of accuracy. But it wouldn't hurt to check.

Clothing

Speed skaters and other high-speed athletes wear special clothing and assume special positions that are designed to reduce the resistance created by the passage of the athlete through the air. The author does not advocate altering one's form to assume a more streamlined shape while running. Running form should be predicated upon those factors that improve performance without regard to the air resistance it might entail. However, once the running form is thus established we should then look to minimize air resistance by thoughtfully selecting our clothing. While runners do not achieve the speeds at which athletes in a few other sports compete, no logical advantage is seen to the wearing of clothing that ignores the aspect of air resistance.

Shoes are available with a zippered flap that covers the laces and thereby smoothes the airflow over them. If your shoes do not have this aerodynamic shroud, you might consider covering the laces with wide packaging tape after they have been pulled finally snug. This takes a little more time than zipping a ready-made shroud, but if carefully done the tape method can be made as smooth as the shroud.

If the weather is not too hot, one might also consider the use of a body suit for optimum smoothing of the exposed body surfaces. If the body suit is not a viable option, panty hose made of lightweight and smooth synthetic fiber can be worn to cover body hair on the legs. Panty hose can also be useful in keeping leg muscles warm on those cool mornings.

An evening spent with needle and thread can take some judicious tucks in a pair of loose-fitting running shorts and convert them into a satisfactory formfitting garment. The loose sleeves of a tee shirt can be streamlined by taking tucks on the inner sides of the sleeves next to the chest. It stands to reason that, as long as you do not impair the body from acquiring its best operating temperature or restrict its flexibility, any smoothing of one's running apparel will lower the turbulence created by moving through the air. In an event that is timed to $\frac{1}{100}$ of a second, energy conserved by the runner in this manner can be used in ways that are far more advantageous.

18

CLOSING THOUGHTS

Take Care of Business

Most of us will never see an Olympic medal in our future. The recipients of that award are extremely rare. We each do not have a body destined for Olympic glory. But there is much we can do with what we have. We must take the body that has been given us, work with it and improve it. Hone it to the strongest and the sharpest we know how. Then couple this with knowledge of good technique and thorough training. This will give us the optimum opportunity to do our very best when we step to the starting line on race day.

To *do* our best, we must *try* our best. This includes not only how *hard* we train, but also how *smart* we train. We must learn to utilize *all* our faculties to their fullest. Proper preparation provides us with the knowledge that we've brought our best to the game. This inspires the inner confidence needed to perform at our highest level. We should be mindful that a desire to excel must precede one's ability to succeed.

If your form is not as smooth as it should be, search to find the trouble spots. Ask for help; it's almost always available. If you choose friends in the running community with similar goals and commitment, your chances of success are further enhanced. With more knowledge and greater awareness of those subtleties that promote higher speed, *and* those that inhibit it, the sprinter will be better prepared to take control and recognize opportunities for improvement, both in oneself and also for one's training partners. However, the best techniques in the world will be of little value to a runner who is not dedicated to implement the proper physical training. When one combines the two, the prospects for success are vastly improved. What is being advocated here is not to train less, but to train smarter. At no time does the author suggest reducing the intensity of one's conditioning program. Training in a group, under the direction of a good coach, is far more conducive to maximizing one's physical capabilities than attempting to do this singly.

Strength and quickness are at the root of each of the running elements. But it is the author's belief that proper balance between arms and legs is an integral component of one's running ability. It is therefore suggested that the runner be aware of this concept throughout one's training routine and strive for the necessary smoothness of form that accompanies it. Without the finesse of a smooth running form, one will not achieve maximum running speed. Strength is then interwoven to further enhance that form. Proper use of these fundamentals will define a person's running style. Work on them; they can open the door to new success. We cannot all be Olympians, but armed with proper knowledge and attitude, we can fulfill the capabilities of the talents we have.

Many of the techniques discussed in this book are so subtle, they will not be readily apparent to an observer. In such an instance, the runner must be ready to assume responsibility for evaluation of a technique being examined. To accomplish this, the runner must first decide what gage will be utilized to judge the effectiveness of the technique under consideration and also what criterion will indicate whether the trial is leading toward success or toward failure. The subject matter contained herein was intended to assist in these determinations. We must be cognizant of the fact that no one technique is right for every runner and that each individual will, of necessity, face some experimentation. But, not blind experimentation. It has been the intent of this book to provide the runner with additional knowledge, and thereby some direction for that experimentation.

It is desirable that one be sufficiently versed in the many techniques that are available to the sprinter so that an informed decision can be made regarding which way to look next in the search for a faster race. Also, knowledge of the basic physics involved will be a valuable tool when mastering the mechanics of each technique. Knowledge can help unlock the mysteries of running, but it will be the runner's feel of increased smoothness and speed that will define when a new technique has been mastered.

After all is said and done, when the various techniques have been explored, mastered and assembled into a smooth and homogeneous form, the final key to speed is *feel*—your *feel* for your form; your *feel* for your speed. It's a wonderful experience of speed and freedom when you *feel* you are running fast. You know you've put it all together and are having a great run. Let's acknowledge the obvious: *fast* is more fun than *slow*.

Now, don't lose sight of what you've done to get yourself on this high.

Make note of what specifics you've utilized and how you've put them together. We need to do this so the great-run-high can be duplicated in the future and yes, improved upon still further. Such is the competitive addiction to speed. Once tasted, we will always want still more. The quest for greater speed is a race without a finish line, so enjoy the adventure.

The Sport of Track and Field

The opportunity to compete with others in one's chosen sport is a unique experience. It provides the setting to bring out the best in each of us. But, if the athlete makes the ill-advised choice to use illegal drugs in an attempt to better one's performance, the result can be demeaning, even destructive, both to oneself and to the sport in which one participates. The competitive nature of the athlete produces a strong desire to win. A nearly indescribable joy and sense of gratification is experienced when one has demonstrated oneself to be the best on a given day. But, how hollow must be that joy if one knows that cheating was resorted to in order to achieve that win.

The purpose of athletic competition is to see who can best accomplish a recognized athletic event. If all competitors were to artificially alter their athletic prowess, we would witness a competition among a field of artificial beings. No human being in the true sense of the word would have earned an award. What a terrible situation that would be. The true meaning of athletic competition would be lost.

The use of illegal drugs to enhance one's performance cannot be tolerated. Those who show a propensity to go that route cannot be allowed a place within the ranks of athletes who choose to compete with honesty and integrity. It is every sportsman's responsibility to help weed out those who would poison our sport, those who would bring illegal drugs to the field of competition and fair play.

Those who are in a position to influence our young and aspiring athletes are in a particularly strong position to favorably influence the choice that each youngster will some day have to make. For the good of future sports, each individual must bear the responsibility of making the correct choice. Better sports through chemistry, is not only the ultimate oxymoron, but is such a dangerous concept that we cannot permit it to coexist with true sportsmanship. Each of us has a responsibility to keep sports clean. *"You do your part; I'll do my part"* should be every athlete's mantra.

Running is truly an individual sport, and you are that individual. You can train as hard as you want, as smart as you want, or as little as you want. It is entirely up to you. You do not have to conform to a team plan or a team schedule. Whatever impetus you put into your training must come from within yourself. In this sport, you are entirely in control of your own program. If you want to try something new today—do it! If you want to hone your start a bit finer today—do it! If you want to explore a different technique for a higher top-end speed today—do it! Whatever you believe is important to you today—do it! You hold the entire deck of cards. Play them as best suits you.

You can do your own thing and take full satisfaction from having done it your way. If you do it well, be proud of what you have accomplished. For it is you who has brought your performance to this level of achievement. Accept every opportunity to learn from others, but do not be constrained by convention. Maintain an open and receptive mind. This is how we advance ourselves—and our sport.

As I've assembled my thoughts about the making of a better sprinter for others to consider, I have taken some grammatical liberties. I trust you have stayed with me all this way. There are things I believe needed to be said about the sport and hope you have kept an open mind as to this book's contents. A determined training and an enlightened application of good technique, which culminate in a display of good sportsmanship, will provide the athlete with a bountiful reward: the knowledge and satisfaction of having done one's best in the endeavor at hand.

Remember, the winning of a medal does not necessarily have to be one's goal. To run well, is itself a challenge. To have run your best on any given day is a victory. And if the challenge has lead to a victory this day, it is nice to have someone with whom you can enjoy your gratification. For the best victories, are the ones we can share.

We are each subject to the laws of the universe. When one attempts to raise the bar of one's performance, the laws of physics that will be encountered have been noted and briefly explained. These laws were included to provide the factual basis for the author's beliefs. Remain cognizant that in the domain of physics, there are no elite, nor are there any under-privileged. The laws of physics are universal and apply with absolute equality to all. They accompany us to whatever realm we may travel. In sports, they provide an equal footing from which to begin the competition. How we proceed from that point is for each individual to decide for one's self.

It has been the author's desire to assist the runner toward a better race, and thereby derive greater enjoyment from the sport. Additionally, it is hoped that by now the reader will also have attained a better understanding of oneself. Understanding oneself is a steppingstone toward improved performance.

Think about yourself	Understand yourself
Think of where you are	Understand where you are
Think of where you want to be	Understand where you want to be
Think of how you will get there	Understand how you will get there
What will you do when you get there?	That's for you to decide

It has been my purpose, not only to express my personal views and to offer a few suggestions for improvement of the sport, but also to furnish factual information and to provide food for thought so that you, the reader, will take a fresh and objective look to see if some different techniques may be applicable to your running form. I have endeavored to provide an insight into various techniques so that you will be in a better position to understand them, thereby increasing your opportunity for success with them. As a sprinter, you have already experienced the thrill of running fast. I now wish you an even greater thrill—that of running still faster.

Do you believe you have a still better race in you?

BIBLIOGRAPHY

Baldwin, David. *Track and Field Record Holders.* Jefferson, NC: McFarland, 1996.

Beyersdorff, Gerald. *Inside Track.* Milwaukee: Advanced Learning Concepts, 1975.

Bowerman, William J. *Coaching Track and Field.* Houghton Mifflin, 1974.

_____, and Hardin Freeman. *High-Performance Training for Track and Field.* Champaign, IL: Leisure Press, 1990.

Bresnahan, George Thomas. *Track and Field Athletics.* Rpt. Textbook Publishers, 2003.

Carr, Gerald A. *Fundamentals of Track and Field.* Champaign, IL: Human Kinetics, 1999.

Condon, Robert J. *The Fifty Finest Athletes of the 20th Century.* Jefferson, NC: McFarland, 1990.

Currie, Stephan. *The Olympic Games.* San Diego: Lucent Books, 1999.

Derse, Ed, Jacqueline Hansen, Tim O'Rourke, and Skip Stolley. *AAF Track & Field Coaching Manual.* Los Angeles: Amateur Athletic Foundation, 2007.

Dintiman, George B., and Robert D. Ward. *Sports Speed,* 3rd ed. Champaign, IL: Human Kinetics, 2003.

Ecker, Tom. *Basic Track & Field Biomechanics.* Los Altos: Tafnews Press, 1996.

_____. *Championship Track and Field.* Rpt. Textbook Publishers, 2003.

Fee, Earl W. *The Complete Guide to Running.* Oxford: Meyer & Meyer Sport (UK), 2005.

Freeman, William H. *Peak When It Counts.* Los Altos: Tafnews Press, 2001.

Gambetta, Vern. *The Athletic Congress' Track and Field Coaching Manual.* Champaign, IL: Leisure Press, 1989.

Gordon, James A. *Track and Field.* Boston: Allyn and Bacon, 1966.

Greene, Ernest, and Audrey Greene-Nesb. *On the Right Track with Maurice Greene.* Bloomington, IN: AuthorHouse, 2006.

Greenspan, Bud. *100 Greatest Moments in Olympic History.* Los Angeles: General Publishing Group, 1995.

Guthrie, Mark. *Coaching Track & Field Successfully.* Champaign, IL: Human Kinetics, 2003.

Guttmann, Allen. *The Olympics: A History of the Modern Games.* Urbana: University of Illinois Press, 1992.

Holst, Don, and Marcia S. Popp. *American Men of Olympic Track and Field.* Jefferson, NC: McFarland, 2004.

Jarver, Jess. *Sprints & Relays.* Los Altos: Tafnews Press, 2000.

Johnson, Michael. *Slaying the Dragon.* New York: Regan Books, 1996.

Joyner-Kersee, Jackie. *A Kind of Grace.* New York: Warner Books, 1997.

Lawrence, Alan, and Mark Scheid. *The Self-Coached Runner II.* Boston: Little, Brown, 1987.

Lawson, Gerald. *World Record Breakers in Track & Field Athletics*. Champaign, IL: Human Kinetics, 1997.

Lewis, Carl. *Inside Track*. New York: Simon & Schuster, 1990.

Macy, Sue. *Swifter, Higher, Stronger*. Washington, D.C.: National Geographic, 2004.

McComb, David G. *Sports: An Illustrated History*. New York: Oxford University Press, 1998.

McNeely, Edward. *Power Plyometrics*. Aachen, Germany, and New York: Meyer & Meyer Sport, 2007.

Miller, David. *Athens to Athens*. Edinburgh: Mainstream, 2003.

Miller, Thomas S. *Programmed to Run*. Champaign, IL: Human Kinetics, 2002.

Olson, Leonard T. *Masters Track and Field*. Jefferson, NC: McFarland, 2000.

Peoples, Maurice. *Sprint Secrets*. Alexandria, VA: Inspired Dream Publishing, 2006.

Price, Robert G. *The Ultimate Guide to Weight Training for Track and Field*. Cleveland: Price World Enterprises, 2007.

Rogers, Joseph L. *USA Track & Field Coaching Manual*. Champaign, IL: Human Kinetics, 2000.

Rosen, Mel, and Karen Rosen. *Championship Running*. New York: Sports Illustrated, 1988.

Schmolinsky, G. *Track and Field: The East German Textbook of Athletics*. Toronto: Sport Books, 2000.

Sears, Edward S. *Running Through the Ages*. Jefferson, NC: McFarland, 2001.

Siddons, Larry. *The Olympics at 100*. New York: Macmillan, 1995.

Squires, Bill, and Bruce Lehane. *Speed with Endurance*. Lexington, MA: S. Greene Press, 2004.

Tricard, Louise Mead. *American Women's Track and Field*. Jefferson, NC: McFarland, 1996.

Wallace, Edward L. *Track & Field Coach's Survival Guide*. Englewood Cliffs, NJ: Parker, 1998.

Wilt, Fred, Tom Ecker, and Jim Hay. *Championship Track and Field for Women*. Englewood Cliffs, NJ: Parker, 1978.

Zarnowski, Frank. *American Decathletes*. Jefferson, NC: McFarland, 2002.

INDEX